A MOST
REMARKABLE
FAMILY

A MOST REMARKABLE FAMILY

A history of the Lyon family
From 1066 to 2014

from
the Normans, King Robert the Bruce, the Scottish Kings
to
HRH Queen Elizabeth II

Michael Hewitt

authorHOUSE®

AuthorHouse™ UK Ltd.
1663 Liberty Drive
Bloomington, IN 47403   USA
www.authorhouse.co.uk
Phone: 0800.197.4150

Image by courtesy of the Earl of Strathmore

Published by AuthorHouse 06/04/2014

ISBN: 978-1-4969-7786-1 (sc)
ISBN: 978-1-4969-7785-4 (hc)
ISBN: 978-1-4969-7787-8 (e)

This edition is published and edited by Michael Hewitt, 12 Milnthorpe
Road, Burtonwood, Warrington, WA5 4PN, England
Tel. +441925220688

There are maybe literally millions of people living in Scotland, England, United States of America, Canada, Australia, New Zealand and the Commonwealth who are proud to have the surname of Lyon. Many hundreds have served their homeland and their adopted countries either in the armed services or in business, education, the sciences, agriculture—all having a common heritage for which they have right to be very proud.

CONTENT

Appendices

This is not an Index but the reader may find it helpful to check these Appendices by page number in the main text of the book —

ACKNOWLEDGEMENTS

The author wishes to thank various people for their help in preparing this book for publication.
To my wife Gillian for editing and correcting all the book several times and for her endless patience.

To friends in alphabetical order;

John Bogin for his help and in writing one article for the book and assistance with the subject of the Knights Templar.

Sylvia Dillon (nee Lyon) for all the encouragement and help inspiration to 'get it right'.

Alan Edwards for writing some parts and helping to make the book readable and suffering for the cause - his time and patience are very much appreciated.

Chris Ure for giving encouragement and helping to rewrite several passages, without his advice and friendship I would have given up many times.

Special mentions;

Reginald Lyon of South Wales whose collection of information about the Lyon family is almost endless. His work is to be found on the website Clan Lyon Association of Canada - and many other sites. *(http://clanlyon.wordpress. com/2012/05/21/lyon-familyhistory/)*

His extensive research has been a help and inspiration and is much quoted because of his relevant knowledge. The reader can assume that most things written as quotes are from Reginald's findings after forty years of dedicated research, these are with his permission. If another quote is identified it is most often by another quoted author or resource.

Also often quoted are; **The Lyon Memorial** books see Bibliography.

MAPS AND ILLUSTRATIONS

Maps & Illustrations

	The Norfolk Line	Years	Age
1	Roger De Leonne	1040	
2	Paganus de Leonne	1080	
3	Hugo De Leonibus	1113	
4	Ernald Lyon	1150- 1175	25
5	John De Leonibus sons Pagan (6) and Walter (7)	1175-	
6	Pagan Lyon (De Leonibus) m. Ivette de Ferrers, sons John (10) and Thomas (11)	1200-1242	42
7	Walter de Leonibus m. Alicia, sons Henry (8) and William (9)	1205-1266	61
8	Sir Henry de Leonibus - land in Sussex - no issue	1230	
9	William de Leonibus	1235	
10	Sir John de Leonne— married Marjory de Ackle (Northampton) sons John (13) Adam (12)	1225-1316	91
11	Thomas Lyon	1230	
12	Sir Adam de Lyons	1255	
13	Sir John de Lyons – sons Adam (14), Richard (15) and John (16) died Warkworth	1250-1316	66
14	Sir Adam Lyon born Norfolk – sons John (18) and Adam (19)	1285	
15	Sir Richard Lyon born Norfolk – daughters Isabella, Cecilia and Christina and Richard (17)	1287	
16	**Sir John Lyon born in Warkworth. Settled in Scotland – see Northamptonshire line for John Lyon born 1314 in Scotland and sister Elizabeth 1324 born Warkworth.**	1289 -1246	57
17	Richard Lyon in London. Sherriff of London 1374. A vintner.	1310-1381	71
18	Sir John Lyon – sons Richard (20) John (21) Henry (22)	1320 -	
19	Adam de Lyon	1325 -	
20	Sir Richard Lyon born of Oxford, Cambridge and Huntingdon	1350 -	
21	Sir John Lyon born Kingsland, Suffolk and Norfolk	1353 -	
22	Sir Henry Lyon born in Norfolk later moved to in Ruislip (Middlesex)	1355 -	'
This line becomes the Middlesex line through Sir Henry Lyon (22)			

The Kings of Scotland	
Robert the Bruce	1306 - 1329
David II	1329 - 1371
Robert II	1371 - 1390
Robert III	1390 - 1406
James I	1406 - 1437
James II	1437 - 1460
James III	1469 – 1488
James IV	1488 - 1513
James V	1513 - 1542
Mary I	1542 - 1567

	The Northamptonshire or Warkworth Line	Years	Age
1	Nicholas de Lyons		
2	John de Lyons arrived from France in 1080		
3	John de Lyons son John (4	1100	
4	John de Lyons was born in married Elizabeth de Warkworth in 1170 – son Richard (5)	1140	
5	Richard de Lyons married Maud from Warkworth, son Roger (6)	1174 - 1205	31
6	Roger de Lyons he married Hawise, son Roger (7	1199 - 1250	51
7	Roger de Lyons married Joan de Napton, sons Richard (8), John (1247 – 1288) unknown.	1225 - 1250	25
8	Richard de Lyons married Emma – son John de Lyons (9)	1242	
9	Sir John de Lyons married Margery de Oakley,– sons Adam (1285 - Norfolk), Richard (11), John (10)	1268- -1312	44
10	**Sir John de Lyons in married Alice de Liz, - son John Lyon (14), Elizabeth (15)**	1289 - 1346	57
11	Richard de Lyons about married Elizabeth de Senlis – son John (12), Elizabeth (13)	1289 – 1349	60
12	Sir John de Lyons – no known issue – he died in Northamptonshire and is buried there	1320 – 1385 or 1371	65
13	Elizabeth Lyons daughter of Richard (11)	1330 – 1371	41
14	**Sir John Baron Of Forteviot Forgandenny and Drumgawan Lyon born in Scotland**	1314	
15	Elizabeth Lyons married Sir Nicholas Chetewode and Richard de Wydeville sister of John (14)	1324	

The Lords of Glamis

	Lords of Glamis	Birth-Death	Father	Dates
1st	Patrick Lyon	1402-1459	Sir John	1380-1435
2nd	Alexander Lyon	1429-1486	Patrick	1402-1459
3rd	John Lyon	1431-1497	Patrick	1402-1459
4th	John Lyon	1452-1500	John	1431-1497
5th	George Lyon	1488-1505	John	1452-1500
6th	John Lyon	1491-1528	John	1452-1500
7th	John Lyon	1521-1592	John	1491-1528
8th	John Lyon	1544-1576	John	1521-1592
9th	Patrick Lyon	1575-1615	John	1544-1578

Lyon crest

Glen Lyon

New England in the 1600's

Map of New Jersey

The Lyon and Lyons at war in the American Civil War

	Lyon	Lyons	Lyon	Lyons		Lyon	Lyons	Lyon	Lyons
State	Unionist		Confederate		State	Unionist		Confederate	
Alabama			37	24	Mississippi				41
Arkansas	3		6	9	Missouri	42	19		
California		6			New Hampshi	5	10		
Connecticut	49	24			New Jersey	21	40		
Delaware		2			New Mexico	2			
Florida		1	1	8	New York	175	244		
Georgia			36	46	North Carolina	1		3	22
Illinois	61	108			Ohio	76	157		
Indiana	41	75			Pennsyvania	94	145		
Iowa	50	34			Rhode Island	10	14		
Kansas	7	6			South Carolina			11	21
Kentucky	23	31			Tennessee			145	76
Louisana			11	65	Texas			118	51
Maine	19	29			Vermont	12	8		
Maryland	4	13	3	2	Virginia			169	32
Massachusetts	26	72			West Virginia	6	40		
Michigan	74	30			Wisconsin	46	27		
Minnesota	4	20			Totals	851	1155	540	397
					Totals	Lyon	1391		
						Lyons	1552		

	1840	1880	1905	1920
Alabama	9	376	4	80
Arizona	0	5	2	13
Arkansas	3	95	3	46
California	0	200	32	385
Colorado	0	70	13	68
Connecticut	150	746	130	192
Delaware	0	7	1	3
Florida	1	11	2	36
Georgia	18	387	10	97
Idaho	0	14	6	42
Illinois	19	808	92	302
Indiana	36	397	39	109
Iowa	2	665	47	156
Kansas	0	405	35	168
Kentucky	41	628	16	174
Louisiana	6	53	0	47
Maine	29	142	47	45
Maryland	26	160	1	72
Massachusetts	64	550	228	241
Michigan	50	890	117	270
Minnesota	0	183	31	94
Mississippi	18	184	9	53
Missouri	13	487	15	144
Montana	0	13	8	39
Sub-totals	485	7482	888	2882

	1840	1880	1905	1920
Nebraska	0	129	36	77
Nevada	0	14	1	7
New Hampshire	3	31	28	11
New Jersey	89	560	92	181
New Mexico	0	5	2	11
New York	433	2515	444	846
North Carolina	31	772	4	227
North Dakota	0	34	6	22
Ohio	113	648	87	263
Oklahoma	0	0	4	87
Oregon	0	27	10	56
Pennsylvania	76	701	119	282
Rhode Island	11	107	20	26
South Carolina	0	95	7	36
South Dakota	0	0	19	18
Tennessee	25	347	5	90
Texas	0	191	4	145
Utah	0	53	0	31
Vermont	60	260	56	73
Virginia	25	267	18	89
Washington	0	0	10	113
West Virginia	0	111	7	44
Wisconsin	9	286	54	77
Wyoming	0	7	0	8
Sub-totals	875	7031	997	2743
Grand Totals	1360	14513	1885	5625

State entry dates from http://americanhistory.about.com/od/states/a/state_admission.htm

A= William, Thomas, Henry, Richard, Peter, John, Abel Lyon families

The Earls of Strathmore & Kinghorne

1st Earl	Patrick Lyon	1606-1615
2nd Earl	John Lyon	1615-1646
3rd Earl	Patrick Lyon	1646-1695
4th Earl	John Lyon	1695-1712
5th Earl.	John Lyon	1712-1715
6th Earl.	Charles Lyon	1699-1728
7th Earl	James Lyon	1702-1735
8th Earl	Thomas Lyon	1735-1753
9th Earl	John Bowes	1753-1776
10th Earl	John Lyon-Bowes	1776-1820
11th Earl	Thomas Lyon-Bowes	1820-1846
12th Earl	Thomas Lyon-Bowes	1846-1865
13th Earl	Claude Bowes-Lyon	1865-1904
14th Earl	Claude George Bowes-Lyon	1904-1944
15th Earl	Patrick Bowes-Lyon	1944-1949
16th Earl	Timothy Patrick Bowes-Lyon	1949-1972
17th Earl	Fergus Michael Claude Bowes-Lyon	1972-1987
18th Earl	Michael Fergus Bowes-Lyon	1987-

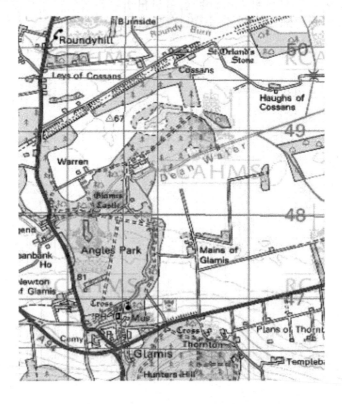

Map of Glamis & Cossins

Dates and origin unknown

Rulers of England

Kings, Queens, rulers of the United Kingdom		House
James VI & I of England	1603-1625	Stuart
Charles I	1625-1649	Stuart
Commonwealth, Oliver Cromwell	1649-1658	Commonwealth
Richard Cromwell	1658-1659	Commonwealth
Charles II	1660-1685	Stuart
James II,	1685-1688	Stuart
William III of Orange and Mary II (Jointly)	1689-1694	Orange
William III alone	1694-1702	Orange
Anne,	1702-1714	Stuart
George I	1717-1727	Hanover
George II	1727-1760	Hanover
George III	1760-1820	Hanover
George IV	1820-1830	Hanover
William IV	1830-1837	Hanover
Victoria	1837-1901	Hanover
Edward VII	1901-1910	Saxe-Coburg-Gotha
George V	1910-1936	Windsor
Edward VIII	1936	Windsor
George VI	1936-1952	Windsor
Elizabeth II	1952-	Windsor

INTRODUCTION TO THE LYON FAMILY

Over a year ago a friend, Sylvia Dillon (nee Lyon), asked me to trace her family history. She had little to work on, a few relevant dates and a photo of her father, one of nine Lyon children and a message handed down to her from her father and his father, that however poor they were, they should "be proud of the name Lyon" and that a Lyon "always put their money into land or property if they could".

When Sylvia asked me to do some work on her father's side of the family I started to discover that there were literally hundreds of thousands of Lyon family members many of them were already undertaking research on the various branches of the family.

The Lyon family turns out to be one of only a handful of famous families in the United Kingdom who have survived over 900 years of history and can be traced back to before 1066 and William the Conqueror.

Historians and genealogists spend much of their time researching monarchs and famous people but few seems to have discovered the riches of tracing a family through hundreds of years of history. Very few families can claim such a colourful history as this family Lyon, yet few people have written about them, despite the fact that they produced a Queen of England and gave service to Scottish monarchs and English monarchs since the eleventh century.

Many members of the family moved to America in the 17th century and played a large part in the settlements in New England, in Massachusetts, Connecticut and New Jersey. There are countless members of the family today in the USA from the East to the West coasts and the Southern states. There are also members of the family in Canada, Australia, New Zealand and other countries in the world.

This book is written primarily for those who are members of the Lyon family, by birth, through marriage or by any other direct or indirect relationship. However I believe that it will have a much wider interest particularly for those interested in the history of a formidable family with roots directly linked to the British Royal family. It may not be possible to follow every branch of the Lyon family tree and neither will every Lyon be able to trace back to connections with the Royal family, as for the first few hundred years, until about 1500 it was often only the eldest male who was documented. So there are undoubtedly other siblings and illegitimate family members who were not recorded for various reasons.

Some obtained the surname from their 'masters' so their bloodline is different and cannot be traced back to a previous Lyon. Most family names can only be traced to the mid-18th century whereas the Lyon family actually goes back to before 1066.

The American Lyon family is very fortunate as they can be traced back to England and Scotland because of three books named "The Lyon Memorial" which were created by collecting and collating data from local records that go back to the early settlers in the 17th century. In the UK with the help of Debrett's Peerage and Burke's Peerage and other historical books the nobles can be traced through to the 13th century and earlier.

European history records that the Vikings were busy invading countries including Scotland, England, Brabant, Normandy and much of northern Europe in the so called "dark ages". From around AD 800 to the 11th century, a vast number of Scandinavians left their homelands to seek their fortunes elsewhere. These seafaring warriors - known collectively as Vikings, Goths, Visigoths or Norsemen - began by raiding coastal sites, especially undefended monasteries, in the British Isles. Over the next three centuries they would leave their mark as pirates, raiders, traders and settlers on much of Britain and the European continent, as well as parts of modern-day Russia, Iceland, Greenland and Newfoundland. The Vikings left behind blue-eyed people with blonde hair. Some genealogists claim that the family descended from the Vikings, whether this is true is unproven, but certainly many of the Lyon family have white blonde hair and blue eyes.

Their story is full of sensational and sometimes bizarre events: murders, burnings at the stake, and deaths on the field of battle and amazing power and ownership of vast estates in Scotland and England. What struck me as surprising was how little attention the Lyon family had received from historians. The Lyon family served the Kings of Scotland from 1099 until 1607 in high office and are barely mentioned and I know of no family that was loyal for so long.

The biggest challenge for genealogists is for them to judge whether the information they have collected and the data that has been provided by other research is true or false. In the end we have to judge whether the data we have is reliable or not and this sometimes requires considerable detective work to reach a reasonable conclusion. Sometimes it is necessary to make an informed guess. These opening chapters have provided a huge challenge for me and I have devoted many months of research to reach a satisfactory conclusion. I could not always rely on the results of other researchers many of whom were eminent in their field. I also have had to re-assess the work of one particular professional genealogist whose work of more than a century ago omits important information that is now available.

There are several lines or branches of the family from 1066 onwards. When researchers explore the Norfolk Lyons most of them conclude that the research undertaken 100 years ago is reliable. As a result they have appended that information into their family trees giving much greater credence than it should have received. Such information is not always to be trusted as will be seen later on. It is necessary for the reader to make their own judgement, having carefully assessed the arguments. This sort of research is the foundation stone of genealogy.

Concerning the origin of the name of Lyon, some research dates back to Roman times. However some of this early history is unreliable and has to be viewed with discretion. I hope to show the reader how centuries old scholarship compares with the more current information that is now available. Over the centuries surnames changed dramatically creating extra difficulties for genealogists. The family is first recorded as 'de Leonne', then 'de Lyons', 'de Leonibus', 'Lyon' and 'Lyons'. In the USA we have; 'Lyne' and other variations. Sometimes people were not literate and inevitably made mistakes.

Many believe that the Lyon name originated in the city of Lyons in the Rhone Valley in France. Some claim a much more ancient lineage from Rome – these various claims cannot be conclusively proved. A large problem for genealogists is the difference between 'Lyon' and 'Lyons'. There is much evidence that the singular form is the spelling of the Royal line but there are also many examples of the plural form belonging in the Royal Scottish line. The spelling 'Lyons' does seem to have been generally used when a part of the family moved to what is now Northern Ireland from Scotland in the 12th or 13th century. Members of the Lyons family are more often from Irish descent than Scottish.

The period from 1066 to the mid-1300s is a difficult one for historians because they rely on uncertain material and it is necessary to carefully determine where errors may have occurred. There are many inconsistencies during this period by researchers both amateur and professional and in this instance Wikipedia retains inaccurate and misleading information on its website.

Enter the site for any search on the early Lyon family history and there will be inevitable errors such as confusing Northumberland with Northamptonshire and Warkworth Castles in both counties, which co-existed at that time. Move to 'Ancestry.com' and other such genealogical sites and there are links that are full of errors. For example a search for 'John Lyon 1289' will reveal that eight out of nine hints will claim his birth place is Northumberland and only one claims that he was born in Northamptonshire, which is correct. There are also many problems even with the 'experts' on the location of births. It does not help when at least half of the records involve the name John. Dealing with the name John, generally I use the date of birth, namely John Lyon (1314) to differentiate one John Lyon from another. In this book I endeavour as best I can to identify these errors and correct any previous research that has been inaccurate or misleading.

Part 1 of the book, covers the early Lyon family history from around the Norman Conquest (1066) to the time just after the execution of Charles I (1649) when some Lyon family members went to America. Prior to the Norman Conquest in 1066 there is no member of the Lyon family living in England? John Lyon was born in Scotland in 1340 and from then on the family history in Scotland is fairly well documented. In between these two dates we have a great deal of family history about two branches of the Lyon family. Unfortunately it is not altogether clear which branch of the family became the Scottish Lyon family. Previous Lyon family histories have undertaken a great deal of work and have discovered a family path that endeavours to resolve this issue. Unfortunately having reviewed their work in the modern day I have found it to contain several errors and in certain cases duplication. In one case one member of the Lyon family appears in both the Norfolk and Northamptonshire lines at the same time.

How to deal with these matters caused a great deal of thought. Certain Lyon family histories have dealt with it by starting their story in 1340 and totally ignoring the earlier period. I have drawn the most reliable conclusions given the data that is available. I do this in the belief that at some point in the future research will result in my findings being amended or modified.

I have also tried in a small way to provide appropriate background information about the life and times when these people lived. The political scene did have an effect on the Lyon Family. This involved several wars notably between England and Scotland, with Wales and France also being involved, and the occasional Crusades to the Holy Land. Civil War later reared its head and caused conflicts and a certain mobility of people around the kingdom. It is also important to take account of social structure, religion, famine and the occasional plague during this period.

The story begins with William the Conqueror and his invasion in 1066. Some members of the Lyon family joined him to settle, primarily in Norfolk and Northamptonshire. William gave them lands in both counties which they inhabited for hundreds of years. Up until the 14th century these members of the family established manors, such as Warkworth in Northamptonshire and inherited Scottish lands through an early member of the Norfolk family. The family did not settle permanently in Scotland until the beginning of the 14th century when one of them moved to Scotland to support King Robert the Bruce.

Part 2 deals with the family in America from 1635 onwards when William landed near Boston at the age of 14. He was followed by cousins and other more distant members of the family later in the century. They settled in Connecticut and New Jersey and helped to found towns and cities in those states. They later participated in the War of Independence from 1776 and later the American Civil War. We trace the families through to the 1940s and the most recent published census in the United States. I have also been in contact with many members of the family through the www.thelyonfamily.org.uk website. The family can be traced west to California and south to Florida and Texas.

Part 3 returns to the UK to trace families in Lancashire who originated from their Scottish ancestry. We also trace the continuance of the 'royal' family line from Scotland through the Earls of Strathmore to the Bowes-Lyons of the present day and the present Queen of England – Elizabeth II.

There are also many appendices with further information for those who wish to delve more deeply into the family and its connections.

Part1

CHAPTER 1
THE NORFOLK FAMILY
•◈•

Life in the Middle Ages. The Norfolk and Middlesex Branches – after 1066

We start the story by painting a brief picture of life in the 'Middle Ages', it was during this time that the Lyon family came to England and eventually to Scotland. What was life like in these early days? They arrived in 1066 and after and came from what is now known as France which was then made up of several monarchies such as the Normans.

Peerages of England and Scotland

Dukes   The highest title in England, the first was the Duke of Cornwall in 1337. The Duke of Rothesey was the first Scottish Duke in 1398).

Earls   The first in England after 1066 was the Earl of Derby in 1485. There had been Earls in Scotland from 1230 onwards. When King James VI became King James I of England in in 1603 the first Scottish Earl in the Lyon family was the Earl of Kinghorne and later Strathmore on the 7ᵗʰ July 1606.

Viscount   This title was rarely used in Medieval England

Barons   There were many Barons - Baron de Ros was the first in 1264. Sir John Lyon (1340) was made a Baron in the reign of King Robert II after he married the King's daughter, Jean.

The first Earl in the Lyon family was the **Earl of Kinghorne.** The title **Earl of Kinghorne** was created in 1606 for Patrick Lyon. In 1677, the designation of the earldom changed to "Strathmore and Kinghorne". The consort of any incumbent would be known as the Countess of Strathmore and Kinghorne. Aside from the Earldom, Patrick held the subsidiary titles: *Viscount Lyon* (created 1677), *Lord Glamis of Tannadyce, Sidlaw and Strathditchie* (1677). Other members of the family owned titles such as; *Lord Glamis* (1445), *Lord Lyon and Glamis* (1607).

> **Elizabeth Bowes-Lyon** (1900–2002), the Queen consort of KING GEORGE VI from 1936 until 1952, and mother of the present Sovereign, was the daughter of the **14th Earl of Strathmore & Kinghorne**.

Knights

William the Conqueror brought over his knights from France and gave them large estates. Knights were not entertainers who jousted for fun at medieval tournaments – they were serious fighting machines, dressed in expensive armour. They raised companies of soldiers from their estates and often built castles to protect themselves from those who would challenge their authority.

The **Lyon** family crest was brought over from France when William invaded in 1066 – it always depicts a rampant lion and changed slightly over the centuries as titles were added.

These Knights sometimes became the noblemen who ran parts of the country for their King or Queen or those in command above them. Their armour was emblazoned with their family crests so that in war or battle their men would rally to their distinct 'colours'. The Knights were primarily land owners on behalf of the Regent at the time. They were expected to pay homage by supporting their rulers and paying their taxes to pay for their battles and other expenses.

We generally have a view of Knights being noble gentlemen, this was often not the case. Some were ruthless rulers of their castles, manors and lands. They exacted tithes and labour from their subordinates and owned their citizens who often had few rights and little choice about who was their master. They were not necessarily honourable men and treated their people as slaves and inferiors.

The story of the Lyon family is replete with members of the family who became Knights and were titled from the early day as we shall see in the rest of this book.

The Church

The Roman Catholic Church ruled parts of Great Britain before William the Conqueror but when he died the Church owned a quarter of the land in England

and much in Scotland and Wales. The Knights and soldiers serving the King were soldiers and needed monks and religious people to pray for them for absolution for their killings of thousands of British people and others. After the Battle of Hastings, for instance, every soldier, including Knights, had to do 120 days penance for every person that he killed. The Church was willing to take over this task and used monks to do penance on the soldier's behalf.

This may sound preposterous in this day and age but this was the practice of the church at that time. William founded abbeys near the site of battles and even as far afield as Selby in Yorkshire. He was indirectly responsible for thousands of deaths in

Yorkshire. He also gave great amounts of money to the abbeys, monasteries and churches to cleanse his conscience. Because of these practices the churches amassed great riches and much land which is still in church hands to this day.

William almost totally Christianized Britain and brought over many French Bishops to head up various dioceses throughout the country. The number of monks grew from, one thousand in 1066, to thirteen thousand in 1215. There were several orders such as Cistercians, Benedictines and other holy orders.

Every village and town eventually possessed a church, the bigger the town or city the more churches it supported. As Normans said they were 'the soldiers of Christ'. The priests started to teach the peasants how to read the Bible in Latin and brought some small amount of education to many. They officiated at feasts and on Sundays and encouraged attendance at their churches, even bringing in laws to fine those who failed to attend.

Some church officials were materialistic, many were humble monks who served their communities and brought comfort in times of troubles. The Church also employed about 10% of the population and had enormous power in the land.

The relationship of the Church with the people changed dramatically in Scotland and England in the 16th century with the arrival of the Reformation.

The Lyon family supported the Church for most of their history and churches in Northamptonshire and Scotland bear witness to their participation in the life of the Roman Catholic Church. The family was split in its loyalty in the 16th century when many followed and some became ministers of religion in the Presbyterian Church. There is no record that I have of a member of the Lyon family becoming a Roman Catholic priest.

The Squires

After the Knights came the Squires who were the shield bearers for the Knights. They were also male attendants, especially on great personages. A squire was a member of the British gentry ranking below a Knight and above a gentleman. He was often the owner of a country estate, usually the principal landowner in a village or town. The word was first used in England in the 13th century. So the hierarchical structure so far was King or Queen, the Dukes, Earls, Barons, the Knights and then the Squires, they made up 20% of the population.

Many of the family were Squires in the early day in particular in England and Scotland where they owned manor houses and sometimes large estates. The first part of the book deals mostly with wealthy members of the family and there are no records of those who lived in poverty.

The Villeins

These were peasants who worked the Squire's or Lord's land and paid dues in return for use of the land. This usually meant labouring for their master; the usage of this land could be passed down but it was never owned by the Villein. He was expected to work for his master for at least three days per week and was attached to a certain manor. The rest of the week he could plant and reap for his own use. To see more about villeins visit the following site.

(http://www.middle-ages.org.uk/villein.htm)

The Peasants

People mostly lived in the country and worked to make 'an honest living'. They worked for the local lord of the manor or the villeins. Most were freemen, as opposed to slaves, they were often poorly paid.

In the 14th century they were often paid 1d (one penny) per day and given up to 3d worth of food for themselves and their families. Contrary to common belief they did not live in one-room houses but evidence recently shows that their houses were made up of three rooms or more often two stories high. Some built their houses with timber provided by their masters and some lived in houses provided by their masters.

They usually paid a rent and were given plots of land to cultivate their own crops. The houses would usually be lived in by the peasant's family and parents if they still lived and some kept cattle or sheep on the ground floor. They were usually crowded and this often caused disease to spread and hygiene was unknown by modern western standards.

The peasants, like the villeins, worked long days for their wages and had only a day or two to themselves and their families, depending on the seasons. Sunday was for worship and religious duties and attendance at church was obligatory at least twice a day on the Sabbath.

Not all of the Lyon family held titles and owned great swathes of lands, some were villeins and some peasants. Some later branches of the family were poor and owned only small plots of land, scraping a living from them. Many are recorded as labourers and some were semi-skilled workers. We do not use the word peasants today but use the term 'working class' or 'underclass' as subservient in status to the 'middle classes'.

The Outlaws

Those who did not conform to the local laws and national laws would be named as Outlaws. These condemned men and women would be driven out of their communities and eventually move to France. They could seek sanctuary in a church for a period of time (usually 40 days) for their personal safety and this enabled those who believed that there had been some injustice would be safe from arrest.

An example of sanctuary is provided in the records of Beverley Minster in Yorkshire where outlaws had to make a full confession of their crimes. When the 40 days were expended they were in mortal danger and had no protection from other citizens. Any citizen who communicated with them could be hanged. Hanging was a common sentence for many crimes which would nowadays earn the perpetrator prison or community service.

Henry II in 1154 brought about many enlightened laws including judging potential criminals before local representatives who formed a jury for a trial. Crimes committed on highways and during feasts and fairs were treated as injuries to the King himself. Travelling judges oversaw the trials and if proved guilty the offender received a sentence.

If a charge was difficult to prove he/she would be tried by water. *(See Terry Jones – Medieval Lives - BBC Books for more information)*

He would be trussed up and thrown into water, and if he sank it proved his innocence and he would be pulled out, but if he floated it proved his guilt and he was given a few days to leave England and never to return. There must have been many criminals in France who didn't speak the local language!

There was no distinction between civil and criminal law and citizens could take others to court for theft or other crimes that demanded restitution. Normally the Lord of the Manor would be responsible for his peasants and villeins and if cases were settled then no further action would be taken. In the 14th century and since the invasion of William the Conqueror, all persons were expected to be answerable to the local lord who took responsibility for his people. The accused would need to obtain the support of local people who would take oaths to support him/her.

In part 3 of the book in more recent times we find a member of the family who was hanged for theft in Lancashire so George Lyon was maybe one of many who would be known today as a 'black sheep' of the family.

Living conditions

The weather dictated the lives for everyone from peasants to Kings and Queens. If the weather was stormy and too much rain fell then the crops would fail for all, despite their status in life. In the 11th century there was such extreme weather either from storms or high temperatures that great numbers died of hunger and disease because of crop failure and the death of cattle and sheep. Starvation across the country was widespread and tens of thousands died. It was so punishing at times that cannibalism was not uncommon. When people lost over 40 per cent of their body mass they usually died in agony having often succumbed to diarrhoea, cholera or dysentery.

For the next two centuries life improved as the weather improved. Tree rings prove the state of the weather in these years and famines almost disappeared for some time. Peasants began eating healthier bread with wholemeal flour that they were provided with and also with enough malt to make several pints of weak or strong beer. Fish was available occasionally if they were near the sea or if they lived near rivers or the Lord of the Manor owned a fish-pond. Cheese was a popular food, as were eels, bacon, meat and sausages at special times.

There was never an abundance of food for peasants at this time and they very much relied on the generosity of their masters and the quality of the strips of land that they husbanded. Infant mortality was high and an agricultural labourer was old at 40. Villeins usually farmed 15 to 30 acres for a fixed rent and were comparatively well off.

The Great Famine started in May 1315 in England having come as a result of years of rain and cold weather across Europe. Crops failed, villages sank into the ground and then disease in the form of the Black Death hit from Europe again. According to some historians maybe more than half the population of the country died between 1315 and 1350. Villages became deserted all over the country and land fell into disrepair. The results of starvation and the Black Death were to damage England in particular for the next century and more. Landless people were able to take over deserted land and wages increased because of general shortage of labourers and skilled people.

These troubles were followed by revolt by the remaining workers famously called the 'Peasants Revolt' led by a man called Wat Tyler. They refused to accept the old system of rule of law and servitude. Land owners realised that they ought to rethink their feudal system of management. They started making their money out of sheep and were able to provide wool and meat for the markets, with far less trouble than employing 'ungrateful labourers'. The owners started to move people off their land and replace the arable land with pasture for breeding sheep and cattle instead. Most villeins disappeared from the land, many moved to become managers of mines and others took up other business opportunities.

The Invasion of England in 1066 by Duke William of Normandy, known as William the Conqueror, who was then crowned King William of England, was one of the most significant events in British history. It influenced history for hundreds of years and was the cause of many wars. It had a significant effect on the relations between England and Scotland. No record exists of any member of the Lyon family in Britain before this date. To see more on the history just prior to the invasion see Appendix A.

William the Conqueror who bore his name for good reason, claimed all the lands he conquered for his knights having scant regard for those who legally owned the land. He ordered his knights to rule these lands on his behalf. They took the local women as ransom and often treated the locals with contempt, stealing their belongings and enslaving them.

When William the Conqueror invaded England he was accompanied by a Leonne 'to whom he gave great honours and lands'. The main sources for this information are in the Battle Abbey Roll and the Domesday Book. The Battle Abbey Roll was a list of all of the followers of King William who came over with him from Normandy. Unfortunately the Abbey where the Roll was kept was burnt down in the 16th Century and the Roll was destroyed. Several historians over the years have tried to re-create this Roll but their results are not consistent with each other.

The Domesday Book was a survey carried out by William the Conqueror in 1086 in which he ordered that the entire country be assessed to see what properties and rights existed, who held them and what they were worth. By this time William had deposed many Saxons from their lands and titles and rewarded his own followers. With the money he accumulated more knights including other members of the Lyon family who were recruited and more land was secured. William's knights played a vital role in supporting the new King of England. They raised companies of soldiers from their estates and often built castles and manors to protect themselves from those who would challenge their authority. By rewarding them with land and titles in England William was protecting himself, honouring those who would give him loyal support, also removing the wealth from many of the Saxon families who might oppose him in future.

It seems to be fairly certain that the first member of the Lyon family to live in Britain was **Sir Roger de Leonne** born in 1040 in Normandy, (first generation). Roger de Leonne is first mentioned in the re-created Battle Abbey Roll as holding lands in Norfolk. The Roll lists several members of the Lyon family.

There are claims that the family dates back to Rome in the third century but I can find no certain proof of that. It seems highly probable that they originated from the French city, Lyons, and Lyons was named by the Romans who built a beautiful amphitheatre there, the Lyons Odeon.

Sir Roger de Leonne, one of the founders of the Norfolk family tree, was born in 1040 in Normandy and came to England in 1066. Roger and his family settled in Norfolk where they held grants of land from William the Conqueror in recognition of their assistance in seizing the English throne. At the time of the Domesday survey a Roger de Leonne was given Melton Constable, a parish in the west division of Norfolk, 5½ miles from Holt. *("MELTON CONSTABLE*

> "This lordship was granted by the Conqueror to William de Beaufo Bishop of Thetford, to be held of him as a lay fee, and in his own right, being his lord chancellour, &c. out of which 4 freemen of King Harold were expelled, and Roger de Lyons held it of the Bishop, with Anschetel the provost, with 3 carucates of land; 2 villains and 32 borderers belonged to it, with 7 carucates and an half; there was paunage in the wood for 60 swine, and 6 acres of meadow, 2 beasts for burden, and 7 cows, &c. and a church endowed with 6 acres valued at 5d. The whole valued formerly at 30s. At the survey at 40s. per ann. and was one leuca long and half a leuca broad, and paid 10d. Gelt".)"

This extract is from William the Conqueror's Doomsday Book. The manor was given by William the Conqueror to the Bishop of Thetford; which was held, under the Bishop, by Roger de Leonne (Lyon); and continued to be held by his descendants for several generations.

Wikipedia says

> "Migration into East Anglia must have been high as by the time of the Conquest and Domesday Book survey it was one of the most densely populated parts of the British Isles. During the high and late Middle Ages the county developed arable agriculture and woollen industries. Norfolk's prosperity at that time is evident from the county's large number of mediaeval churches: of an original total of over one thousand, 659 survive, more than in the whole of the rest of Great Britain. The economy was in decline by the time of the Black Death, which dramatically reduced the population in 1349. Over one-third of the population of Norwich died during a plague epidemic in 1579. By the 16th century Norwich had grown to become the second largest city in England, but in 1665 the Great Plague again killed around one third of the population.
> During the English Civil War Norfolk was largely Parliamentarian". *(http://en.wikipedia.org/wiki/Norfolk#History).*

Norfolk is in eastern England with Cambridgeshire to the west and Suffolk to the south. This branch of the family continues for hundreds of years and eventually merges with other branches of the family namely the Middlesex and Northamptonshire branches as well as many other lines.

A transition in Britain

Both England and Scotland had been ruled by kings and queens for many centuries before the Roman invasion. After the Romans left, Britain was invaded by the Vikings and various other northern tribes from Scandinavia, northern Europe and France. These invaders brought new cultures and laws that still affect our western nations today. The Angles, Saxons and Jutes and others left an imprint on Britain that is still clearly obvious in place names such as *Nottingham*, and hundreds of villages, towns and counties such as *Norfolk* and *Suffolk*. After the Romans left Britain this period became known as the 'dark ages'.

Following the invasion of William the Conqueror in 1066, a new direction towards Christianity and a new system of law ensued. Britain was certainly not a land of barbarians but the 'dark ages' tag referred mostly to pagan beliefs and standards that generally reigned over the land. In recent decades great hoards of treasures have been uncovered showing the advanced cultures that prevailed after the Romans left.

William brought over many French priests and bishops who were ordered to bring the Christian message to the people. He built monasteries, cathedrals and churches in every area of Britain that was reachable. At this time it was common for land to be held by the Church on behalf of the King. The Roman Catholic Church ruled, without opposition, for several hundred years. Rules were enforced that insisted that all members of society should attend mass and other religious practices or be fined. These same laws are still on the books today, but obviously are not enforced.

The Norfolk Family line from the Norman Conquest

This period is fairly well documented in the Memorial books about the Lyon family history published about 100 years ago. Surnames of individuals varied considerably from 'De Leonne' to 'Leonibus', to 'de Lyons' and also 'Lyon'. This is how the information has come down to us. I assume that some used French derivations of the family name, whereas others used Latin and eventually the more English 'Lyon'. It was probably down to the individual as to how they wished to be known.

(1)   **Roger de Leonne** was the first generation of this line. He had lands in Norfolk and his son Paganus (2) was born in 1080. Roger would become the first Lyon to be involved with Scotland.

Malcolm III had ruled Scotland from 1057. After Malcolm's defeat by William I (the Conqueror) in 1072 he still had hopes of gaining land from England. In 1087 William I died and his son William II (known as William Rufus) became the King of England. Malcolm could not settle his border disputes with William Rufus so in 1093 he made hostile raids into Northern England. On his return he was ambushed by the Earl of Northumbria at what is known as the Battle of Alnwick. At this battle both Malcolm and his eldest son Edward were killed. His wife Margaret died within a few days. The Roman Catholic Church later made her a saint and she became Saint Margaret of Scotland.

Glen Lyon

From 1093 to 1097 the throne of Scotland was held by a variety of relatives of Malcolm, many of whom did not live very long. However in 1097 Edgar a son of Malcolm became the King with English support. Roger de Leonne was part of that English support. He went to Scotland and as a reward for his services to King Edgar, the King gave Roger the use of land in Perthshire which was later called Glen Lyon.

Glen Lyon is a very beautiful Glen running from Fortingall for twenty five miles to Loch Lyon. Its river passes through Invervar and Bridge of Balgie. Its main historic features are Meggernie Castle and a 5000 year-old yew tree. There is no evidence that any of the family lived in Glen Lyon at any time but it had value as it was very fertile in places.

See Maps and Illustrations at the beginning of the book.

Glamis

Roger de Leonne was also given other lands in Perthshire which are now known as Glamis (pronounced Glarms). Glamis was also the name of a village founded in the 8th century. Both village and Glamis were at that time in Perthshire but are now in the next county in Angus which is only a few miles from Perth and Kinross County. At that time Glamis was a Hunting Lodge which had been frequented for many years by the Kings of Scotland for hunting deer and other wild animals and for fishing. It was not at that time a Castle but obviously provided accommodation for several days at a time for the sportsmen who used it. It is not known whether Roger lived there at that time or if he lived elsewhere awaiting his next call of duty. It had been a Royal hunting lodge from as early as the 11th century, when King Malcolm II (1005-1034) is thought to have been murdered there on November 25th 1034.

This gift of land to the family has caused problems for professional and amateur historians ever since. The three volumes of the Lyon Memorial refer to the fact that historically the Lyon family are from Glen Lyon in Scotland, others are quick to point out that the Lyon family has never inhabited the area which has caused some friction between genealogists and historians. When the Memorial books indicate that Thomas, Henry and Richard were all from Glen Lyon, this is not meant to indicate that they were actually born there. It is true however that Glen Lyon was the official land of the family at the time of King Edgar. The relationship with Glamis and the surrounding area has continued for hundreds of years up to the present day.

After serving in Scotland for several years Roger returned to Norfolk

(2)   **Paganus de Leonne** was born in 1080, most likely in Norfolk. He claimed to be 23rd in descent from Atulph, King of the Goths in Spain and the brother of Alaric who sacked Rome in 409 AD

Alaric was born in Dacia in the Danube delta to a noble Goth family. The Goths had previously moved from Scandinavia. A description of them recounted that they "all have white bodies and fair hair and are tall and handsome to look upon. They used the same laws and practice a common religion." Many Goths had converted to Christianity before they entered the Roman Empire and a previous bishop, Ulfila, had translated the Bible into Gothic. This is a colourful claim to greatness that would be difficult to prove beyond doubt but it is possible. Paganus, despite his name was a descendant of the Goths and the Vikings, as were his family in Normandy. *(http://ancienthistory.about.com/od/alaricthevisigoth/p/AlaricTimeline.htm)*

It is also claimed that Paganus went to the Holy Lands with Geoffrey Plantagenet, presumably as a Knight Templar or in association with them. Geoffrey Plantagenet was born August 24th 1113 in France. He became a Plantagenet through his marriage to Matilda (1102-1167) who was the only daughter of King Henry I. He became the Count of Anjou (1131-1151). Geoffrey ruled Normandy for a few years then passed it to his son Henry II of England in 1150. Geoffrey died September 7th 1151 at Le Mans. Geoffrey's father Fulk V was the King of Jerusalem from 1131. Paganus would have been 51 years of age and Geoffrey 18 years of age making the trip possible for Geoffrey.

There was around that time a person named Paganus in the Holy Land. This 'Paganus the Butler' built the fortress of Kerak around 1120 He remained as the butler for King Fulk until 1136, in the Holy Land. The Fulk family was related to King Henry II (1154-1189) of England. Geoffrey was the brother-in law of Henry II through marriage.

The question of whether Paganus went to the Holy Land with Geoffrey Plantagenet still remains unanswered. It seems possible that if Geoffrey went to see his father when he was the King of Jerusalem, Paganus could have met him there and sailed back with him to Norfolk. At the moment there is no date offered for the death of Paganus Lyon. King Fulk died in 1143 and Paganus the Butler died in 1148. All this is conjecture, but possible – we shall never know for certain.

(3)   **Hugo de Leonibus** was born in 1120 and was the son of Paganus (2). We know a little about Hugo who is sometimes referred to as Hugh. We are told that he owned lands in Norfolk at the time of Henry II and also lived at the same time as Richard the Lionheart. There is every possibility that Hugo was a Knight and served his superiors, maybe even the King, to obtain lands and favours which was a common practice in those days. Because of his past royal connections in Scotland he would have been acquainted with courtiers such as Ida Isabel de Toeny, Countess of Norfolk, reputed mistress to Henry II and Henry III.

(4)   **Ernald de Leonibus** (1150) was the son of Hugo (3), he also living in Norfolk. He had one son whom he named John (5). "He seized land in Kettleston in Norfolk in the time of King John I (who started his reign in 1199).... The same land greed was a passion with his knights and it besets their descendants even to this day". *(Lyon Memorial II page 11).* This makes Ernald's given date of death in 1175 as incorrect or the information about the possession of this land improbable.

(5)   **John de Leonibus** was born in Norfolk in 1175 and owned many lands in many counties according to the records and he had two sons Pagan (6) and Walter (7). The Memorial does not tell us at this stage which counties, or when or why the Lyons moved to them. Where there are specific records of counties inhabited these have been capitalized the first time mentioned.

(6)   **Pagan de Leonibus** (1200) was born in Norfolk and married Yvette de Ferres who came from Cambridge. They had two sons Sir John (10) and Thomas (11). This is the last time we will see the name Pagan used.

(7)   **Walter de Leonibus** (1205) was also born in Norfolk and he had two sons Henry (8) and William (9).

(8)   **Sir Henry Leonibus**, the son of Walter (7), was born in 1230 in Norfolk - he had no children so this becomes the end of that part of the family line.

(9)   His brother **William de Leonibus**, the son of Walter (7) was born in 1235 in Norfolk and he is also the end of his line.

(10)   **Sir John De Leonne**, son of Pagan (6) was born in 1225 in Norfolk and had lands both in Norfolk and in NORTHAMPTONSHIRE according to the records. He served in the army for Edward I against the Scots in 1294. The records state that he married Margery de Ackle of Northampton.

Edward I (1239–1307) became King of England in 1272, he was often known as Longshanks because he was particularly tall. Edward was a great law-maker and a warrior who fought battles all over England and Wales and Scotland. Sir John de Leonne was knighted at this time continuing the custom of the family to become knights and warriors. Sir John died in 1314 in the reign of Edward II.

(11)   **Thomas Lyon**, son of Pagan (6) was born in 1230 in Norfolk and lived in Woodward, ESSEX, in the time of King Edward I so he would have joined his brother John in serving his King.

(12)   **Sir Adam Lyons** was born in Norfolk in 1255, the son of Sir John (10) and had no family.

(13)   **Baron John de Lyons** was born in Norfolk in 1250 the son of Sir John (10). He had three sons; Adam (14), Richard (15) and John (16). He died in 1316 in Warkworth Castle in Northamptonshire. It is noteworthy that a member of the Norfolk line went to die at Warkworth with the Northamptonshire family which infers that associations between the two branches of the family had been going on for some time.

(14)   **Sir Adam Lyon** was born in 1285 and was the eldest son of Baron John (13). He owned lands in Norfolk and CAMBRIDGESHIRE and had two sons John (18) and Adam (19).

(15)   **Richard Lyon** son of Baron John (13) was born in 1287 in Norfolk and had three daughters Isabella (1336), Cecilia (1338) and Christina (1345) and a son Richard (17).

(16)   **John de Lyons son of Baron John (13)** born 1290 in Warkworth, Northamptonshire. John married Alice de Liz (13001374) and died in 1346. This is a duplication as the same John de Lyons was also recorded in the Northamptonshire (Warkworth) line see the chart in the Maps section at the beginning of the book. John was of the Norfolk line which merged with the Northampton line at this time, hence the duplication. They had two children; John (1314) and Elizabeth (1324) – their record should be followed on the Northamptonshire line in the next chapter to avoid further confusion.

(17)   **Richard Lyons** born in 1310 in Norfolk, the son of Richard (15). I am not certain that the following is correct but it makes a good story!

" .. Richard Lyons, who was killed by Wat Tyler ... At the time of his death he held the Manor of Overhall in Liston." --- An eminent lapidary (a cutter, polisher, or engraver of precious stones usually other than diamonds - Merrian-Webster dictionary) and wine-merchant in London, and one of the sheriffs in 1374. It is said that Wat Tyler, leader of the insurgents by whom the city was infested in 1381, had been the servant of Mr. Lyon, Tyler was beheaded during the rebellion. --- Wat Tyler is thought to have travelled to France in the service of Richard Lyons, a merchant from London --- On the 12th June 1381 a detachment of Essex men led by a priest, John Wrawe, came over Ballingdon Bridge and were met by the Vicar of All Saints, Geoffrey Parfrey and a group of Sudbury men.

They made their way to Liston Hall, about three miles north of Sudbury, which belonged to Richard Lyons a wealthy merchant and notorious moneylender and destroyed it. --- The first move of John Wrawe was to march to the Manor House of Liston, wreck it and burn all the records. This was not a haphazard choice, for the Manor belonged to Richard Lyons, wine merchant, financier and lender of money to the Royal family. Lyons was not liked by the East Anglians as he sat in Parliament for Essex during 1379-80 he had achieved little for his constituents.

And before that, in 1376, he had been impeached by Parliament for fraud and for other misdemeanours and his goods and land taken away from him-to be given back to him a little later through, it is thought, the help of Alice Perrers later."

(http://www.foxearth.org.uk/ListonMiscellany.html)

Richard died in London in 1381.

(18) **Sir John Lyon** son of Adam de Lyons (14) born 1320 – sons Richard (20) John (21) Henry (22)

(19) **Sir Adam Lyon** son of Adam de Lyons (14) born 1325

(20) **Sir Richard Lyon** son of Sir John (18) born 1350 with lands in OXFORD, CAMBRIDGE and HUNTINGDON.

(21) **Sir John Lyon** son of Sir John (18) born in 1353 with lands in Kingsland (MIDDLESEX), SUFFOLK and Norfolk.

(22) **Sir Henry Lyon** son of Sir John (18) born 1355 with lands in Norfolk and later Ruislip, Middlesex. He is also the **head of the Middlesex** line of the family.

The Norfolk line then becomes the Middlesex line. See the Maps and illustrations at the beginning of the book.

Genealogy

Members of the Lyon family have started to research their family in the UK, USA and many other countries. Most have taken their information from the Web and various sources such as Ancestry.com and all other genealogy sites. This saves time and provides an immediate database of millions of entries from other researchers. There are estimated to be over one million members of the family who have used Ancestry alone, not to mention many other providers of data.

My own research endeavours to evaluate and cross-check those sources, so what I hope to deliver to you is a well-researched, composite conclusion from the many and often contradictory sources that currently exist.

The generally accepted view is that the Norfolk family tree from 1066 is the most reliable and that it provides the proof of the parentage of Sir John Lyon (1340) who became the Chamberlain of Scotland under King Robert II of Scotland towards the end of the 14th century. He is believed to be the son of John Lyon who was born in 1314 in Scotland who in turn was the son of Sir John de Lyons (1289/90) who is generally claimed to be from Norfolk but I believe is from the Northamptonshire Warkworth line.

See entry No 16 Sir John Lyon (1290) on the table at the front of the book. For those wishing to delve more deeply into these genealogical issues please move to Appendix B where an attempt is made to resolve these matters.

John Lyon (1340) the Chamberlain of Scotland was married to the granddaughter of King Robert the Bruce. Because of this marriage Glamis became the home of the family to this day and the present Queen and her family are all descended from the Lyon family and particularly from a John Lyon born in 1314 in Scotland.

The Middlesex Lyon family line

Genealogists claim that a Sir Henry Lyon who was born in 1355 in Norfolk was a son of Sir John (1314). However Sir John Lyon (1314) is recorded as only having had one son namely Sir John Lyon born in 1340 in Scotland who was later to marry the daughter of King Robert II of Scotland. See Chapter 3 for more information on the matter.

An inspection of my list of the Norfolk line will show that Sir Henry (1355) (entry No 22) was the son of Sir John Lyon (18) born in 1320 in Norfolk. He had two brothers Sir Richard (1350) of Oxford, Cambridge and Huntingdon and Sir John (1553) of Kingsland, Suffolk and Norfolk. This business of sorting out the Johns from the Johns has caused so many mistakes by genealogists that can be challenged now that we can see so much information available on computers.

It is not possible after all these years to verify the claim for Sir Henry but possibly sufficient to say it is doubtful that Sir John (1314) went to Norfolk for Henry's birth when in fact his family were from Northamptonshire and he was in Scotland at the time. There is no record either in Scotland or in England of a Sir Henry as the son of Sir John (1314) and I can only surmise that this is a false claim made to claim to be part of the Royal family line in Scotland.

For those wishing to look at the complete Middlesex line in detail go to Appendix C.

The Middlesex line – achievers of the family line

The names in brackets are the known ancestors from the father back to the verifiable records.

John Lyon (Sir Henry) was born 1380 in Ruislip, Middlesex and died in 1425.

Henry Lyon (John, Sir Henry) born in 1410 in Ruislip, died in 1460 in Perifere, (Perivale), London. He married ELIZABETH DENNIS BERKLEY who was born in 1412.

They had four children;
1   **Henry Lyon** 1440-1477, Norfolk.
2.   **John Lyon** born 1450, Preston, Middlesex.
3.   **Thomas Lyon** born 1453-1550
4.   **William Lyon** born 1460-1508 – no children. EOL (end of line)

I have only noted below those members who are of interest because of their achievements.

John Lyon (John, Henry, John, Sir Henry) was born in 1500. His father John was born 1450 and married John's mother EMMA HEDDE born about 1470.

He founded Harrow School, one of the top private schools in the country – he is described as a wealthy landowner who started the school for poor children in Harrow, Middlesex. The story is worth telling:

"The **Free Grammar School of Harrow**, an establishment which has gradually acquired such high reputation for learning and good conduct as to rank at present amongst the eight great schools of England, (The eight principal Public Schools of the kingdom are considered to be those of Winchester ; Westminster; Eton; Harrow ; The Charter House ; Merchant Taylor's ; Saint Paul's; and Rugby.) Like most foundations of a similar nature, proceeded from a small beginning. In the 14th year of Queen Elizabeth I, **John Lyon** a wealthy yeoman of Preston, in this parish, procured letters patent, and special license from the crown, for perpetuating his benevolent intentions with respect to gratuitous instruction, and other pious and charitable purposes. He drew up, with most minute and elaborate care, a code of Regulations for the government of his Foundation.

This curious document is entitled;

Orders, Statutes, and Rules, made and set forth the Eighteenth day of January, in the three and thirtieth yeare of the Raigne of our Soveraigne Lady Elizabeth, &c. by me, John Lyon, of Preston, in the parish of Harrow on ye hill, in ye county of Middlesex, yeoman, Founder of ye Free Grammer Schoole in Harrow, to be observed and kept by the Governors of ye Lands, tenements, goods, and possessions of ye said Free Grammer Schoole. Within the towne of ye Hill, meete and convenient Roomes for the said Schoole Mr. and Usher to inhabite and dwell in; as also a large and convenient Schoole house, with a chimney in it. And, alsoe, a celler under the said Harrow upon Roomes and Schoole house, to lay in wood and coales ; which said Celler shall be divided into three several Roomes; ye one for ye Mr. the second for the Usher ; and ye third for ye Schollers.

He directs that if such intention should not be carried into effect previous to his decease, the sum of 300 L. (pounds) should be appropriated to that purpose by certain Governors, the appointment of whom he then regulates."

John Lyon was a member of the Middlesex Lyon family. The differences between the branch of the Middlesex Lyon family and the more Scottish branch of the family will become quite evident.

The Middlesex line is no doubt correct in many ways but towards the end of the 4th Generation there seems to be a preponderance of Richards, Henrys, Johns and Williams, all vying to be the future emigrants to America. It is strange that the dates often differ from the most common hints and leads when doing searches.

There is even doubt cast by some websites over whether William (1620) who was the first Lyon migrant to America was the William of the Middlesex branch. I think there will always be a vested interest in claiming an ancestor who is important but most of us have to be satisfied with a family tree leading us nowhere. Illegitimacy was common and must account for many faults for genealogists to sweat over.

Lords of the Manors in Scotland and England employed many people and as surnames were not common in the middle-ages. People were often referred to as John the ploughman or John of Glamis and sometimes John Lyon, adopting the name of the Lord of their manor. This causes immense problems to historians and record keepers through the ages. Without birth certificates, marriage or death certificates, there is little evidence of father and mother. Many hidden and seemingly lost records are in local parish and church registers but this requires a visit to the church of local library and is time consuming.

There can be little doubt that all the Lyon and Lyons families are related to the original members of the family in Scotland. When we study the family in the USA we can see how very quickly the name Lyon or Lyons appears all over the country and in Canada, Australia and even Germany and all over the rest of the world. Just as many families like my own came from France at the turn of the Millennium and have grown enormously since then with many variations so it is so with the Lyon family. With the census entries we find Lyon spelled in many ways, either because the census taker did not hear correctly, or wrote down the name incorrectly or the copiers for the census could not read the writing.

Sir John Lyon - Lord Mayor of London - 1554

He was voted as the Lord Mayor of London in 1554, in the reign of Queen Mary (1553-1558). He was a Grocer by trade. Little is known about him except these bare facts on the list of past Mayors of London.

The claim to be the first emigrants to America according to the Middlesex line genealogical supporters.

William Lyon II (William I, John, John, Henry, Henry, John) born in 1580 in Stanmer Parva, Middlesex. He married ANNE CARTER, born in 1594 in London and they both died in 1634 in London. He had 3 children:

Katherine Lyon born 25th October 1616 in London, died 1720 in Picardie, France,

John Lyon (1617-1617) died as infant.

William Lyon III who was born 13th December 1620 in Cambridge (?) This is not proved., He died on 16th May 1692 in Roxbury, Massachusetts, USA?

Richard Lyon (brother of William II) (William I, John, John, Henry, Henry, John) born 1590 in Heston, died 17th October 1678 in Fairfield, Connecticut, USA. Married MARGARET unknown who was born in 1630 in Fairfield, Connecticut, she died 23rd March 1705 in Fairfield. They had 8 children all born in Fairfield; Connecticut, America; Samuel (1644 - 1723), Richard (1653-1740), Esther (1658), Elizabeth (1659), William (1660-1699), Hannah (1661-1743), Samuel (1665-1733), Abigail (1673-1698)

The ages of some of these children are uncertain as Abigail would have been born when Richard was 83 years of age! My belief is that this is an attempt by persons unknown to claim that their ancestors were part of the royal line.

Summary of the Middlesex line claim

Many of the facts are correct but Sir Henry Lyon (1355) was not the son of John Lyon (1340) the first Lord of Glamis or of John's father John Lyon (1314). Also the line seems to disappear into obscurity after the early 1600s. We know some went to America but most became lost in history.

The largest concentration of the Lyon family in England after 1650 was in Lancashire, Yorkshire and possibly London and there were many members of the family who remained in Scotland.

CHAPTER 2

THE NORTHAMPTONSHIRE FAMILY

──────•◦❀◦•──────

The Warkworth Line of the Lyon family – after 1066

We have already considered what is known as the Norfolk family. We will now look at the Northamptonshire side of the family often referred to as the Warkworth line.

A **Nicholas de Lyons** arrived in 1080 from France and settled in Northamptonshire. The recognised founder, **John de Lyons**, of the Northamptonshire branch of the family came over with his father Nicholas. He was the first of over one hundred others named John in the future generations of the Lyon family. In French his name would have been Jean de Lyons.

The two Warkworths

Throughout the next few chapters the name Warkworth will appear many times. A presenting problem is that there were two Warkworths, one in Northumberland and one in Northamptonshire. 90% of genealogy entries on the web list Northumberland as the home of a branch of the Lyon family which in my view is incorrect. Northumberland is in the north east of England on the Scottish border whilst Northamptonshire is in central England.

Some previous histories of the Lyon family have stated that some of them settled in a Warkworth Castle in Northumberland. A ruined Warkworth Castle does still exist in Northumberland, however that Castle was granted to Roger Fitz

Richard by King Henry II of England (1154-1189). This was mentioned in a Charter dated 1157 to 1164.

When in 1345 the last of this family died, the Castle was passed by King Edward III (1327-1377) to Henry de Percy. It has been owned by the Percy family for hundreds of years and never owned by a member of the Lyon family. The Percy family have been the Earls and Dukes of Northumberland for many generations until the present day.

They have historically supported the English Royal families because Northumberland was often invaded by the Scots and Warkworth Castle was built as a defence against such attacks. The Lyon family have, on the other hand, usually supported the Scottish cause. It is inconceivable that the Lyon family would ever have lived in the Percy family home, Warkworth Castle in Northumberland.

I think the confusion has arisen because there is another Warkworth, in Northamptonshire. As much of the history of the family is in Northamptonshire this was almost certainly the home of the Lyon family at that time. In fact there was a Baron Lyon of Warkworth, Northamptonshire in the 1400s.

The cause of such confusion can be readily seen with the similarity of the names of the two counties. Adding some family histories describe a Marston St. Lawrence as being in Northumberland, there was never a place by that name in Northumberland. But there is a town of that name in Northamptonshire. It is about 4 miles to the east of Warkworth. These types of errors are easily made when people do not know the geography of a country and make assumptions about a location and blindly follow previous researchers.

Warkworth Castle - Northamptonshire

"Warkworth Castle, in the parish of Warkworth, was formerly the seat of the Woodhulls and the Chetwoods. Little or nothing can be found about the Woodhulls at this time, the Chetwoods were also an ancient family who came to England at the time of William the Conqueror. This handsome castellated mansion consisted of a body and two wings, forming three sides of quadrangle and the centre was flanked with two Bastion Towers, rising to the height of the building, one on each side.

It stood in the large park decorated with fishponds and plantations. On the death of the late owner, Francis Eyre Esquire, the estate was sold, the house pulled down and the pleasure grounds etc. were destroyed (possibly in 1806) ....The Chetewode family is mentioned regarding tomb inscriptions in the local church of people who died in the 1400s."
(Taken from an article in the

Northampton historical records for Warkworth.)

There are comments about Warkworth Castle but generally the evidence is that it was a Manor with mock battlements was maybe not a castle in the accepted meaning of the word. It was earlier the seat of the members of the Lyon family. There are few records of the castle because it was demolished in 1806 as "surplus to requirements – the family had plenty of other property".

(http://lh.matthewbeckett.com/lh_complete_list.html).

This site is so useful because it lists hundreds of explanations of the demise of sites in every county in the country whether castles or manor houses.

The Village of Warkworth

Warkworth in Northamptonshire is today only a small village about 3 miles east of Banbury. The population at present is 5 persons! There is absolutely nothing left of a Warkworth Manor. Drawings do exist which seem to show it, but the building shown is of a far later period than a Norman Castle. It is possible that no medieval castle existed but rather the family occupied a Hall or Manor House.

However in the local Church of St Mary in Warkworth is the tomb of a Sir John Lyons who died circa 1350. This physical evidence should settle the dispute as to whether the family were in Northumberland or Northamptonshire. The recreated Battle Abbey Roll does mention a Sir John de Lyons as Lord of Warkworth in Northamptonshire in 1322. The village itself had a very small population in the 19th century of 25 persons. For more information and pictures visit the website; *www.thelyonfamily.org.uk/warkworth*

The Northamptonshire (Warkworth) Lyon family

This branch of the family is harder to piece together than the Norfolk line because on occasions there is a general lack of information about the whole Warkworth family.

1. **Nicholas de Lyons** was a Norman, from what is now France, who arrived in 1080. His father was Jean Lyons. We know nothing more about Nicholas but we do know that the family was well known in Normandy and Brabant. We have this basic information from the *Battle Abbey Roll Volume II*. Nicholas was the father of Sir John (2)

2. **Sir John de Lyons** also arrived in England in 1080. He had one son John de Lyons (3).

3.   **John de Lyons** born in 1100 had a son named John de Lyons (4). During his lifetime a civil war was fought in England between the Empress Matilda (the daughter of King Henry I) and Stephen who was her cousin. Matilda carried on the struggle for many years before retreating to Normandy in 1148. She had married Geoffrey V, Count of Anjou and had a son Henry. Henry later became King Henry II (1154-1189) of England. These were difficult times to live through and one had to be very careful which side one supported. Note that this Geoffrey is alleged to have travelled to the Holy Land with another Lyon from the Norfolk line – Paganus Lyon.

4.   **John de Lyons** was born in 1140 in Bushby, Leicestershire. Bushby is about 60 miles from Warkworth. He married an Elizabeth de Warkworth in 1170. She was born in 1145 in Warkworth. John died in 1204 in Frampton, Leicestershire. There is no explanation why they lived in Leicestershire but knights travelled around in those days because of civil wars and somehow he met Elizabeth from Warkworth and continued his family there with his son Richard (5).

5.   **Richard de Lyons** was born in 1174 in Banbury near Warkworth and married a Maud (1178–1224), she was also born in Warkworth they had a son Roger (6). Richard died in 1205 in Banbury.

6.   **Roger de Lyons** was born in 1199 in Warkworth. He married a Hawise (1203–1225). They had a son named Roger de Lyon (7) in 1225, it is therefore possible that his wife Hawise died in childbirth.

    It can be assumed that Roger lived at Warkworth where he would have acquired estates and would have employed many workers either in his residence or looking after his lands. This would have at least made him the Lord of a Manor that would have befitted his title. His days as an active Knight may have been over but he would have made sure that he trained his son to follow his own example, serving whichever ruler happened to be in charge of his domain at the time.

    This would have created the pattern for future generations over hundreds of years where the Lyon family would have been adept at providing a service for their rulers, many of them ending up by having very high office in Scotland. Roger died in 1250 in Warkworth Manor.

7.   **Roger de Lyons** born in in 1225 in Marston St. Lawrence in Northamptonshire. Roger married Joan de Napton (1227-1278), she came from Plumpton in Northamptonshire. They had two children; Richard (8)

and John. Nothing is known about this John and every site fails to mention him as far as I can discover.

8. **Richard de Lyons** was born in 1242 in Banbury Northamptonshire, he married Emma who had been born in Warkworth in 1244. They had one son John de Lyons (9).

9. **Sir John de Lyons** was born in 1268 in the reign of King Henry III (1216–1272). He married Margery de Oakley in Northamptonshire. They had three known children Adam (1285), Richard (11) born 1289 and John (10) born 1290.

    "An interesting legal case in Northamptonshire states that a Richard de Seyton had married his ward, Margery de Okley, and had been in possession of her and her land for four years and more when **John de Lyons** (9) carried her off by force against her will and still holds her and her lands. He requested a remedy from the King and Council in 12th October 1284".
    (SC8/256/12792F Northamptonshire Records.)

    Margery died in Great Oakley in either 1297 or 1323. John died in 1312 in Warkworth.

    If a check is made with the Norfolk line it will be noticed that one of its leaders, Sir John (13) (1250-1316) died at Warkworth bringing reconciliation to the Lyon family after years of separation.

10. **Sir John Lyon was born in 1289/90 in Great Oakley in Northamptonshire he married Alice de Liz also known as Alice de Elizabeth or Alice St. Liz in Warkworth in Northamptonshire, the daughter of Sir William de St. Liz. She was born in 1290 in Grafton Regis, Northamptonshire. Sir John moved to Scotland sometime before 1314 when his son John (14) was born at or near Glamis.**

11. **Richard de Lyons**, the brother of John de Lyons (10) was also born in 1289 in Warkworth Northamptonshire and he married Alice de Senlis in about 1315. Alice was born about 1300 in Warkworth and she died young in 1323. Richard next married Elizabeth de Warkworth who was born in 1324 and they married in 1348. They had two children John (12) who was born in 1320 and Elizabeth (13) who was born in 1325. Richard died about

1371 in Warkworth. This was not the John Lyon of Scottish fame as claimed by many genealogists.

12.   **John Lyon** born in 1320 the son of Richard (11). "John de Lyons (12) was born 1320 in Warkworth Northamptonshire. In 1336 Sir John de Lyons donated a carucate of land [the area a plough team of eight oxen could till in a single annual season] to St Leonard's Hospital near Banbury. In 1376 Sir John de Lyons granted further possessions to Robert, the chaplain of the hospital, he died 1385 without issue, the estate passed to his sister Elizabeth. He married a Margaret St John".

13.   **Elizabeth Lyon** born in 1330 daughter of Richard (11) and died in 1371

14.   **Sir John Baron of Forteviot, Forgandenny and Drumgawan Lyon, the son of John (1289) (10) was born in 1314 in Scotland.**
       See Chapter 3 for more details of his life.

15.   **Elizabeth Lyon** was born in 1324? She was the daughter of John (10) and married Sir Nicholas Chetewode born about 1300 (some say Sir John Chetwode). She later married about 1339 Richard de Wydeville who died about 1371.

Northamptonshire in the 14th century

Northampton became the third largest town in England at that time. Many villages were abandoned because of the Bubonic Plague (1348-1350) and many starved to death because of the Great Famine from 1315 to 1317 earlier in the century. The result of these and other calamities reduced the population by about 40 percent. Because of so many deaths and therefore a shortage of labour, the wages were largely increased and many landlords left their estates because this did not help them to prosper. It could well be that the Lyon family found Scotland more hospitable and many left England for good.

Great Oakley, Northamptonshire

Sir John de Lyons (1268) married a Margery de Oakley in Northamptonshire and died there in 1323, she was the mother of Adam (1285), Richard (1289) and John de Lyons (1289), sometimes recorded as 1290.

From the 11th century Great Oakley probably had a resident Lord of the Manor. The Oakleys and their successors -- the **"Lionses"** (presumed these are the **Lyon** family), Imworths, Druells, and Lovetts -- were relatively minor land-owning families with few interests elsewhere, who exercised power and authority on a parochial rather than on a regional or a national stage. Some took a close interest in village and manorial affairs, witnessing local charters and entering into agreements with other landholders.

Changing economic and social conditions in the 15th century enabled some tenants to accumulate land, suggesting that differences in wealth and status widened as the population declined. Migration was fairly common and there is little indication of sustained depopulation.

Manor Courts and Officers

Regular manor courts were probably held by the Oakleys and their successors from the 13th century. This court could impose fines for misdemeanours and a tenth of the proceeds were sent to the King, the remaining proceeds would be kept by the lords of the manor. In 1329, following the division of the manor between the daughters of Richard of Oakley, both Nicholas de Tolthorp and **"Richard de Lions" (Lyons)** were summoned to respond to a plea of quo warranto - (an English writ formerly requiring a person to show by what authority he exercises a public office, franchise, or liberty). It is likely that one or more courts continued to be held, the profits of which were divided between the two lords.

Family sizes

It may have been noted that according to the records few families had more than one or two children. Roger's family is noted as having three children whereas most records provide the names of only one child. The possible reason for this custom was to only publicise the eldest child or the one who would inherit the estates. In the next generation we will see more children listed. Normally family trees can grow very large over six generations. Later on in the book we will see that families of over 12 children and sometimes as many as 18 children are recorded.

In the Northamptonshire chart we have a duplicated claim that Sir John's (1289) father was a Sir John de Lyons who was born in 1268 and died in 1312. He had married a Margery de Oakley and they had three sons; Adam, Richard and John (1320). The birthplace of the three sons is not generally recorded. This MUST be the same Sir John (1289) so the records have been duplicated as both Johns are recorded as having been married to an Alice de Liz (1300-1374 in Norfolk line and (1290-1374) in the Northamptonshire line.

"The tomb of this Sir John Lyons (1320) is in the parish church. He
is in plate armour; each elbow gusset is decorated with a lion's face; his
shield, charged with a lion rampant, is on his left arm: and the upper

part of it is sustained by a small lion seated on his breast: his feet rest on a couchant lion. He reposes on his helmet, surmounted by his crest, a talbot's head issuing out of a ducal coronet."- *George Baker, Northamptonshire Records.*

Sir John de Lyons (1320) died in 1371 in Warkworth, Northamptonshire, this Sir John was the nephew of Sir John (1289) and is the son of Richard de Lyons (1289).

The move to Scotland for Sir John Lyon (1289)

In my research I can find no historian who has tried to explain this important move and it has taken many months of my time to reveal plausible reasons for the change of direction from England to Scotland for Sir John and Alice. As far as I am aware this is the first time that this possible explanation has been mooted.

Sir John was the son of a Knight, either Sir John de Lyons (1250) from Norfolk or Sir John de Lyons (1268) from Northamptonshire, during reigns of Edward I (1272-1307), Edward II (1307-1327) and Edward III (1327-1377).

Why did Sir John de Lyons leave England for Scotland as a young man? His son John Lyon was born in Scotland in 1314. His wife Alice de Liz was the daughter of William de Liz who was born in Scotland in 1274 but who was from a family from Banbury, Northamptonshire. Despite his family being established in Northamptonshire for several generations, Sir John moved back to Scotland where his family owned lands in Perthshire, given to them by King Edgar in 1097. Some reasons need to be provided as to why Sir John moved to Scotland before the birth of his son there in 1314. It is necessary to see the importance of King Edward I of England and his son Edward II, to clarify this story.

Edward I (reigned 1272 to 1307) was a warrior of immense physical strength. His knights called him 'Longshanks' because of his long legs. He was also a great churchman, he was an associate of Popes and Cardinals and was an efficient administrator. He was quite conventional but used the feudal observances to his own great advantage – "he was playing with feudalism, not against it".

He left for a crusade in 1270 and went by ship to the Holy Land where he was remembered for slaughtering the entire population of Nazareth. He heard about his father's (Henry III) death when he was in Sicily but it took him almost 2 years to find his way back to England where he returned for his own coronation in Westminster Abbey. When Edward returned he demanded that his Knights provide warriors to fight in France. The Scottish Parliament at Scone angrily rejected the English demand for Knights service in France.

The forfeiture of all English barons holding lands in Scotland was announced. This concerned Sir John whose family still owned Scottish land given to his family by King Edgar in 1097. In 1295 John Balliol, who was briefly the King of Scotland from 1292, signed an alliance with Philip the fourth of France each undertaking to help each other against any English aggression.

The forfeiture of Scottish lands would have directly affected the family of John de Lyons (1289) of the Northamptonshire line as the family still owned lands in Perthshire gifted by King Edgar (1097-1107) in 1099 to John's family who were in Norfolk at the time. In 1296 the English attacked the French, in support the Scots attacked the English in Cumbria. Edward I invaded Scotland with a huge English army including 11,000 Welshmen. They captured Edinburgh and continued north to Elgin. John Balliol was beaten and the Stone of Destiny, the Scottish regalia and other relics were carried off to London. The King of England, Edward I, presided over the Scots Parliament at Berwick.

The first fact to be noted is that King Edward was antagonistic towards the Scots and he had already taken all Scottish lands from John's father. His son Edward II joined in the persecution of those associated with the Knights Templar, and it is my belief that this caused even more havoc for the Lyon family in 1307. Both John (1289) and his father (1268) could have been associated with the Knights Templar like their forebears in Norfolk. They would have had to flee to Scotland to safety. Sir John's move to Scotland before the birth of his son could also have been as a result of his relationship in the past with Robert the Bruce, both being of Norman stock.

After researching the Knights Templar and their history it became evident that there was another likely reason for John's move to Scotland. It was noted previously that some of the Lyon family had been to the Holy Land and it is very possible that Sir John Lyon was either a Knights Templar or Hospitaller and was driven out of England with his father by King Edward II in 1307. We also know that his father lost their lands in Scotland to Edward I. King Edward II plundered the assets of the Templars in England and any who left for safety in Scotland would have been stripped of their belongings even if they were Hospitallers or Knights of St John.

Sir John de Lyons (1289/90) and King Robert the Bruce

Sir John Lyon was born in 1289/90 in Great Oakley in Northamptonshire he married Alice de Elizabeth (St. Liz) in Warkworth in Northamptonshire, the daughter of Sir William de St. Liz. Sir John moved to Scotland sometime before 1314 when his son John was born. We still need to consider how it was that John Lyon was born in Scotland in 1314. This was the time of the Battle of Bannockburn.

The Battle of Bannockburn

"The Scottish force was composed largely of infantry, with few archers and little cavalry. Bruce placed his men between two stretches of uneven and boggy ground, so the English had to attack against a narrow front. This negated the English superiority in numbers, which has been estimated at three to one.

Bruce's tactics worked to perfection. The English cavalry hurled charge after charge against the massed spears of the Scottish front, to little effect. The Scottish cause was aided when a large group of their camp-followers was mistaken by the English for fresh Scottish troops, and the English army broke ranks and fled. The flight of the English troops was hampered by the boggy ground, and many were cut down by the pursuing Scots. The lack of Scottish cavalry limited pursuit, however.

Bannockburn was the decisive blow in establishing the independence of Scotland from England. Although the English refused to recognise the fact until the treaty of Northampton 14 years later, Bannockburn set the seal on Scotland's bid for freedom. Robert the Bruce is rightly remembered as a national hero for his role in ridding Scotland of the English yoke, at least for a time".

(http://www.britainexpress.com/History/battles/bannockburn.htm)

The influence of the Knights Templar on the Lyon family.

The Knights Templar arrived in Scotland in 1307. There is a possibility that Sir John de Lyons was a member of the Knights Templar, maybe a Serjeant by rank, who had to flee from England to escape King Edward II (1307-1327) in 1307. He most likely returned to England when the Knights Templar had been given back their seized lands in 1321.

The Knights Templar, or as they became later, the Hospitallers or Knights of St John might have been involved in the upbringing of John (1314) and taught him the essentials of finance, diplomacy and manners of court. John would have learned discipline from an early age and learned how to address his elders and to behave seemly at all times. He would have learned the rudiments of knighthood and its privileges, he would have learnt the art of swordplay, archery and hunting. He would have learned about the history of the Kings of Scotland and France and England and been fluent in French and Latin besides English.

John Lyon (1314) was also no doubt friendly with the young King David, the son of King Robert Bruce. David himself was looked after at one time by the Earl of Mar who was acting as Regent after the death of King Robert the Bruce in 1329. He may also have looked after young John Lyon as if he was part of the Royal family.

King Robert had offered protection in Scotland and would have been pleased to invite the Templars with their riches, knowledge of finance and organisational skills to help him in his fight against the English King. As he had been excommunicated from the church he would have been more than happy to welcome these persecuted men who were suffering at the hands of the King of France and the Pope. Some of their leaders had been put to death and burned at the stake in France. Some escaped to England and then to the Highlands and all over Scotland where they were made welcome.

Masonry was not new to Scotland, King Malcolm III in 1031 had been made the first Grand Master of the Masons Guilds, Alexander I, David I had all been Grand Masters prior to Robert coming to the throne. For more details of the old Masonic guilds in Scotland read Appendix J.

The return to England

Having come from Northamptonshire in the first place John (1289) would want to return to his family when the opportunity arose. We also know that he was called to service by the English King Edward II in 1322. We know that John de Lyons died in Northamptonshire in 1346 at the age of 56. After his sojourn in Scotland he received the following writ to serve his English King.

"In Oxfordshire, John de Lyons of Begbrooke (Begbroke in Oxfordshire is about 20 miles from Warkworth), received a writ of military summons in 1322 (Palgrave's Parliamentary Writs). This was Sir John de Lyons, Lord of Warkworth in Northamptonshire, whose genealogy is furnished by the county histories. He was sixth in descent from Nicholas de Lyons, and the son of another Sir John, who had married the co-heiress of Great Oakley and Preston Capes (Margery de Oakley).

His own wife, Alice, had a share in the inheritance of her father, Sir William de St. Liz; and in 1319 he made over to her "all his goods moveable and immoveable in his manor of Beckbroke, with investiture or livery of his lands and their daughter and sole heiress, Elizabeth, married first Sir Nicholas (others say Sir John) Chetewode, and secondly Richard Widville".

John and Alice had a daughter Elizabeth Lyon born in 1324 in Warkworth.

It is extremely likely that Sir John Lyon (1289) helped King Robert to formulate and sign the Treaty of Edinburgh and Northampton because he obviously knew the territory and would have friends in the area of Northampton who could help them to make the arrangements for the signing of the Treaty that was signed on

17th March 1328. Obviously the fact that he spoke French fluently, the language of the court at this time, would have been a great advantage.

Another advantage enjoyed by Northamptonshire, it was on a very direct route to London and Edinburgh and a path well-trodden by both King Robert and King Edward II. As a large town in its day it was a good choice for signing the Treaty of Edinburgh and Northampton which hopefully provided peace between the two kingdoms for some time.

CHAPTER 3

SCOTLAND, THE KNIGHTS TEMPLAR
AND ROBERT THE BRUCE

—•❀•—

The Lyon family in Scotland from John Lyon (1314) until King Robert II and John Lyon (1340) - the Royal Chamberlain

At the time of the Norman Conquest of England, Scotland had generally had good relations with the Wessex rulers of England. In 945 AD King Malcolm I had annexed Strathclyde in Scotland as part of a deal with King Edmund of England. His successor was Malcolm II who was reputedly murdered at Glamis in 1034. This is of interest to members of the Lyon family because in the future Glamis would become the heart of the family. However in 1034 it was just a Royal hunting lodge, not the Castle that it would later become.

Following Malcolm, in 1034 Duncan I became King of Scotland. His reign was marred by failed military adventures. He was eventually defeated and killed by Macbeth who became King in 1040. Macbeth is the subject of 'the Scottish play' by William Shakespeare who had his main character reside at Glamis Castle, even though at that point in history the Castle had not been built and Macbeth had no connection with Glamis. Macbeth ruled for seventeen years until he was overthrown by Malcolm III in 1057.

King Robert the Bruce (reigned 1306-1329)

According to most historians, Robert the Bruce was born on July 11th 1274 at Turnberry Castle, Ayrshire. He had married Elizabeth in 1302. His father was Robert VII de Brus, who died in 1304. His mother was Margery Countess of Carrick. As a young man Robert the Bruce had family connections with Louvain and Brabant in what is now Belgium but was then part of France. The Brus (an original spelling) name could well refer to the City of Brussels, now the capital of Belgium, in Brabant. Some historians believe that the name originated from Vikings who invaded France many years earlier and inhabited Brussels and Normandy.

"Robert VIII the Bruce (1274-1329) was the latest of eight generations of French barons bearing the same name. Robert I from Breaux, Normandy (died 1094), he was a companion of the William the Conqueror and was given a new family seat at Skelton in Cleveland. Robert II (died 1141), was a companion of David I of Scotland (reigned 1124-1153). Robert VI (died 1295) known as 'the competitor' was a companion of Henry III (r. 1216-1272) at the battle of Lewes in Sussex and was an opponent of John Balliol who claimed the Scottish throne. Robert VII (died 1304) had accompanied Edward I (r. 1272-1307) on a crusade in 1269 to 1274 and had asked for John Balliol's Crown. He was very firmly refused by the King". *(The Isles by Norman Davies — the outline of some of this information is used from this excellent book.)*

Robert VIII, as the Earl of Carrick, paid homage to Edward in 1296 for his Scottish lands. He later helped William Wallace in his opposition to the King in 1297 and again in 1303. On a trip to London to visit the joint Anglo-Scottish Parliament he saw the head of Wallace still hanging on London Bridge and like many Scottish lords was disappointed by the meetings at Parliament.

On 10th February 1306 Robert the Bruce met John Comyn of Badenoch at Greyfriars Kirk in Dumfries. A fight broke out, daggers were drawn and Robert the Bruce killed Comyn by the altar. The Pope excommunicated Robert the Bruce but Robert Wishart, Bishop of Glasgow, absolved him and made plans for Bruce to quickly take the throne. Robert the Bruce came to the throne on 10th February 1306 and was invested at Scone near Perth on 27th March 1306.

In 1306 King Robert the Bruce eventually took the throne back after ten years of rule by the English. This was an extremely significant move for the Lyon family.

The question of why John moved to Scotland at this time has never been completely answered to my satisfaction. He may have been asked to come to Scotland by King Robert the Bruce, because of previous family connections, to give him support and advice in running the court. John would have been fluent in the language of the court, which would have been French. It could be that he had met King Robert on one of the King's many forays in England. Their family backgrounds were very similar, both had come from Normandy and Brabant in what is now Belgium. Also as the lands and estates of the Lyon family had been taken by Edward I, John would have seen the possibility of regaining them from King Robert.

It does, however, seem certain that Sir John Lyon moved to Scotland at about this time when he was in his twenties because his son John Lyon was born in 1314 in Scotland and it is claimed lived at Glamis where his son's adventure would change the family's history.

The history and importance of Scone
(http://en.wikipedia.org/wiki/Scone_Abbey)

Scone Palace, originally, Scone Priory was a home of Augustinian canons, and church leaders, based at Scone, Perthshire. The earliest mention of Scone is in 710, at which date, and probably for some time earlier, it was the capital of Pictavia, a territory that is supposed to have been that part of Scotland lying north of the river Forth. Scone continued to be the Pictish capital at least up to AD 843, when the Pictish kingdom came to an end, and was by conquest (the battle of Scone) amalgamated with that of the Scots under Kenneth McAlpin. Under its various Kings it lasted two centuries, or until the dynasty became extinct in 1029 under Malcolm II. Kenneth McAlpin was the most powerful man of his time, he lived and died at the Palace of Forteviot, a Royal residence that has long since disappeared.

It is recorded that Hallhill, near Forteviot Church, was a summer residence of Malcolm Canmore (1058–1093) and other Scottish Kings. The Mill of Forteviot, mentioned by some writers, was a place of some note. The miller's daughter is said by tradition to have been the mother of King Malcolm. On the night before the battle of Dupplin, 31st July, 1332, Edward Baliol with his troops encamped on the miller's acre close to Forteviot. Malcolm was buried at Iona in 860; all the Kings down to Edgar in 1098 were interred there. They regarded Iona as the Holy Isle, where it was thought essential that their bodies should rest if they expected happiness in a future state.

The Abbey was not founded till 1115, Scone was an important place long before that period. The most ancient Council in Scotland of which we have any record was held on the Moothill of Scone in 906, at which date it received the title of the Royal City. Skene, a well-known historian, is of the opinion that Scone was a Royal city before the reign of Kenneth.

The history of Scotland, up to the Reformation, may be divided into four periods;

(1)   the Roman period, terminating in 420;
(2)   the Pictish period, terminating in 843;
(3)   from this date to the Norman Conquest of 1066;
(4)   and from the Norman Conquest to the Reformation of 1560.

"From 843 to 1066 there were nineteen Kings under the new monarchy, and some of these evidently resided at Forteviot Palace, Scone, and the Castle of Perth. Scone, however, continued to be a place of great importance, on account of the ordinance of Kenneth McAlpin appointing the Scottish Kings in future to be crowned there, in the chair which it is alleged he brought from Dunstaffnage, and which he ordered to be kept perpetually at Scone."

(http://www.electricscotland.com/history/perth/vol1chapter5.htm)

This ordinance was observed up to 1651, when the last coronation took place; but all the Kings were not crowned at Scone. It was believed that no King had a right to reign in Scotland unless he had first, on receiving the Royal name, sat on the sacred chair. An ancient myth identifies it with the stone which Jacob used at Bethel for his pillow, and anointed with oil, which was afterwards removed to the Second Temple and served as a pedestal for the Ark. This is, of course, mere tradition.

Brief timeline history of Scotland and Scone;

843   King Kenneth McAlpin defeats the Picts to become the ruler of Scotland. It is said he brought with him the Stone of Scone.

906   King Constantine II holds the first ever national council on Moot Hill – Scone. Here he affirms the laws of the Christian faith. Scone was known as the Pictish capital before the amalgamation of the Picts and Scots.

1040   MacBeth becomes the King of Scotland. Contrary to modern popular belief, he ruled wisely and well for 17 years until he is slain by Malcolm III.

1114   Alexander I founds an Augustinian priory at Scone. The priory later becomes an Abbey within the Bishopric of Dunkeld.

1210   The first parliament is held at Scone. These parliaments continue to make the laws of Scotland until the 1450s.

1249   Alexander III becomes the first King of Scotland to be crowned on the Stone of Scone, rather than simply enthroned.

1292   Edward I of England chooses John Balliol to take the crown of Scotland at Scone Palace.

1296   John Balliol rebels. Edward's troops force Balliol to surrender the crown and Royal regalia and remove the stone to Westminster.

1306   Robert the Bruce (Robert I) is crowned twice at Scone, first by Bishops, two days later by the Countess of Buchan, sister of the Earl of Fife.

1329   Robert I's son, David II, becomes the first King of Scotland to be anointed with sacred oil as part of the crowning ceremony.

1390   Robert II is buried at Scone. Robert III is crowned at Scone.

1398   Robert III creates Scotland's first dukedoms, Rothesay and Albany, at Scone Abbey. Future Kings' eldest sons now become Dukes of Rothesay.

1424   Released by the English 18 years after his father's death **James I** is finally crowned at Scone. He bans football in favour of archery practice.

1488   James IV, 'the ideal Renaissance prince', takes the throne at Scone.

1559   Scone falls victim of the Reformation when, despite the intervention of John Knox himself, 'a riotous mob from Dundee pillaged and burn it'.

1580   Scone Abbey lands are given to the Ruthvens of Huntingtower, who rebuild the abbey palace. Lord Ruthven becomes the Earl of Gowrie in 1581.

1600   The Gowries are disgraced for their alleged conspiracy against James VI. Scone is given to Sir David Murray of Gospetrie, James's cupbearer.

1604   Sir David Murray is created Lord Scone. He is later made Viscount of Stormont, an administrative area in the vicinity of Scone.

1651   Charles I is crowned at Scone. Within months he is defeated by Cromwell at the Battle of Wor cester and forced to flee.

(Scone palace – the crowning place of Scottish Kings. ISBN 085101 3775)

Persecution of the Templars in 1307

There were rumours about the Templars' secret initiation ceremony and King Philip IV of France who had borrowed large sums from the Templars took advantage of the situation. In 1307, many of the Order's members in France were arrested and tortured into giving false confessions, and then burned at the stake. The abrupt disappearance of a major part of the European infrastructure gave rise to speculation and legends, which have kept the 'Templar' name alive into the modern day. The organization had existed for nearly two centuries.

The Knights Templar were occasionally in conflict with the two other Christian military orders, the 'Knights Hospitaller' and the 'Teutonic Knights', and decades of feuds between then weakened their Christian positions, politically and militarily.

After bullying from King Philip of France, Pope Clement then issued the papal bull 'Pastoralis Praeeminentiae' on 22nd November 1307, which instructed all Christian monarchs in Europe to arrest all Templars and seize their assets. Pope Clement called for papal hearings to determine the Templars' guilt or innocence, and once freed of the Inquisitors' torture, many Templars recanted their confessions. Some had sufficient legal experience to defend themselves in the trials, but in 1310 Philip blocked this attempt, using the previously forced confessions to have dozens of Templars burned at the stake in Paris.

The Escape to Scotland of the Knights Templar

When Pope Clement V and King Philip of France affected the successful dissolution of the Templars on 13th October 1307, many knights escaped and some managed to take refuge in the highlands of Scotland. The Scots were currently embroiled in a struggle for sovereignty against their neighbours, England. A significant number of Templars found refuge in Scotland, the only monarchy in 14th century Europe that didn't recognize the authority of the Catholic Church.

Reorganizing under the protection of King Robert the Bruce, they soon found the perfect camouflage to hide their existence in the British Isles. Apart from the state and local governments, the Mason's Lodges were the most powerful organizations of the time, and the Templars first infiltrated them, then brought them under control. Lodges that had been professional bodies were turned into ideological and political organizations, which eventually, centuries later, led to the Freemason Lodges of today.

Another Masonic source estimates that between 30,000 and 40,000 Templars escaped the Inquisition by wearing Mason's clothes and mingling with them, others obtained and used the 'Laissez passer' (free passage) given to Masons. Another large group of Templars is known to have joined the 'Hospitallers'. In England, the Templars were arrested and interrogated, but quickly released again.
(http://www.bibliotecapleyades.net/sociopolitica/templars/knights_templars01.htm.)

Their emerging leader, Robert de Bruce, was then under an order of excommunication issued by the Pope and was at war with Edward II of England and his allies. Consequently, having nothing to lose, Robert gave his approval for the outlawed Templars to be sheltered and merged into the Knights Hospitaller or to take refuge in the Highlands of Scotland, thus enabling them to live out their lives.

The current position of the Roman Catholic Church is that the medieval persecution of the Knights Templar was unjust, that nothing was inherently wrong with the Order or its Rule, and that Pope Clement was pressed into his actions by the dominating influence of King Philip IV, who was Pope Clement's relative.

"Scotland...was at war with England at the time [1307], and the consequent chaos left little opportunity for implementing legal niceties. Thus the Papal Bulls dissolving the Order were never proclaimed in Scotland - and in Scotland, therefore, the Order was never technically dissolved. Many English and, it would appear, French Templars found a Scottish refuge, and a sizable contingent is said to have fought at Robert

Bruce's side at the Battle of Bannockburn in 1314. According to legend and there is evidence to support it - the Order maintained itself as a coherent body in Scotland for another four centuries."

(Baigent, Leigh and Lincoln, the Holy Blood and the Holy Grail.)

The legend of Bannockburn 1314

Seven years later, in 1314, a Sir Henry St. Clair, who was allegedly a member of the Knights Templar, and his two sons, William and Henry, took part in the famous Battle of Bannockburn where the Scots were able to regain an independent Scotland for the King, Robert de Bruce.

An exciting and romantic legend links the Templars to the battle of Bannockburn. The legend tells us that Scots were outnumbered three to one and were struggling desperately against the forces of Edward II, losing men and ground rapidly, when there appeared on the horizon a well-equipped and obviously highly professional band of knights in full armour and mounted on heavy horses. The knights, although superbly equipped and obviously experienced in military battle tactics, bore no markings on their shields and carried no battle standards flying their colours.

These mysterious soldiers joined the battle on the side of King Robert and quickly turned the tide in favour of the Scots who won the battle and freedom for Scotland. The knights then rode off over the horizon without making known their identities or from whence they came.

More recent growth of Templarism

In more recent times there was a large Masonic ceremony near Stirling in remembrance of Robert the Bruce and the battle of Bannockburn which I have included here.

"Corn, as token of Liberty: wine, as an emblem of Courage: and oil as a symbol of Peace — were poured at a masonic ceremony on Wednesday evening at the Borestone on to the foundation stone of the giant granite plinth upon which is to be erected the Statue of King Robert the Bruce at the Field of Bannockburn. The ceremony was attended by about 1000 Freemasons from all over Scotland and was witnessed by a large gathering of people.

The ceremonial was carried out by Lord Bruce, Grand Master, Mason of Scotland, after a silver casket, within a lead one had been placed in a cavity in the foundation stone. The silver casket contained coins dated 1314 and 1964, along, with a message on parchment from the Grand

Lodge of Scotland. The Freemasons, in full regalia and headed by three pipers, had marched in colourful processions from the Whins of Milton School to the Borestone.

The Ceremony was watched by Mr C. d' O. Pilkington Jackson, sculptor responsible for the equestrian statue of Robert the Bruce, which is to be transported here soon and unveiled on 24th June of this year – the 650th anniversary of the Battle.

Her Majesty the Queen will be inaugurating the rotunda, now in process of completion, at Borestone on that day. The procession was headed by Lord Bruce, Grand Master Mason, and the Grand Lodge office-bearers. A former Grand Master Mason, Lord Elgin, was also present at the ceremony". *(http://www.lodge76.wanadoo.co.uk/the_bruce_statue.htm)*

The birth of a form of Freemasonry in Scotland

There is some other evidence to sustain the probability of this early commencement of Freemasonry in Scotland. It is very generally admitted that the Royal Order of Herodem was founded by King Robert Bruce, at Kilwinning. Thory, in the Acta Latomorum, gives the following chronicle:

"Robert Bruce, King of Scotland, under the title of Robert I, created the Order of St. Andrew of Chardon, after the battle of Bannockburn, which was fought on the 24th of June, 1314. To this Order was afterwards united that of Herodem, for the sake of the Scottish Freemasons, who formed a part of the thirty thousand troops with whom he had fought an army of one hundred thousand Englishmen. King Robert reserved the title of Grand Master to himself **and his successors forever,** and founded the Royal Grand Lodge of Herodem at Kilwinning. Doctor Oliver says that the Royal Order of Herodem had formerly its chief seat at Kilwinning; and there is every reason to think that it and Saint John's Masonry were then governed by the same Grand Lodge."

(http://www.phoenixmasonry.org/mackeys_encyclopedia/k.htm - a very useful site for finding Masonic information.)

Robert became a hero in Scotland and in 1320 encouraged his nobles to unite and make Scotland independent with the **Declaration of Arbroath.**

The Declaration of Arbroath was probably written by churchmen at Arbroath Abbey. The Abbot of Arbroath was King Robert the Bruce's head of administration. The document is strongly biased toward Bruce's cause. It attempted to lift King Robert the Bruce's sentence of excommunication and to get the Pope to agree that Scotland was an independent nation from England, to recognise the Scots as a united people and have Robert the Bruce as the King and the leader of the Scots.

King Robert the Bruce had a son David in 1324. David's mother died in 1327.

King Robert's dream was realized in 1328 when King Edward III came to the throne and the **Treaty of Edinburgh and Northampton** was signed, confirming the independence of Scotland. (For those wanting more information visit - *http://iainthepict.blogspot.co.uk/2011/05/treaty-of-northampton.html.*)

As it turned out, the year after the signing of the treaty King Robert the Bruce died of leprosy in his beloved country and his body was taken to Dunfermline Abbey for burial on the 7th June 1329.

The Great Famine

England was in the grip of a great famine and immense poverty was common at the beginning of the 14th century. For most people there was often not enough to eat and life expectancy was relatively short since many children died of starvation. Almost one third of the population died in most of England. The average life expectancy in 1276 was 35 years. Between 1301 and 1325 during the Great Famine it dropped to 30, while between 1348 and 1375, during the Black Death and subsequent plagues, it went down to only 17 years. The Great Famine was restricted to northern Europe, including Britain, northern France, the Low Countries, Scandinavia and Germany.

Stores of grain for long-term emergencies were limited to the lords and nobles. Because of the general increased population, lower-than-average harvests meant many people would go hungry; there was little margin for failure. People began to forage for wild edible roots, plants, grasses, nuts, and bark in the forests. Edward II, King of England, stopped at St Albans on 10th August 1315 and no bread could be found for him or his entourage; it was a rare occasion in which the King of England was unable to eat.

In the spring of 1316, it continued to rain on a European population deprived of reserves to sustain itself. All segments of society from nobles to peasants were affected, but especially the peasants who represented 80% of the population and who had no reserve food supplies. To provide some measure of relief, draft animals were butchered, seed grain was consumed, children were abandoned to fend for themselves and some elderly people voluntarily refused to eat in order to provide food for the younger generation to survive. The chroniclers of the time wrote of many incidents of cannibalism.

The height of the famine was reached in 1317, as the wet weather continued. Finally, in the summer the weather returned to its normal patterns. By now, however, people were so weakened by diseases such as pneumonia, bronchitis, and tuberculosis, and so much of the seed stock had been eaten, that it was not until 1325 that the food supply returned to relatively normal conditions and the population began to increase again. While the Black Death (1338–1375) would kill more people, it often swept through an area in a matter of months whereas the Great Famine lingered for years, drawing out the suffering of the populace.

John Lyon 1314 and King David II

John Lyon (1314) was thought to have been friendly with the young Prince David, the son of King Robert the Bruce. In 1328 at the age of four, David was married to Joan, sister of King Edward II of England (she was seven) as Robert the Bruce tried to establish better relations with England. This was part of the agreement at the Treaty of Edinburgh and Northampton. David's mother had died in 1327.

Following the death of Robert the Bruce in 1329, David was crowned at Scone on 24th November 1331, holding a small sceptre specially made for him, he was only 7 years of age. David himself was looked after at one time by the Earl of Mar who was acting as Regent after the death of King Robert the Bruce in 1329. He may also have looked after young John Lyon as if he was part of the Royal family.

Edward Balliol (son of King John Balliol of Scotland who had been overthrown by King Robert), supported by a number of nobles who had been disinherited by Robert the Bruce, soon started a rebellion. In August 1332 at the Battle of Dupplin Moor, near Perth, Balliol defeated the Regent, Earl of Mar. In September, Balliol was crowned at Scone and thereafter there was a see-saw battle for the throne. He was deposed by supporters of David II in December 1332, restored in 1333 (after the Scottish army led by Archibald, Lord of Douglas, attacked Balliol besieging Berwick Castle and lost at the Battle of Halidon Hill. Balliol was deposed again in 1334, restored in 1335 and finally deposed in 1341.

The young King David was driven into exile in France in 1334, he was 10 years old at that time, but returned from there in 1341, deposing Edward Balliol for the last time. In 1342 John Lyon (1314) would receive the lands of Forteviot and Forgandenny in Perthshire and the lands of Curteton and Drumgowan in Aberdeenshire. He also received the Thanedom of Glamis and its lands. Glamis did not have a castle at this time but was a very popular hunting lodge for the royal families for several generations. He also received the Thanedom of Thaneds, now Tannadyce in Forfarshire.

"The John de Lyons (1314) who in 1334 was summoned to attend the King with horses and arms at Roxburgh *(Rot. Scot., I. 306)*, and in 1343 had charters for lands in Perth and Aberdeen, who obtained the reversion of Glamis, and whose son (John 1340) was Grand Chamberlain of Scotland, was a descendant of Richard of Northampton (1242) - King David had possessions there — and may have been a cousin of the last Sir John." *Lyon Memorial — Thomas Lyon, page 19*

In response to an appeal for help from France, King David invaded England in 1346 but was captured at the Battle of Neville's Cross, remaining a prisoner at the English court until the Treaty of Berwick in 1357. He was returned to Scotland on payment of a large ransom.

Forteviot

A University of Aberdeen team has uncovered startling evidence at Forteviot of a massive Neolithic ritual complex, as well as evidence for the origins of Scottish kingship.

"Forteviot also preserves a much deeper, and hidden, history. The fields around the modern village contain one of the largest concentrations of prehistoric ritual monuments hitherto identified in Britain. Almost nothing of these monuments, built of earth and timber, is visible on the surface, but aerial reconnaissance since the 1970s has recorded the tell-tale crop-marks. The most spectacular is a huge circular palisaded enclosure more than 250m in diameter just to the south of the modern village.

Did early Scottish Kings use a prehistoric ceremonial centre to build their power?"

(http://www.archaeology.co.uk/issues/ca-231.htm.)

On a recent trip to Scotland I visited Forteviot which is near Perth and was rather surprised to find a very small village in a beautiful valley which seem to have no memory of its past. This is a common occurrence with places which were famous in their day but are past that time of distinction and have become ordinary places again.

Sir John Lyon (1314). Some records state that he was born at Glamis, Angus but we have already seen that Glamis was only given to John Lyon in 1342. He married MARGERY ST JOHN, born 1330? Some records state that she was born in Plumpton in Northamptonshire but it is more likely that she was born in

Scotland as her father was on record as living in Scotland at the time of her birth. The records probably indicate the family connection to Plumpton. Her father was descended from another Brabant family, an interesting coincidence because of the Lyon family and Robert the Bruce connection. Some historians have said that her father, John St John III was the son of Jean II "The Peaceful" de Brabant (Duke) and Princess Margaret Plantagenet of England, but records do not support this. John St. John was born in 1296 in Scotland and died on 5th December 1355.

Sir John Lyon (1314) had a son John in 1340 born at Glamis according to the records. I suspect that **John Lyon** (1314) never left Scotland. Some historical records and nearly all genealogical records show the same date of death for both John (1314), the father and also for John (1340), on the 4th November 1382 at Balhall, Forfarshire.

There was a duel recorded between Sir James Lindsay of Crawford and John Lyon (1340), resulting in his death and it is generally presumed that this was John, the younger (1340). It is unlikely that he should have been killed on the same day and in the same place that his father died. So it is probable that we will never know the true date of the death of John Lyon (1314). For those wishing to see genealogical notes about the three Johns and the ensuing contradictions see Appendix B.

Summary to date

The Lyon family had come to England and Scotland from France and had established themselves up to this point in time as respected, upstanding gentlemen and titled land owners. The records available are very limited and there are often inaccuracies, prejudice, poor scholarship and untruths. There is little or no information on the families of the other branches of the Lyon family apart from the heirs to titles and honours.

It should be recognised that these records cover around two hundred years of history and at this time printed records were still many years away in the future. There were of course manuscripts, church documents and personal records of educated families but for ordinary families, many of whom were illiterate, little remains but tales and memories passed down from generation to generation.

Trying to imagine the life that John Lyon (1314) lived is difficult. Sir John (1289) and his mother it seems had returned to England because we know that they died there. They had a daughter, Elizabeth Lyon, born in Warkworth in 1324. The father had returned to Warkworth by then because he was at Northampton in 1328 for the signing of the Treaty of Edinburgh and Northampton. We also have a record of his being called to serve his King Edward II of England.

We can guess that John Lyon (1314) was left in Scotland at the request of King Robert the Bruce or other friends. He was possibly educated there and taught the rudiments of politics as his son John (1340) obviously inherited the ability to confer with King Robert II and eventually became the Lord High Chamberlain of Scotland. John (1314) had been friendly with the young King David, the son of Robert the Bruce. The Earl of Mar who was acting as Regent after the death of King Robert the Bruce in 1329 had looked after young John (1314) as if he was part of the Royal family.

This is all obviously conjecture but if John was found in this position his education would have been considerable, with tutors and advice from his elders and some remaining Knights Templars. He would have been the right man, when he was older, to bring his talents to the household of King Robert II. He married Margery St John who had been allegedly born in Scotland in 1330, there may be an error here; Margery must have been very young when their son John Lyon was born in 1340. It is highly probable that this date of birth for Margery is totally wrong even though in those days people did marry young. There is always another possibility and that is that his real mother is unknown.

There is little doubt about the birth of John Lyon in 1340 as this date is well established by genealogists over the centuries. The very sad thing about all this is that few people have come up with any records about the history of the Lyon family in Scotland and it is disappointing that there is no concrete evidence of much that has been written. I cannot imagine why this should be, because there is much substantiated history about the Lyon family from the Norfolk line and Northamptonshire line.

Sir John Lyon (1340) – the Lord Chamberlain of Scotland

Before we start on the life of John Lyon (1340) we need to understand his relationship with King Robert II of Scotland because he married into the family.

The Children of Robert II – the first King of the House of Stewart

King Robert II had more children than any other King of Scotland, in all 15, by his two marriages. The King's first wife, ELIZABETH MURE OF ROWALLAN, daughter of Sir Adam Mure, had formerly been his mistress. He married her in 1336, but this marriage was said to be 'uncanonical'. Robert and Elizabeth were remarried in 1349 and all of their 10 children were legitimated at this date:-

(1)   **John,** Earl of Carrick (later ROBERT III) c.1340-1406
(2)   **Alexander,** Earl of Buchan 'The Wolf of Badenoch' - 1343-1394
(3)   **Margaret Stewart** m. John Macdonald, Lord of the Isles
(4)   **Walter Stewart** died 1362
(5)   **Robert,** Earl of Albany 1339-1420
(6)   **Marjorie Stewart** m. (1) John Dunbar, Earl of Moray (2) Alexander Keith

(7) **Jean (Johanna) Stewart** married (1) Sir John Keith (2) **Sir John Lyon** (3) Sir James Sandilands

(8) **Isabel Stewart** married (1) James Douglas, Earl of Douglas (2) David Edmondstone.

(9) **Katherine Stewart.**

(10) **Elizabeth Stewart** married Sir Thomas Hay, Lord High Constable of Scotland

The King had a further 5 children by his second wife, EUPHEMIA OF ROSS, daughter of Hugh, Earl of Ross.

(11) **David**, Earl of Caithness died before 1389

(12) **Walter Stewart**, Earl of Atholl died 1437

(13) **Margaret Stewart**

(14) **Elizabeth Stewart** married David Lindsay, Earl of Crawford

(15) **Egidia Stewart** married Sir William Douglas of Nithsdale

He also had 8 illegitimate children by various mothers.
(http://www.englishmonarchs.co.uk/stewart.htm.)

John Lyon (1340), the son of John (1314), became the most famous of the Lyon family and the start of the family line to the present Queen Elizabeth II. There is possibly a problem of his date of birth, some genealogists even say that he is the same John (1314) as his father and miss out a generation. Because of this the deaths of the two Johns is recorded as November 1382, an unlikely coincidence. See Appendix B for an explanation.

The mother of John is recorded as Alice de Liz (1330-1395) it is unlikely that she was his mother as she was only 10 years of age at the time of his birth so either his mother was not Alice or he was born later than 1440 or she could have been born earlier or he had another mother who is not recorded.

He was in the service of the Crown prior to 9th July 1368, and appears in the Charter of Courtastoune granted to him in that year, but the earliest recorded reference to his official position at Court is on January 1368-69, when he is described as 'clericus domini nostri regis' (clerk to his master our King) on his appointment as one of the auditors to examine the accounts of the Chamberlain of Scotland. He remained an auditor until his own full appointment as the Chamberlain. In the same year (1369) he was dispatched on a mission to London, and in the English state papers he is referred to as the 'Clerk of the Privy Seal of the King of Scotland'.

There is a remark about him; "He was a young man of very good parts and qualities, a very graceful and comely person and a great favourite of the King".

This was said by King Robert II in 1372. It is unlikely he was describing his father John (1314) who would have been 58 years of age at the time!

A document, dating from 1372, recorded that John Lyon was appointed **Thane of Glamis** and his fortunes were enhanced still further when he married JEAN STEWART, one of the daughters of King Robert II (1376). He was then made a Royal Chamberlain.

A new ruler King Robert II

On the accession of King Robert II in 1371 John was appointed Keeper of the Privy Seal. On 10th October 1375, Queen Euphemia, the second wife of King Robert II gave him the duty to collect revenues from the Castle of Edinburgh, of which he was then Keeper and made them payable to her. There is an order by the King dated at Dunfermlyn 25th June 1380, directing the auditors of the Royal accounts to allow to John Lyon the whole expenses disbursed by the Chamberlain in fortifying and furnishing the Castle of Edinburgh with provisions, instruments of war and all other necessities.

Where David II's council had been dominated by court knights and esquires whose power and influence were largely dependent on Royal favour, Robert's council seems to have been made up of major regional leaders who exercised authority in their own areas by virtue of their status. John Lyon owned many lands in Perthshire and at that time in Angus with the Glamis estates.

"The financial effectiveness of Robert's administration reflects the one area of obvious continuity from David II's reign, with Robert employing most of the former King's bureaucrats and clerks after 1371. Indeed, some of David's administrators, such as Sir John Lyon, enjoyed 'spectacularly successful careers under the first Stewart King'."

(To read more about the history of this time in Scottish history I recommend the article in the web:

http://www.oxforddnb.com/templates/article.jsp?articleid=23713&back)

On 18th March 1372 Robert II granted John (1340) the lands of Glamis in the sheriffdom of Forfar, for the service of one archer in the King's army. A confirmation of the charter of Glamis was granted on 7th January 1373 by the King's three sons, John, Earl of Carrick, afterwards Robert III, Robert, Earl of Fife and Menteith, afterwards Duke of Albany and Governor of the Kingdom, and Alexander, the 'Wolf of Badenoch', wherein they declare that;

"Considering the deserts of **John Lyon** and his very faithful services, they confirm and ratify the grant for themselves and their heirs, and promise that never in any future time shall they impugn or revoke the same, even if any of them shall attain the Royal dignity."

Glamis becomes the chief seat of the family

From the date of the Royal grant Glamis became the chief seat of the family. Malcolm II had died at Glamis on 25th November 1034, and the national records, in existence; prove that it remained a part of the Royal patrimony until 1372.

On 4th October 1376 King Robert II granted "to his dearest son **John Lyon** and Johanna his wife, the King's beloved daughter", the thanedom of Tannadyce in the sheriffdom of Forfar. *(clanlyon.wordpress.com/2012/05/21/lyon-family-history/)*

On 20th October 1377 he was appointed Chamberlain of Scotland, then the most important office at the disposal of the Crown. This position he retained until his death. A Chamberlain is an officer in charge of managing a household. In many countries these are ceremonial posts associated with the household of the sovereign. In the spring of 1382 he was again engaged in a mission to England.

Sir John Lyon received many lands from the King; Thutiston, Wodhall, Wodely, Haddington, Kinghorne, Doune in Banffshire, Glendowachy, parts of Perth, Fothros and Schenevale, and other lands not listed in the document.

If the reader wishes to examine the source of this information please turn to Appendix D.

Sir John Lyon's wife

Sir John's wife was the PRINCESS JOHANNA (JEAN) STEWART, one of the daughters of King Robert II by his first wife ELIZABETH, daughter of Sir Adam MURE of Rowallan. The Princess had three husbands. On 17th January 1373 she was married to Sir John Keith, eldest son of Sir William Keith, Marischal of Scotland, and she was left a widow on 27th December 1375.

Her marriage to Sir John Lyon took place between 27th June and 4th October 1376, on which latter date the King refers to him as "his dearest son". The dowry of the Princess was the thanedom of Tannadyce. After Sir John's death she married Sir James Sandilands of Calder. The only recorded child of the union between Sir John and the Princess was his son and successor, **Sir John Lyon**, born in 1380.

Sir John Lyon (1340) was slain on 4th November 1382 by Sir James Lindsay of Crawford. The only contemporary narrative of the event is contained in the accounts of Robert, Earl of Fife and Menteith, who succeeded Sir John in the office of Chamberlain and who states that his death took place on the 4th of November, 'suddenly and unexpectedly'.

The deed was done at night when the victim was in bed and unsuspecting. All the early references to the catastrophe indicate the belief of the writers that there was foul play, and Lindsay was compelled to flee from Court to elude the vengeance of the King. The event marked the beginning of a feud between the families which remained unhealed for centuries. Sir John was only 42 years of age when he was murdered.

Brief summary of his life

It would be difficult to imagine how many other honours would have been bestowed upon him had his life not been taken at this time. His father John Lyon (1314) laid the foundation in Scotland for the ensuing members of the family to serve Kings in both Scotland and England over several centuries by training his son in the art of politics and finance. His son John whom we have been studying rose to dizzying heights in such a short lifespan and it was fortunate that he left the family to carry on their service in Scotland.

He had begun to build Glamis Castle, and his wife continued the work after his sudden murder. His heirs have used this glorious memorial to his life up until the present day. This John was truly a great man and was married long enough to produce a family that he would have been proud of who became the Lords of Glamis for hundreds of years and eventually the Earls of Strathmore to this present day.

The great tragedy for Sir John and his King were that the feuds between the Norman rulers and the local clans were never settled and bitterness like poison ran through the veins of some of the Scots for many generations. This would not be the place to name those clans or any members of them, except those who are directly involved in the story of the Lyon family.

Lifestyle of a person in high office at that time

From what we know of John Lyon he must have been a very committed man and have been able to take great responsibility. Being so close to the King would be like being a loyal son who was willing to do anything to protect him against any enemies in the royal household or outside. He was a Knight and would have given his life to protect his benefactor.

He would have had to take on many great responsibilities with all the lands and properties that had been bequeathed to him. He must have organised all the building works at Glamis as the Castle took shape. This would mean employing hundreds of workers and craftsmen. He would have had to find the means to pay the cost of such a large task. Glamis was his family home but he also had responsibility for the vast estates and the thousands of people who would have lived from Aberdeen in the North down to Perthshire. He would have to arrange for people to collect the tithes from the locals and would have had to enforce law and order in those vast areas. To do this he would have had to appoint judges or magistrates to carry out these duties and they would have been answerable to him.

Life at court would have been an important part of his life, especially as his wife Jean was part of the Royal family. There would have been banquets and balls to arrange for the entertainment and visiting Royalty and Lords of the Manors, clan chiefs and other titled people and he would have had to arrange all these, not necessarily personally, but be responsible and be in charge of all the preparations. Whether he had time to pursue any other interests must be open to question. One of the gifts he received from the King mentions fishing rights in various places so he might have spent some time fishing for relaxation. No doubt the King enjoyed hunting which was the custom and the beautiful countryside around Perth and Glamis and further north would have provided hunting opportunities with wild deer and birds such as pheasants available on the moors.

The Lyon family have historically been involved in farming and agriculture to this day. There is a very interesting agricultural Museum in the village of Glamis that is worth visiting to get a picture of the land in that vicinity and the farming methods used in the old days. Even the Lyons who migrated to America have been 70% farmers and continued the family traditions which were started at the time of William the Conqueror and possibly before, in France.

The history of the Knights Templars offers a solution to the mystery about the Lyon family for several generations. When John (1340) married the daughter of King Robert II he was given many titles the highest of which was the Lord Chamberlain of Scotland. How he reached these dizzying heights, apart from the fact that he married the King's daughter, are somewhat mysterious unless one takes into account the following information:

> "Having amassed huge wealth, they were the most powerful bankers of their time and also the largest fighting force in the West. The Templars commissioned and financed cathedrals, mediated in international transactions, **and even supplied court chamberlains to the ruling houses of Europe**".
> *(www.bibliotecapleyades.net/sociopolitica/.../knights_templars01.htm)*

History shows us that the Templars had, before their dissolution, trained court Chamberlains in financial matters and there is no reason to believe that the Hospitallers and Knights of St John did not carry on the same practices. Young John Lyon (1340) would have been trained in these skills and he and his family held the post of Chamberlain and Court Treasurer for several generations, until Thomas Lyon (1549-1608), the Master of Glamis.

History of the Court of the Lord Lyon

"The Lord Lyon is the sole King of Arms in Scotland. He is Head of the Heraldic Executive and the Judge of the Court of the Lord Lyon which has jurisdiction over all heraldic business in Scotland.

The office of Lyon King of Arms dates from the 14th century. The position may incorporate the much older Celtic office of royal Seanchaidh or of King's Poet with responsibility for keeping the Royal genealogy and attending the inauguration (later coronation)   of the King."
(http://www.lyon-court.com/lordlyon/221.185.html)

This office continues until the present day and must have been named after one of the John Lyons who served the Kings of Scotland in the 14th Century. If the reader wishes to know more about heraldry or clans or Scottish families the above website is of some use.

CHAPTER 4

SCOTLAND AND THE KINGS

The Lyon family in Scotland from 1380 onwards
serving the Kings of Scotland up to James VI.

The Lords of Glamis

King James and Sir John Lyon 1380-1435

In the charter-room at Glamis there is an instruction by King Robert II addressed to the Abbot and convent of Dunfermline, charging them to enter a statement that John Lyon, son and heir of the deceased John Lyon, Knight (1340) was heir of his father who owned the lands of Fothros and Schenevale.

On 18th October 1388 the King issued his protection, taking John Lyon (1380) 'nepotem nostrum,' (our favoured one) his lands, men, and whole possessions under his peace and protection, etc., and directing all his debtors to make payment to him of their debts without delay; thus avoiding the hardships inflicted on the youthful heir because of the murder of his father. John was knighted on or before 1404. On the 4th December 1423 his name occurs in a list of the hostages to be delivered for the exchange and ransom for King James I of Scotland (1406-1437). A few days afterwards Sir John received a safe conduct to meet with King James at Durham, and there is little doubt he formed one of the company of Scots notables who conducted King James from Durham to his own Kingdom in April 1424, his son and successor Patrick taking his place as a hostage in England.

James I of Scotland's story

James was born July 25th, 1394 at Dunfermline, Fife. His father was King Robert III of Scotland and his mother was Annabella Drummond. He was of the House of Stewart. He ascended to the throne April 4th, 1406, aged 11 years and was crowned May 2nd or 21st, 1424, at Scone Abbey, Perthshire. He married Joan Beaufort, February 13th, 1424 and they had 2 sons and six daughters. He died February 21st, 1437, assassinated in the Monastery of Friars Preachers, Perth, aged 42. He was succeeded by his son James II. He was the 15th great-grandfather of Elizabeth II.

In 1406 James' father, King Robert III, fearing for his infant son's safety, as others wanted control of the Kingdom, attempted to send the child to safety in France. The boat was intercepted by the English and James the future monarch of Scotland was taken captive and held to ransom. His father King Robert III is said to have died from shock on hearing the news. For the next 18 years James would be a prisoner of the English King, Henry IV (and later Henry V).

The Scottish court was administered by Robert Stewart the first Duke of Albany, on behalf of the young James. He failed to pay the ransom demanded by Henry IV. It is thought that he hoped that his own son would rule after him if James did not come back. While he was a captive James interested himself in writing poems such as *The Kingis Quair* and *Good Counsel*. He received an education appropriate for a King and by the time of his release James was well schooled in philosophy, theology and the law. James was interested in architecture and was instrumental in the building of Linlithgow Palace in Scotland.

After the death of Robert Duke of Albany the ransom due to the English was finally paid. In 1424 James returned to Scotland to take revenge on the Albany Stewarts and he executed the leading members of the family. James tried to bring reform to Scotland with his knowledge of law, finance and politics. James still needed an answer to the question of his legitimacy and his right to be King. James's grandfather, Robert II, had married twice and had numerous children. The children from the first relationship (from which James was descended) were widely held to be illegitimate. The question of the validity of James's rule became increasingly heated until it finally resulted in open rebellion. In 1437 supporters of Walter Lord of Atholl, son of Robert III's second marriage, attacked and killed James in the Dominican Monastery in Perth. His wife Joan escaped with their son, James, to Stirling Castle.

Sir John Lyon (1380) continued;

John Lyon married his first cousin once removed, ELIZABETH GRAHAM (1385-1435), youngest daughter of Euphemia, Countess Palatine of Strathearn and her husband, Sir Patrick Graham of Dundaff and Kincardine. Their common ancestor was King Robert II, the bridegroom being a grandson of that monarch and the bride a great-granddaughter. They both lived in Glamis all their lives as far as we know, Elizabeth was buried there. They had three children;

1.   Patrick (1402-1459) who became the 1st Lord of Glamis,
2.   David (1404-1459)

3.   Michael (1406-) the date of his death is unknown but we believe he died in Picardy, France, in a battle.

John's own death is said to have taken place in 1435, being of the blood-royal he was interred at Scone.

Sir John Lyon (1380) was not the last of the Johns who achieved greatness in their lives, some refer to them as John I, John II and this one John III etc. The next Lyon was to be a Patrick, named after the patron saint of Ireland. He became the 1st Earl of Glamis, to be followed at various times by five other Earls who were named John.

It must have been a hard task to follow the great achievements of his father John who set a standard for the family to follow. John (1380) also died quite young at 55 but at least we have the record that he and his wife Elizabeth brought three children into the world, there may also have been daughters but unfortunately for genealogists they were rarely recorded for posterity unless they achieved greatness.

The Lords of Glamis

It might be surprising to learn that in the early years after the arrival of William the Conqueror in 1066, the common language of the court in much of Scotland was in fact French. This was also the case in England because so many people arrived from France and occupied significant positions of importance and power within the country. So for those members of the Lyon family who moved from France to Scotland, they did share a common language.

As you may have already gathered, there are a number of family members named John Lyon and this has created real confusion in researching and reporting on the family. There were at this time many branches of the original Lyon family in England. Other first names commonly in use by the family at that time were Patrick, Alexander, George, Richard and William.

An account of the death of the **King James I** is as follows quoted from Wikipedia;

"The King's cousin Sir Robert Stewart, heir to his grandfather Walter, Earl of Atholl, was Chamberlain of the royal household and used his privileged position to allow a small band of former Albany adherents led by Robert Graham to enter the building. James was alerted to the men's presence after servants discovered their approach giving the King time to hide in a sewer tunnel but with its exit, recently blocked off to prevent tennis balls getting lost, James was trapped and killed.

Although wounded, the Queen managed to escape and sent a directive ahead to Edinburgh for the now James II to be shielded from any widening of the conspiracy and had the boy King's custodian, the pro-Atholl John Spens, removed from his post and replaced by the trusted John Balfour.

The regicide of King James came so unexpectedly that a period of disorder took hold before James II was crowned at Holyrood Abbey on 25th March 1437 but it was not until early May that the main conspirators, Walter of Atholl, his grandson Robert Stewart and Robert Graham were gruesomely executed. King James' embalmed heart was likely taken on pilgrimage to the Holy Land following his interment at Perth Charterhouse, as the Exchequer Rolls of Scotland for 1443 notes the payment of £90 to cover the costs of a Knight of the Order of St John who had returned it to the Charterhouse from the Island of Rhodes."

(http://en.wikipedia.org/wiki/James_I_of_Scotland)

Patrick Lyon 1st Earl of Glamis was born in 1402 in Glamis Castle, Angus. Patrick married ISABEL OGILVIE in 1427 in Lintrathen, Angus. Isabel was born in 1402 in Glamis.

King James II – of the Stewart (or Stuart) Line

Because of **Patrick Lyon's** loyalty and service he was rewarded by King James II (1437-1460). On 23rd September 1440 Patrick Lyon acquired the lands of Fothros and Schenevale, in the royal estate of Dunfermline. In 1442 he was given the ancestral estates in Forfar and Fife. On 30th September 1444 he was titled "Patrick Lyon of Kinghorn, Knight". He was created a Lord of Parliament under the title of Lord Glamis on 28th June 1445.

Lord Glamis appears as 'Master of the Household'. The office of **Master of the Household** is one of the Great Offices of the Royal Household in Scotland. He held the office for the usual period of two years, his attendance at Court was almost unbroken during that time. In 1450 and the following year he was one of the Lords Auditors of the Treasury. In 1451 he received the lands of Cardani-Berclay, Drumgley and Drumgeith, in the sheriffdom of Forfar.

He had a safe-conduct into England as one of the Commissioners appointed for settling violations of the truce between the Kingdoms on 17th April 1451. In 1455 he was again Ambassador to England. Here we have Patrick, in his fifties, travelling all over Scotland and England having served two Scottish Kings carrying out diplomatic duties to keep the peace whenever possible between the Kings of England and Scotland. This was during the reign of Henry VI of England. His promotions continued for several years and he amassed more lands and titles.

In 1456-59 he was Keeper of the Royal Castles of Kildrummy, Kindrocht and Balveny, and various payments for the repair and maintenance of these fortresses were made to him during that period. In 1457 he was nominated one of the Lords of Session on behalf of the Barons of Scotland, being the first of seven Judges of the Supreme Court. Lord Patrick Glamis died at Belhelvies on 21st March 1459 and was buried at Glamis, there is an inscription on his tomb there. After her first husband's death Isabel, Lady Glamis married Gilbert, first Lord Kennedy, whom she also survived. She was a determined woman who fought her sons, her tenants, her neighbours, and her creditors, and had a tough struggle with the representatives of her second husband for the possession of the family fortune.

In her widowhood, she finished the old House of Glamis, built the two stone bridges, and the aisle in the Kirk of Glamis, wherein, with her first husband, she was interred in 1484 as the inscription upon the tomb bears witness. They had several children;

1. Alexander Lyon born 1429, died 1486 – he became the 2nd Earl of Glamis,
2. Janet Lyon born 1430, married James Scrymgeour.
3. John Lyon born 1431 became the 3rd Earl of Glamis,
4. William Lyon of Pettanys, born 1433.
5. Patrick Lyon born 1435 and died in 1481.
6. Elizabeth Lyon born 1437, Elizabeth, married Alexander Robertson of Strowane.

Isabel, Lady Glamis, died 1n 1484.

William obtained a charter of Easter Ogil, in the parish of Tannadyce, from his elder brother Alexander, and on 26th June 1498 his right to the possession of the estate was vindicated in a litigation with his nephew John, 4th Lord Glamis.

Daughters as well as sons now become recorded. Many daughters marry titled persons and we can imagine the amount of lands in the hands of the family grew quite rapidly.

Alexander Lyon 2nd Lord Glamis

Alexander Lyon 2nd Lord Glamis was born in 1429. He married AGNES CRICHTON born around 1425 from Crichton Castle, Pathhead, East Lothian, she died about 1448. They had no known children. In 1460 he was given the lands of Glamis and Tannadyce by King James II. In 1478 he was in possession of the lands of Redeplowland, originally granted to the Chamberlain.

Land-holding in Scotland was feudal, i.e. there was an overlord or superior and his vassal who received the right to occupy the lord's land. Each time land changed hands; permission had to be obtained from the superior in the form of a 'precept' (letter). The letter was then shown to the 'bailie' (official) of the particular lands who then gave title to the new owner. This took place on the actual property, where the new owner was given a handful of earth and stone or if in a burgh, took hold of the handle of the door and thereby became 'infeft' or 'seized' the property. Ownership of property was then recorded in the Register of the county in which the land lay.

In 1461 Alexander was appointed Keeper of the Castle of Kildrummy and Kindrocht in succession to his father, Patrick. In 1463 his name was included in the list of Barons present in Parliament, and from that time onwards he was a leading figure in the administration of the Kingdom. He was nominated one of the Lords of Council. One of Alexander's colleagues in the exercise of his duties was his younger brother and successor, Mr John Lyon of Courtastoune, afterwards 3rd Lord Glamis.

It is hard not to be impressed by the success of the Lyon family over many years. They had obviously built up trust with various Kings over this period since King Robert the Bruce. This has to be noted as most unusual in the annals of British history. To please a King or Queen for a while was common with the nobility but to continue in such favour seems extraordinary. There must have been a common trait in the family to enjoy service and the rewards of land ownership.

In 1464 Alexander was one of the Barons appointed to attend the King at Berwick, to meet the English Ambassadors summoned to Newcastle to conclude a truce. He died in 1486. There were no children of the marriage, and on his death his widow married, after 20th October 1487 Walter Ker of Cessford.

John Lyon - 3rd Lord Glamis was born 1431 during the reign of James I of Scotland. He married ELIZABETH SCRYMGEOUR the daughter of John Scrymgeour and Isabella Oliphant, she was born in 1435 in Dunhope, Angus. In 1464, John Lyon received payments from the Crown for the upkeep of the castles of Kildrummy and Kindrocht, of which his father Patrick, 1st Lord Glamis, had been the Keeper, and he made measurable additions to the possessions of the family. On 14th October 1472 under the reign of James III, he was made Coroner within the areas of Forfar ad Kincardine. In 1483-84 he appears on the bench with the Lords Auditors and also with the Lords of Council in deciding civil cases and continued to act in these roles for ten years.

On 11th January 1487 King James III nominated him one of the "Great Justices" on the south side of the Forth. A great opportunity to display his qualities as a statesman was granted to him. After the death of King James III at Sauchieburn, a Parliament met at Edinburgh on 16th October 1488. There was some question as to why the King had died in battle and whether it was a genuine accident or was he left to be killed by the English troops.

The attitude maintained by the **3rd Lord Glamis** throughout this grave crisis as to who was responsible secured him the respect and the confidence of both sides.

He was peculiarly fortunate in obtaining the friendship of the young King, and during the early years of James IV's reign his attendance at court was continuous. In Parliament he was, with Lord Gray and the Master of Crawford, appointed a Lord Justice for Angus.

On 15th February 1489 he was appointed one of the Crown Auditors and on the 26th of June following became a member of the King's Privy Council. In 1490, when he was appointed a Commissioner under the Privy Seal to let the Crown lands, the King appointed him "Our Justice"; the ordinary title being simply "Justiciar". In 1491 he was one of the Lords who attended the young King James IV at Berwick to conclude, if possible, a truce with England, and in the same year he was Ambassador from Scotland to the Courts of France, Castile, Leon, Aragon and Sicily. In 1495 his name occurs as one of the two Justiciars on the south side of the river Forth.

On 20th October 1491 King James IV, at the request of Lord Glamis, made the town of Glamis in the sheriffdom of Forfar, into a free burgh for ever, with power to elect bailies and to hold a cross and market on Friday in each week, and a public fair every year on the feast day of St. Fergus, and for the four days following, with the right to impose tolls.

On the map Glamis Town and Glamis Castle are located on the centre left. Above is possibly Cossins written Coβins. Otherwise the place is not notified on any other map that I can find. The β is actually used in German for words like 'strasse' for street and replaces a double s. Cossins must have been an important place at the time as it is referred to in hundreds of references, especially the book – *The Lyons of Cossins and Wester Ogil, Cadets of Glamys by Andrew Ross*. This book, published in 1901 traces a large branch of the Lyon family. John and Elizabeth had the following children;

1. **John Lyon** was born 1452 at Glamis and died 1500. He was to become the 4th **Lord of Glamis**.

2. **George Lyon**, was born in 1453 in Glamis. He died on 9th September 1513 in the **Battle of Flodden** Field, Branxton, Northumberland.

3. **David Lyon**, was born in 1454 in Glamis. He died on 9th September 1513 in the **Battle of Flodden**, along with King James IV. There will follow more about David of Baky.

4. **William Lyon**, was born in 1455 in Glamis, Angus. He died on 9th September 1513 in the **Battle of Flodden** in Branxton, Northumberland.

5. **Janet Lyon**, was born in 1461 in Glamis. Janet, was married to GILBERT HAY of Templeton.

6. **Agnes Lyon**, lived from 1465-1529 in Glamis. She married, first to ARTHUR, 5th LORD FORBES, who died in 1493.

7. **Mariota Lyon**, was born in 1469 in Glamis. Mariota, married WILLIAM, son of Sir James Ochterlony of that Ilk.

8. **Elizabeth Lyon**, was born in 1471-1509 in Glamis. Elizabeth, married to WILLIAM FORBES, son of the Laird of Echt. She died before 24th September 1509.

9. **Christian Lyon**, was born in 1482 in Perth, Perthshire. She died on 30th April 1529.

10. **Margaret** born 1487 died 1507. Margaret, married to JAMES RYND, younger of Broxmouth; dowry 400 merks.

This completes the family of John Lyon (1351-1497) the 3rd Lord Glamis.

Elizabeth died on the 20th October 1492, on which date her husband gave a gift, in remembrance, of two acres and a plot of land in the barony of Glamis to the parish church of Glamis. The last reference to John, 3rd Lord Glamis, is in the Scottish Treasurer's accounts for 1496. He died 1st April 1497 and was buried at Glamis.

The Battle of Flodden

The Battle of Flodden or Flodden Field or occasionally the Battle of Branxton was a conflict between the Kingdom of England and the Kingdom of Scotland. The battle was fought in the county of Northumberland in northern England on 9th September 1513, between an invading Scots army under King James IV and an English army commanded by the Earl of Surrey on behalf of King Henry VIII. It was an English victory. In terms of troop numbers, it was the largest battle fought between the two Kingdoms. James IV was killed in the battle, becoming the last monarch from the British Isles to suffer such a death to date. Henry VIII of England had opened old wounds by claiming to be the overlord of Scotland which angered the Scots and their King.

To read more about the battle visit Wikipedia. *(http://en.wikipedia.org/wiki/Battle_of_Flodden)*

The Lyon family lost three sons in the battle along with their King James IV.

This tragedy must have had many consequences in the future years. Many other great families lost many members at this important battle where so much Scottish blood was shed.

John Lyon 4th Lord Glamis was born in 1452 in Glamis. He married ELIZABETH GRAY, daughter of Andrew Gray and Janet Keith on 18th May 1487 in Glamis. She was born in 1456 in Huntly, Aberdeenshire.

Castle Foulis and Huntly Castle

The Electric Scotland website records that "the Castle of Foulis by this time had become too small for the accommodation of the numerous Gray families; and Lord Gray selected a site on the plateau near the river, a little south-west of the Foulis Castle. The second Lord Gray died in 1469, and it is likely that he had begun the new Castle before that, but it was not completed in his time. The successor was his grandson, Alexander, third Lord Gray, who increased his influence by two prudent marriages, connecting him with the Keiths, Earls Marischal, and the Earl of Atholl, and was the Justice-General of Scotland. At his death in 1514 he left a large family. His eldest son, Patrick, became fourth Lord Gray, after he had reached the age of manhood."

It was the lot of this Lord Gray to see the completion of the Castle, probably during his father's life-time. He had been married to Lady Janet Gordon, daughter of the Earl of Huntly; and as the Castle had not then been named, he devised the name of 'Castle Huntly', which it still bears today. This Castle was sold in 1614 by Andrew Gray, eighth Lord Gray, to the first Earl of Kinghorne, when the name was changed to 'Castle-Lyon' after that Earl's family.

It remained in the possession of the Lyon family, the Earls of Strathmore and Kinghorne until 1776, when it was sold to Mr George Paterson. He was married to the Hon. Anne Gray, and he resumed the old name of Castle Huntly, bestowed on it by her ancestors. This splendid baronial pile still (1927) belongs to the Patersons.

The castle has in modern times become a prison. *(http://www.electricscotland .com/history/castles/fowlis.htm)*

John and Elizabeth had the following children:

1. **George**, fifth Lord Glamis was born in 1488 in Glamis. He died in March 1505. He never married.
2. **John,** sixth Lord Glamis was born in 1491 in Glamis. He died on 8th August 1528 in Leith, Midlothian.
3. **Mr Alexander,** was born in 1491 in Glamis. He died in 1541. He was the Chantor or Precentor of Moray. He was tutor to his nephew
4. **John, seventh Lord Glamis**. He was a benefactor to the church of Aberdeen. He died in 1541, and was buried in the choir of Turriff, which he built.

The 4th Lord Glamis died in 1500 of a wound received in an encounter with the Ogilvys, for which compensation was paid to David Lyon of Baky, as tutor to George Lyon, who would become 5th Lord Glamis. *(http://wc.rootsweb.ancestry.com/cgi-bin/igm.cgi?op=GET&db=aet-t&id=152509).*

In Scottish law, damages were awarded to a relative of a murdered person from a guilty party, who has not been convicted and punished any other way. His wife, Elizabeth Gray Lyon died on 29th January 1530 in Rothesay, Elgin, and Bute Island. Through Elizabeth the house of Lyon claimed right to the estate of Foulis, and the dispute on this point between the two families was not finally settled until 1575.

George Lyon 5th Lord Glamis, was born in 1488 in Glamis, Angus. He never married. He died in March 1505 at the age of 17.

The History of Glamis

The history of the village of Glamis is legendary, dating as far back as the 8th century when it was the home of St. Fergus who lived in a cave and it was considered to be a holy place. Later it is recorded that a Royal Hunting Lodge was built there for the Kings of Scotland who frequented it for hundreds of years although the location of it is unknown.

The entrance of the Lyon family onto the scene

In 1372 the land was granted to Sir John Lyon (1340) by King Robert II (13711390) and eventually became the family seat of the Earls of Strathmore & Kinghorne. The titles given to John Lyon Laird and Thane of Glamis became even more numerous. He and LADY JEAN had raised a son, John who was born at Glamis in 1380. Life centred on Glamis for the Lyon family up until the present time.

By 1376 a castle was being built at Glamis, since in that year it was granted by King Robert II to Sir John Lyon, Thane of Glamis, who was the husband of the king's daughter. Glamis has remained in the Lyon (later Bowes-Lyon) family since that time. The castle was rebuilt as an L-plan tower house in the early 15th century. In 1376, Sir John Lyon, had married Princess Joanna or Jean, the widowed daughter of King Robert II. The Lyon family prospered over the centuries. By 1606 the Lyon family was regarded as the wealthiest in Scotland.

Glamis Castle has a fascinating and exciting history. Legends and myths have grown around it; King Malcolm II was said to have been murdered here in the 11th century. Lady Janet Douglas, widow of Lord Glamis, was burned at the stake as a witch in 1540 by James V. Glamis today looks more like a French Chateau than a medieval fortress, because it was extensively restored in the 17th and 18th centuries. The original tower house remains at the centre of the castle today.

Glamis Castle is the historic seat of the Bowes-Lyons family, the lands were presented to the Lyon family as a gift by King Robert II in 1372. The Bowes-Lyons family now own the castle as the Earls of Strathmore. Alexander the 2nd Lord of Glamis (1429) is quite likely to be responsible for one of the wild stories about Glamis Castle, which it is worth recalling:

The first and most well-known legend is of the secret room or chamber that is hidden deep within the castle walls

"In the 15th century the 2nd Lord of Glamis (known as Earl Beardie) was an avid card player. Earl Beardie and the "Tiger" Earl of Crawford were playing cards late on a Saturday night. According to the story, a servant came to remind Earl Beardie that it was nearing midnight.

The servant urged them to stop playing. It was sacrilege to play cards on the Sabbath. Lord Glamis shouted for all to hear they would play until Dooms Day if they wanted and ordered the servant out of the room. The game continued and at five minutes to midnight the servant again warned his Lord of the time. Earl Beardie said he would play with the Devil himself and ordered the servant out. At the stroke of midnight there was a knock on the door and a tall stranger dressed in black entered asking to join the game.

The stranger sat down and placed a handful of rubies on the table. Earl Beardie and Earl Crawford did not object to his company. Soon after, an argument was heard to erupt between the two Earls. When the servant peered into the room he saw the two men engulfed in flames. It is said that Earl Beardie had played cards with the Devil and for playing on the Sabbath he was condemned to play until Dooms Day. His ghost still roams the halls trapped for eternity doomed to play cards with the Devil. Sounds of stamping, swearing and dice rattling are heard from the tower where Earl Beardie is said to have cursed God and played with the Devil.

So great were the resulting disturbances that the room was sealed up 300 years, later permanently. The secret chamber is thought to be located deep in the thickness of the crypt walls"

(http://www.hauntedcastlesandhotels.com/Scotland/glamis.htm)

John Lyon the 2nd Earl of Kinghorne (1596-1646) helped to finance the army of the Covenanters and became impoverished as a result. The Covenanters were those people in Scotland who signed the National Covenant in 1638. They signed this Covenant to confirm their opposition to the interference by the Stuart Kings in the affairs of the Presbyterian Church of Scotland.

(http://www.covenanter.org.uk/WhoWere/)

Patrick Lyon the 3rd Earl (1643-1695) recovered the family fortunes, however, and became Earl of Strathmore and Kinghorne (a title which has survived to this day). In the 18th century, Thomas the 9th Earl of Strathmore (1704-1753) married a wealthy heiress, Mary Eleanor Bowes. He later became Lord Bowes and inherited estates in England. He adopted the present name of Bowes-Lyon as the family name.

Today the castle is home to the 18th Earl of Kinghorne and is famous for its many ghosts. The author Sir Walter Scott once spent the night at Glamis and wrote of his experience, 'I must own that when I heard door after door shut, after my conductor had retired, I began to consider myself as too far from the living, and somewhat too near to the dead'.

John Lyon 6th Lord of Glamis was born in 1491, in the reign of James IV, in Glamis, Angus. He became Lord on the death of his brother George who died at 17 in 1505. He married LADY JANET DOUGLAS, a woman of rare beauty, daughter of Sir George Douglas Angus and Elizabeth Drummond, in 1515 in Glamis. Lady Janet was the third daughter of George, Master of Angus who was slain at Flodden, and sister of Archibald, sixth Earl of Angus. She was born in 1495 in Angus.

The children of **John, 6th Lord Glamis** and JANET DOUGLAS were:

1.   **Elizabeth**, 1516-1537. Married first, before 30th June 1535, to JOHN, MASTER OF FORBES, who was denounced by the Earl of Huntly for treason, was tried before the High Court of Justiciary and beheaded at Edinburgh on 17th July 1537,
2.   **Margaret**, born 1518 died at Glamis, unmarried, 15th June 1610.
3.   **John Lyon 7th Earl of Glamis** was born in 1521
4.   **George**, born 1522 was born at Glamis he was imprisoned with his brother in Edinburgh Castle.

John Lyon, 6th Lord Glamis, survived the battle of Flodden, and lived to fight another day. John died on 8th August 1528 at the age of 37 in Leith, Midlothian. The cause of his death is not recorded to my knowledge.

John Lyon 7th Earl of Glamis born in 1521 in Glamis.

The tragedy of Janet, Lady Glamis

On 1st January 1532 Janet was indicted by the King accused of poisoning her late husband John Lord Glamis. A month later she appeared to answer the accusation, but the jury who were summoned were mostly Angus gentry, they refused to countenance such a charge, and were fined for non-appearance at the trial. A second jury summoned from a wider circle three weeks later also refused to appear and were likewise fined.

James V was not a pleasant man. He seemed to want revenge on the Douglas family for past actions that had offended him. Janet was a Douglas, she was reputed to be both beautiful and virtuous and there were benefits to be obtained by his taking over the castle of Glamis. It was not her property, but belonged to her son John, the young 7th Lord Glamis, which seems not to bother the King. Because of his hatred of the house of Douglas, James V decided to eliminate Lady Glamis, the sister of the banished Earl of Douglas. But her conduct was so faultless that years elapsed before the King was able to carry out his revenge.

At length on 17th July 1537 she was accused of taking part in a traitorous conspiracy to destroy her husband by poisoning him with the help of the Earl of Angus and George Douglas her brother. She was also accused of plotting to kill the King of Scotland, James V. She was found guilty and condemned to be burned at the stake on Castle Hill in Edinburgh, and the despicable sentence was carried out that same day. At the same time her son-in-law, John, master of Forbes, was beheaded on a charge of conspiring to shoot James V with a pistol in the course of a visit to Aberdeen 'that the Douglas's might be restored to their ancient possessions, titles and honours'. Her husband Sir Alexander, who, together with her two sons, had been arrested, died in attempting to escape from Edinburgh Castle – sometimes a polite way of saying they were murdered or executed.

She was burnt at the stake on the Castle Hill, with the great sympathy of the people because of her noble blood and being so young and beautiful. She died with great courage on 17th July 1537 in Castle Hill, Edinburgh, Midlothian. The English ambassador wrote that Lady Glamis was put to death 'as I can perceive without any substantial ground or proof of matter'.

Young Lord John Glamis the 7th Earl and his brother George, born 1522 at Glamis were detained in Edinburgh Castle until such time as they were old enough to be executed in their turn.

There John was compelled to witness the sufferings of his clansmen who were tortured on the rack in the vain attempt to force them to say words which should implicate his mother. On the 18th of July 1537 he was brought before the Lords of Justiciary and a confession obtained under torture was produced against him.

"The brothers were released immediately after the death of James V, on 18th January 1543. Five years, however, of close imprisonment in a fortress had proved too great a strain on George's constitution and he died shortly after. The seventh Earl started to recover his estates. The next ruler on the throne was the infamous Mary Queen of Scots and

John presented a claim to her at Edinburgh on 12th March 1343. He was well supported by friends of the family. The Queen immediately gave an order that all the lands belonging to John Lyon should be given back to him including one that was to honour his family later - the Barony of Kinghorne. After having difficulty retrieving these lands he eventually won the battle and later became the Earl of Kinghorne.

Lord Glamis sat as a member of the Privy Council 18th February 1544, and up to 3rd May 1547 his name appears in the lists of meetings. He supported the Queen of Scots in her opposition to Henry VIII and his bullying ways and was in Parliament in 1545 when it was agreed to invite the French to help Scotland in their fight against England."

(http://clanlyon.wordpress.com/2012/05/23/the-story-of-the-family-lyon/)

Much of this quotation is questionable as Mary was still in France until 1561 and returned to Scotland at that time, Henry VIII died in 1547 when Mary was 5 years of age. John married JEAN (JANET) KEITH in 1543 whose father was the fourth Earl of Marischal. He disappears from public life on 4th October 1548 when he left Scotland and went for many months abroad. John and Janet had the following children;

1. **John Lyon** 1544-1578, who became the 8th Lord of Glamis.
2. **Margaret** 1547-1626. Born in Glamis. She first married a GILBERT KENNEDY on 30th September 1566, who was the son of the fourth Earl of Cassillis, dowry 10,000 merks; then 30th December 1577), to John, first MARQUESS OF HAMILTON. She died at Evandaill in 1626.
3. **Sir Thomas Lyon of Auldbar**, 1549-1618. The Master of Glamis.
4. **William Lyon** born in 1555 in Little Stanmore, Middlesex, England and died in 1624.

John became a very keen follower of the pro-English Protestant party led by the Earls of Angus and Lennox. This was the time of the great Reformation which would change the destinies of England, Scotland, Wales and Ireland.

He could have found himself uncomfortable with the way the Reformation affected Scotland and maybe this is why he left his home country to live in Middlesex in England.

In 1555 he fathered a son called William Lyon who was born in Little Stanmore in Middlesex in England. I have attributed William's birth to Janet Keith who may have followed her husband to London. The records state that a Janet Keith died in Scotland in 1559 and John lived until 1592 before his death in Ruislip in Middlesex.

John Lyon, 8th Lord Glamis was born in 1544 and took over the title before his father's death because his father had moved to Middlesex in England. John inherited the family estates on the 17th April 1550 at a very young age. Subsequently he gave up any right or claim to his estates in Forfar, Perth and Aberdeen and these were passed to the following members of the family;

1.   **Thomas Lyon** of Auldbar his brother;
2.   **John Lyon** of Haltoun of Eassie;
3.   **John Lyon** of Easter Ogil;
4.   **John Lyon** of Culmalegy;

John Lyon (1544) married on 11th April 1561 an ELIZABETH, daughter of William, fifth Lord ABERNETHY of Saltoun, widow of William Meldrum of Fyvie. She was born in 1540.

The record shows John and Elizabeth had three daughters and one son:

1.   **Jean Lyon** (1556?-1610). There is a problem here John her father was only 12!
2.   **Elizabeth**, born 1558 (before her parents were married!) married on 18th May 1575) to PATRICK, afterwards sixth LORD GRAY, whom she divorced for adultery 21st May 1585. Elizabeth then married, 14th February 1586-87 WILLIAM KER, otherwise Kirkcaldy of Grange, second son of Sir Thomas Ker of Fernihirst. They had four children of which there seems to be no record.
3.   **Sibilla**, (1566 – 1579
4.   **Patrick**, (1575 – 1615) ninth Lord Glamis.

Mary Queen of Scots

Mary, Queen of Scots (8th December 1542 – 8th February 1587), also known as **Mary Stuart** or **Mary I of Scotland**, was born at Linlithgow Palace daughter of James V and Mary of Guise. She was the Queen of Scotland from 14th December 1542 to 24th July 1567 and Queen Consort of France from 10th July 1559 to 5th December 1560.

This Mary is not to be confused with Queen Mary I of England, often referred to as 'Bloody Mary' because of her persecution of Protestants. Queen Mary I of England was born in 1516 (to Henry VIII and Catherine of Aragon his first wife) and ruled England from 1553 to 1558 when she died at the age of 42. She was a Tudor whilst Mary I of Scotland was a Stuart.

The Lyon Memorial book says; "the wheel of history was making some dizzy revolutions in Scotland, carrying the **Lyon** family onward in a rush of peculiar events. The widow, Queen Mary Stuart, had come home from France to a career of capers and intrigues, of conspiracies and crimes. The thunder-bolts and powerful preaching of John Knox could not frighten her back from self- destruction.

Her ill-advised marriage with her cousin, Lord Darnley, the birth of her son, the heir to the throne, the murder of David Rizzio, the retaliatory murder of Darnley, and the suspicion of the Queen's consent to the death of her husband,

Bothwell's indecent wooing when the Royal dead was just buried. Queen Mary's mad marriage with the Black Earl, the rebellion of her outraged subjects and the escape from Lochleven Castle were the extraordinary happenings of seven years of Scottish history. The Lyons decided to wisely keep their heads below the parapet."

John Lyon the 8th Lord Glamis does not again appear until 17th March 1565, on the eve of Queen Mary's marriage with Darnley. He held a command in the Queen's forces assembled in October of that year to defeat the plans of Murray (the Earl of Moray) and his associates, when the Royal army chased their opponents from pillar to post in such a fashion that the campaign came to be known as the "Run-about-Raid". Queen Mary married her cousin Lord Darnley and shortly after his death she married James Hepburn, 4th Earl of Bothwell, who was generally believed to have orchestrated Darnley's death, but he was acquitted of the charge in April 1567.

Queen Mary's son by Darnley was James VI of Scotland and James I of England who was born on 19th June 1566 in Edinburgh Castle. After the death of Lord Darnley, **Lord Glamis** still adhered to the cause of Queen Mary, and he was present at the marriage of the Queen with Bothwell, but he soon joined her opponents not being able to support her extreme Catholicism.

Following an uprising against the couple, Mary was imprisoned in Loch Leven Castle. On 24th July 1567, she was forced to abdicate in favour of James, her one year-old son by Darnley. After an unsuccessful attempt to regain the throne, she fled southwards seeking the protection of her first cousin once removed, Queen Elizabeth I of England.

Mary had previously claimed Elizabeth's throne as her own and was considered the legitimate sovereign of England by many English Catholics, including participants in a rebellion known as the 'Rising of the North'.

Perceiving her as a threat, Queen Elizabeth I had her confined in a number of castles and manor houses in Northamptonshire. After eighteen and a half years in custody, Mary was found guilty of plotting to assassinate Elizabeth, and was subsequently executed. Queen Mary of Scotland was beheaded in 1587.

John Lyon (1544) the 8th Lord Glamis was appointed as a member of the Privy Council by the Regent Murray, and from 22nd December 1567 onwards his name occurs as a regular attender at the meetings of Council until within a month of his death. The Regent was selected to protect and be responsible for the young King until an agreed time when he would be capable of ruling his people. On 23rd February 1568 John entered into an association with James Scrymgeour, Constable of Dundee, Thomas Maule of Panmure and other Forfar barons, who wanted to protect the King's authority (James VI) and to jointly protect themselves if they were attacked.

John was nominated by the Regent Lennox, as an Extraordinary Lord of Session, 30th September 1570, resigning that post on 8th October 1573, when he received a commission from **James VI** with consent of the Earl of Morton as Regent, appointing him as the Chancellor of the Kingdom and Keeper of the Great Seal during his life. In 1571 he was one of a quartet of nobles entrusted with the guardianship of the King's person and in the same year he was one of the Commissioners appointed to meet those from England at Berwick to deliberate on the subjects in dispute between the realms, and to establish a peace.

At this time he corresponded with Beza, the famous theologian on questions of church government, supporting the maintenance of Bishops.

For more information on Beza see Appendix E.

John Lyon the 8th Earl of Glamis (1544) was not present at Stirling on 8th March 1577-78 when the **King (James VI)** took upon him the government of the kingdom, and the statement made by his enemies that he sided against his old friend is disproved by his attendance up to the last at the meeting of Council over which Morton, the Regent, presided. John Lyon (1544), was killed at Stirling on 17th March 1577. Contemporary narratives with one exception agree as to the accidental nature of the catastrophe. While John Lord Glamis was coming down from the Castle of Stirling to his lodging in the town, the Earl of Crawford was going up, and the parties met in a narrow street. Each noble bade his company give way, but in passing two attendants jostled, swords were drawn, and almost immediately Lord Glamis, conspicuous by his stature, was shot by a pistol in the head.

The event naturally aggravated the feud between the families. The elaborate praise of the Chancellor recalled the tribute paid by the old friend to his ancestor the Chamberlain. 'The death of the Chancellor', wrote Spottiswoode, 'was much lamented falling out in the time when the King and country stood in most need of his service. He had carried himself with much commendation in his place and acquired a great authority; most careful was he to have peace conserved both in the country and the church'.

'A learned, godly, and wise man', wrote Calderwood; 'a good justiciar', observed Scotstarvet; 'a good learned nobleman' was James Melville's observation. The English ambassador described him at one time as 'of greatest revenue of any baron in Scotland', and at another 'very wise and discreet, wealthy, but of no party or favour'. The General Assembly which met at Edinburgh in April 1578 passed a resolution of regret at the event, and ordered a general fast to be kept throughout the land.

Summary of the life of John Lyon 8th Lord Glamis

John lived in turbulent times and it seems that he must have been a wise man being able to play the dangerous political game that allowed him to survive but only to the age of 33. He is not the first member of the Lyon family to have been killed or murdered; his grandmother had been burned at the stake. Being involved with Kings and rulers was obviously a bit like walking on a tightrope and despite the risks he seems to have achieved very much in his lifetime.

A very interesting situation arose during his life; that was the beginning of the Reformation which took hold in Scotland very early on. We don't know how much Beza and his writings influenced the young man but Calvinism and Beza's teachings made an enormous impact on Scottish history. From this time on, the Lyon family, for the most part, would be Protestants and the next century would see some of that number migrate to America during and after the time of Oliver Cromwell.

The other important thing that happened at this time was that James VI of Scotland, who ruled from 1567 to 1625 in Scotland would become **James I of England** ruling from 1603 to 1625. His predecessor in England was **Elizabeth I** who ruled from 1558 to 1603 and became the greatest Queen England had ever known, up to Queen Victoria and Elizabeth II.

He was succeeded by his brother **Thomas Lyon.**

Sir Thomas Lyon

Sir Thomas was born in 1549, the younger brother of John Lyon the 8th Earl of Glamis. He was heir presumptive to the title and was known as the **Master of Glamis**, except for the period 1575-78 which intervened between the birth of his nephew Patrick, and the death of John, 8th Lord Glamis (1578). Patrick became the 9th Lord Glamis and Thomas again became Master of Glamis.

On 10th March 1567, he was designated chaplain of the Chapel of St John at Baky by his brother John. He also possessed many other titles and honours. To write even briefly about the career of this great statesman, which covered the stormy period of the minority of **James VI**, would be to attempt a history of Scotland. The briefest outline of a few incidents must suffice.

Thomas Lyon (1549) was employed in March 1578 in the negotiations which led to Earl Morton's resignation of the regency. With the Earls Mar and Gowrie he entered into an agreement for the overthrow of the Earls of Lennox and Arran, and was one of the principal actors in the 'Raid of Ruthven'.

> "The **Raid of Ruthven** was a political conspiracy in Scotland which took place on 22nd August 1582. This was organised by several Presbyterian nobles, led by William Ruthven, 1st Earl of Gowrie, who abducted King James VI of Scotland. The nobles intended to reform the government of Scotland and limit the influence of French and pro-Catholic policy. Their short-lived rule is known as the 'Ruthven' or 'Gowrie Regime'.
> *(http://en.wikipedia.org/wiki/Raid_of_Ruthven)*

If the reader wishes to know more about the following chapters in detail then I recommend that you search the above website to explain the details which basically boiled down to further problems between the Protestants and the Roman Catholics.

After the Raid of Ruthven the united nobles, as the holders of the King's person were termed, were installed in power, and on 12th October 1582 Thomas Lyon the Master of Glamis appears as a Privy Councillor. He was the one individual connected with the Raid of Ruthven for whom the King entertained a personal regard, having been a companion of his boyhood days in Stirling Castle. The King unexpectedly gave his guardians the slip at St. Andrews on 25th June 1583. Arran returned to power and did his upmost to inflame the King's mind, but James showed little animosity against his captors and was more inclined to pardon than to prosecute them.

History of the relationship with the Crawford family

The youngest son of the 4th Earl of Richmond (who was descended from the Duke of Brittany) was granted lands in the Barony of Craufurd (from 'crow ford') in Lanarkshire, Scotland, in the 12th century by King David I and the family took the surname from the place name. In 1127 Sir Gregan Crawford was involved in the legendary incident when King David was saved from a stag and as a result, in gratitude, founded the Abbey of Holyrood.

In 1296 Sir Reginald Crawford was appointed sheriff of Ayr. His sister married Wallace of Elderslie and thus became the mother of William Wallace the great Scottish patriot. Needless to say, the Crawfords rallied to his cause. The main branches of the family were Crawford of Auchinames (in Renfrewshire) who received a grant of land from Robert the Bruce in upper Clydesdale and Sir William Craufurd of Craufurdland who was a brave soldier and who was knighted by King James I and fought for King Charles VII of France.

History of the relationship of the Lyon family and the Crawford family goes back to the 1st Lord of Glamis Sir John Lyon (1340) who died in 1382 'as result of a duel between himself and Sir James Lindsay of Crawford on the 4th November 1382 at Balhall, Forfarshire'. This is not strictly true – he was murdered in his bed.

The next thing we find is the 2nd Lord of Glamis (1380) playing cards; "in the 15th century the 2nd Lord of Glamis (known as Earl Beardie) was an avid card player. Earl Beardie and the 'Tiger' Earl of Crawford were playing cards late on a Saturday night. According to the story, a servant came to remind Earl Beardie that it was nearing midnight'. So here it seems that some reconciliation had been made, despite the death of his father by a Crawford.

The next known contact is in the reign of James III when; 'In Parliament he (the 3rd Lord of Glamis) was with Lord Gray and the Master of Crawford, appointed a Lord Justice for Angus'.

Then the 8th Earl was killed by a Crawford supporter at Stirling on 17th March 1577, it was reported to be accidental.

Attempts were made to heal the feud between the Lyon family and the Crawfords but without success, and ultimately, disregarding an order to keep himself (Thomas) in Dumbarton Castle. Thomas Lyon the Master of Glamis (1549) travelled into England, a penalty naturally followed. Stirling Castle was seized by the Master and his friends on 17th April 1584. But they were unable to make headway against the Earl of Arran. Thomas and his friends were compelled once more to seek shelter in England.

They re-crossed the Borders on 24th October 1585, Arran fled, and after a ten day's campaign the Master and his friends were in power, the King accepting his new Councillors with little protest. On 7th November 1585 the Master became once more a member of the Privy Council, and on the same day Captain of the King's Bodyguard.

On 2nd December he was appointed the **Treasurer of Scotland**. A pension of £1000 per annum was attached to the post. On 20th January 1586-87 he was nominated one of the commissioners for considering grants out of the Crown lands, on 9th February following one of the Extraordinary Lords of Session. On 28th November 1588 he was supplanted in the post of Captain of the Guard by the Earl of Huntly and in the following year he was surprised and taken prisoner at the House of Kirkhill by Gordon of Auchindoun, but was released on the early payment by the King in person.

King James VI of Scotland

"His childhood and adolescence were unhappy, abnormal, and precarious; he had various guardians, whose treatment of him differed widely. His education, although thorough, was weighted with strong Presbyterian and Calvinist political doctrine, and his character – highly intelligent and sensitive, but also fundamentally shallow, vain, and exhibitionist – reacted violently to this. He also sought solace with extravagant and unsavoury male favourites who, in later years, were to have a damaging effect on his prestige and state affairs.

A suitable Queen was found for him in ANNE OF DENMARK and they were married in 1589. As King of Scotland, he curbed the power of the nobility, although his attempts to limit the authority of the Kirk (Church of Scotland) were less successful".

(http://www.britroyals.com/stuart.asp?id=james1)

Thomas Lyon was knighted at the coronation of Queen Anne on the 17th May 1590. On the 9th January 1595 he resigned from the Treasurership, though his resignation did not take effect till May the following year. On 30th January 1597-98 he was excused from further attendance as a Lord of Session but his name appears in the minutes of the Privy Council up to 18th May of that year, when he disappears from public life.

Thomas Lyon married AGNES, third sister of Patrick, fifth Lord GRAY sometime after 1575. She was the widow of Robert Logan of Restalrig, and then of Alexander, fifth Lord Home. Thomas and his wife had a dispute with the Home family regarding the keeping of the Castle of Home, which was seized on 7th November 1578, by Andrew Home. Thomas declared that the castle had been granted to him and his spouse to be kept in the King's name. Thomas Lyon and Agnes Gray had the following children;

1. **Anna,** born around 1578, was still alive on 16th November 1636, on which date William Dick of Braid, merchant burgess of Edinburgh, granted a discharge of her debt.
2. **Mary,** born about 1579, was married, first in 1617 to SIR ROBERT SCOTT of Cruikstoun, then to ROBERT SEMPILL of Beltrees.

Thomas was married again in 1586 to EUPHEMIA, daughter of William, fifth Earl of Morton and had the following children:

1. **John,** born 1587, served as heir to his father in Auldbar 6th August 1608. He married 16th February 1611 EUPHEMIA GLEDSTANES, daughter of George, Archbishop of St. Andrews, her dowry was £11,000. There were no children of the marriage. In the course of a few years he dissipated the fortune so painfully acquired by his father, and by 1619 such of his lands as were not sold were held by the Earl of Kinghorne in trust.

2. **Thomas** was born 1589. He attained his majority in September 1615 and he contracted many debts. In 1618 he was denounced for an attack upon his brother-in-law Mr James Stewart of Tullos. In 1619 he is noted as one of a small band of young and insolent "lymmaris" (A person of prominence) who infested Brechin, and were denounced as rebels, and in the following year he disappears from record.

3. **Margaret,** born 1591, married before 11th August 1609 to Mr James Stewart, afterwards Sir James of Eday and Tullos, Gentleman of the Bedchamber to James VI, fourth son of Robert Stewart, Earl of Orkney. On 29th November 1625 he and his wife received a pension of £900 per annum from the Crown, this slender provision coming in lieu of a liberal income provided to him by his brother the Earl of Orkney which had been forfeited.

4. **James** of whom I can find no record.

Thomas died 18th February 1608 at the age of 59. When the King heard of the event he is said to have observed that **"the boldest and hardiest man in his dominions was dead".**

Summary of life of Sir Thomas Lyon

Sir Thomas was another of the great achievers in the history of the family Lyon. Circumstances were in his favour when he became the Master of Glamis because of the early death of the previous leaders of the family. A successful father does not guarantee the same success for his children, his sons must have been a great disappointment to him as they frittered away the riches that had been built up over very many generations. It would seem that they had turned out to be spoiled brats, in modern parlance, who never appreciated how well off they were and how irresponsible was their behaviour.

Since the beginning of the 13th century the Lyon family were very successful and some outstandingly so. There were failures and tragedies in the family over the period of time but there is nothing new about having sons who show no respect for their elders. The family had gone through much suffering and many trials and I'm sure this must have had an effect on members of the family and might have been the cause of so many failures amidst all the success.

The Protestant Reformation

Christians in Western Europe belonged to one church before the year 1500, the Roman Catholic Church which was ruled by a Pope. The church had become extremely wealthy and influential in the political life of all the countries in Europe. There is no record in the family history of a Lyon being either a priest or other officer in the Roman Catholic Church. If the reader wishes to read more about the importance of William Tyndale and his translation of the Bible into the English language please read Appendix F.

The claims that a large team of scholars translated the King James Version of the Bible in 1611 is questionable as 84% of the translation had been written by William Tyndale. His translation is in very Basic English language and employs hundreds of idioms that we use today and we have much to be grateful for if we support the Reformation.

Martin Luther and the European Reformation

In 1517, a German priest by the name of Martin Luther protested against some of the practices of the church such as charges for indulgences from its members so that they could be forgiven for their past sins. He also objected to the theology of the Mass and other doctrines of the church. He soon had many followers and they were called Protestants because they protested against the church and its teaching and practices. This became known as the Protestant Reformation and soon spread across Europe.

The church tried to make changes but failed to dampen the enthusiasm of the protesters and soon began torturing and killing people because of their heresies. Some countries in Europe became Protestant and this encouraged men like John Calvin in Geneva to take matters further and he founded churches in Switzerland that were openly Protestant.

Christianity in Scotland

Scotland was one of the last countries in Europe to reform its church. The Catholic Church had for years helped the sick and the poor and provided education for many of its citizens.

The church however became very wealthy in Scotland and during the reign of James V (1513-1542) for example, the church had an income of almost £300,000 a year while the King himself only had an income of £20,000 to pay for governing the country. The Kings and nobles tried to find ways of getting more money from the church and the King started to tax the church with the result that many people who would otherwise have been priests felt they were unable to afford to continue to serve the church on such low wages.

In 1528 Patrick Hamilton while attending the universities of Wittenberg and Marburg I Germany, became influenced by the Lutheran theology. He became the first Protestant martyr when he was burned at the stake for his heresy at St Andrews, this was under the reign of James V. Hamilton brought some of these teachings to Scotland with him and these were later to influence more people to become Protestants. About this time in England King Henry VIII had broken with Rome and had been excommunicated. He had allowed the reading of the Bible in English and eventually supported the Reformation in England where great progress was being made.

Henry VIII decreed that the Pope was to be removed as the head of the church in England. In the Reformation Parliament in 1529-36 various laws were passed taking all power from the Roman Catholic Church. In 1534 the King and Parliament created an independent and separatist Church of England with the monarch as its head. The act of the Dissolution of the Monasteries in 1536 led by Thomas Cromwell sealed the fate of the Popish church which would to this day have no political power in England.

The English Parliament was called the 'Reformation Parliament' because it passed and enabled the major pieces of legislation leading to the English Reformation.

The act of supremacy declared "albeit the Kings Majesty justly and rightfully is and ought to be the supreme head of the Church of England and so is recognised … yet nevertheless for corroboration and confirmation thereof, and for increase of virtue in Christ's religion within this realm of England, and to repress and extirpate all errors, heresies and other enormities and abuses… be it enacted… that the King, or our Sovereign Lord, his heirs and successors… shall be taken, accepted, and reputed the only Supreme Head on earth of the Church of England, called Anglicana Ecclesia".

In 1541 in Scotland, Parliament passed laws protecting the Mass, prayers to the Virgin Mary and images of Saints and the authority of the Pope. Private meetings were outlawed for any 'heretics' among the people who opposed Roman Catholicism. After the death of Edward VI of England in 1553, the Scottish adherents of the Reformation who had taken refuge in England had to go abroad or return home to escape the persecution of Mary Tudor (1553-1558). The powerful preachers, Harlow and Whitlock and John Knox organized the church in Scotland and the ministers of the Congregation (Presbyterian) Church were planted in various towns and cities. A pledge drawn up in 1557 by the nobles; Argyle, Morton, Lorne and Erskine 'to defend the whole Congregation of Christ and every member thereof against Satan and all wicked powers,' became the **First Covenant** and generally people accepted this.

It was only in 1560 that Protestant who had been outlawed made a break with the Catholic Church's laws. Churches were from that moment on called Kirks and Roman Catholicism was outlawed. The Reformation was also a political move and would give the King more power to rule his people and change the laws of the land.

James VI was raised as a Protestant by the nobles at Stirling Castle. He was well educated and was taught the skills of diplomacy and was made head of the Kirk 'as appointed by God'. The Presbyterian Kirk was formed in Scotland; it was ruled by Bishops and elders who were at that time appointed for life. The country was organised into 13 Presbyteries with oversight of different areas of the country. Inbuilt into the organisation of the Presbyterian Kirk was the belief that it was independent of secular government and therefore able to concentrate on spiritual matters. John Knox, who was the leader of the new church, decreed that all Abbeys or Friaries that resisted the Reformation would be demolished and all evidence of Catholic idolatry should be removed from all churches in Scotland.

The Parliament of that year (1560), called the great Reformation Parliament, was attended by the Nobles, Bishops, Lesser Barons, Landed Gentry, and representatives. On August 10th the Confession of Faith was sanctioned by the estates, and on August 24th an act was passed prohibiting the rites of the Church of Rome, such as the Mass, Vestments and Indulgences. Athole, Summerville, Caithness and Bothwell alone of all the nobles voted against the Confession, and the power of the State was in the hands of the party of the Reformation.

The sons of **John Lyon**, 7th Lord Glamis, **John Lyon**, 8th Lord Glamis, and **Thomas Lyon**, Master of Glamis, must have stood in line with the Covenanters and accepted the new order of things. It should be noted that all the wrangling between fellow nobles encouraged **John Lyon** the 7th Earl to flee south to Middlesex (this was the reason why John appeared in Ryslippe, Middlesex and handed over his title to his son). He had lived a very perilous life in Scotland because of the accusations against his mother and the Reformation and its dangers after so many centuries of Roman Catholic domination.

The 8th Earl had meetings with Theodore Beza, the theologian and leader of the Protestant movement in Europe, who had a great influence on him.

The Reformation in England caused differences between the people that have not healed to this day. The Church of England, or Anglican Church as it is also known, was divided between High and Low churches, the Puritan faction gained ascendancy in Oliver Cromwell's time. The Puritans were supportive of the colonisers who migrated to America.

High Church supporters wanted to retain some Roman Catholic practices in their services with the use of high altars, candles, incense and vestments for the priests. They still call their priests 'father' and decorate their altars. Low Church still exists although Puritanism is practised by the Fundamentalists and is very strong in the USA, usually in denominations such as some Baptists, Congregationalists and some of the independent churches.

One of the tragedies of the Reformation is the large number of denominations that formed throughout the world as congregations split from each other over doctrinal differences. There are possible as many as 40,000 different denomination of Christians throughout the world, apart from Roman Catholics, according to Wikipedia. Some of these are very small and independent and many suffer persecution, whereas some are large such as the Southern Baptists in the USA. The growth of Pentecostalism in the last century has been phenomenal throughout the world.

(http://en.wikipedia.org/wiki/List_of_Christian_denominations

The Lyon family and the Reformation

There is little evidence of a wholesale conversion to Protestantism by the members of the family in the early days of the Reformation. In the next several generations there was a clear decision by many of the family to support the Presbyterian Church in Scotland or the Anglican Church in England. Within the next hundred years things would change quite dramatically as persecution rocked the country driving many Protestants to escape by going to America.

Many members of another branch of the family such as Lyon's of Cossins and Wester Ogil would enter the Presbyterian ministry and over the next few hundred years would remain Protestant leaders. Before the Reformation there was little evidence of any of the family being deeply committed to the Roman Catholic Church except to give the church land and tithes. The most we can say is that they were nominal Christians possibly because of their family history when they left France in the time of William the Conqueror partly because of the attitude of the church in France.

The Reformation itself has continued and most members of the Lyon family in America joined churches such as the Congregational, Anglican, Baptist, Friends and Methodist churches after John Wesley had gone through New England preaching his particular variety of Christianity. Many became ministers of religion and elders of the church in America and one branch of the family in Lancashire and Cheshire became ministers of religion.

The Lyons of Cossins and Wester Ogil

Much of the information regarding this part of the family comes from a book written in the 19th century and published in 1901. The book was written by Andrew Ross and has been reprinted as recently as 2010. Despite my reading of the book several times I often find the information it contains confusing. The page references bear no relation to the information contained on them. This does not mean that the information is worthless but it has chronological problems throughout that are sometimes irreconcilable. However I will make an attempt to bring some kind of order to the facts. For the maps of Cossins and Glamis see Illustrations & maps at beginning of book.

This is a large part of the story of a branch of the Lyon family that stayed in Scotland for some time and lived within easy reach of Glamis, the Earls of Glamis and the Earls of Strathmore. Many people of this branch of the family became ministers of religion and were highly educated men. Some left Scotland for various reasons.

David Lyon of Baky line, born 1454, was the third son of **John Lyon 3rd Earl of Glamis**. He was the lay Rector of Forbes and the tutor of **George, fifth Lord Glamis**. He purchased the lands of Cossins from Thomas Cossins of that Ilk, in three portions, in 1500, 1504 and 1511, from which the family made their living for many generations. David married LADY ELIZABETH LINDSAY in about 1479, she was born in Crawford, Lanarkshire in 1455. They had one son John. David fell at the battle of Flodden on 9th September 1513.

John, 1st of Cossins (1st Generation) was born in 1512 in Sutherland. MARJORIE OGILVIE who was born in Banff, Banffshire in 1507. They married on 5th November 1544. In 1524, he purchased Haltoun of Eassie. John and Marjorie had one son John in 1553. His descendants continued to be styled 'of Cossins', holding the lands until 1684.

John Lyon of Haltoun of Esse & Cossins (2nd **Generation**) he was born in 1553 in Cossins, Angus. He married MARGARET DRUMMOND on 11th February 1580. She was born in 1555. John and Margaret had the following children;

1. **George Lyon** was born in 1586 in Balmuckety, Angus. He died in 1640.
2. **John Lyon** of Wester Ogil was born in 1587. He died on 22nd May 1637. He married CATHERINE OGILVY. She was born about 1660.
3. **James Lyon** was born about 1598 in Wester Ogil, Angus.
4. **Sylvester Lyon** was born about 1598 in Wester Ogil, Angus.

John died in 1585 and date of death of Margaret is unknown.

John Lyon (2ⁿᵈ Generation) later married the DAUGHTER OF GARDYNE OF GARDYNE. She was born in 1563. There is no record of any children. He died in 1610.

George Lyon (3ʳᵈ Generation) was born in 1586 in Balmuckety, Angus. He married CATHERINE WISHART in 1618 in Angus. She was born in 1592 in Balgarrick. George and Catherine had two children;

1. **Baron John Lyon of Ogil** was born on 16ᵗʰ June 1622.
2. **Thomas Lyon** was born in 1626 in Scotland. He married DOROTHY who was born in 1630. He died in 1694 in Warrington, Lancashire.

He started a new life in Lancashire, England and was the father of a large dynasty whose story is told in Chapter 14, Part 3. Catherine died in 1635 and George died in 1640.

Baron John Lyon Of Ogil (4ᵗʰ Generation) was born on 16ᵗʰ June 1622 in Balmuckety, Wester Ogil, Angus. He married CATHERINE OGILVY of Balfour on 22ⁿᵈ October 1654 in Libertoun, Midlothian. She was born in 1625 in Balfour, Isles of Orkney. Baron John and Catherine had the following children;

1. **Sylvester Lyon** was born in 1640 in Wester Ogil, Angus. He died on 01ˢᵗ May 1713 in Kirriemuir, Angus.
2. **Elspeth Lyon** was born in 1643 in Kirriemuir, Angus.
3. **Frederick Lyon** was born in 1652 in Kirriemuir, Angus. He died on 4ᵗʰ August 1700.
4. **George Lyon of Ogil, Baron,** was born in 1658 in of Wester Ogil. He died on 2ˢᵗ January 1703. He married JEAN NISBET in 1673. She was born in 1650 in Craigentinnie. She died on 6th October 1704.
5. **Alexander Lyon** was born in 1647 in Kirriemuir, Angus.
6. **John Lyon** was born about 1660 in Ogil, Angus. He died in June 1702 in Kirriemuir, Angus.

Baron John died on 4ᵗʰ November 1672 in Edinburgh, Midlothian.

Frederick Lyon (5ᵗʰ Generation) was born in 1652 in Kirriemuir, Angus. He married ISOBEL CRAMOND in 1683. She died on 4th August 1700. Frederick was educated at the University of St Andrews and became MA (Master of Arts) on 23ʳᵈ July 1672. He was ordained into the Presbyterian Church on 12ᵗʰ May 1682.

(This and other notes about ministers of religion taken from www.donjgrant. me.uk/lc00.htm) Frederick and Isobel had the following children:

1. **Geillis Lyon**. She died on 4th August 1700.
2. **Helen Lyon**. She died on 4th August 1700.
3. **Patrick Lyon**. Born 2st June 1689. He died in 1733.
4. **John Lyon**. Born 27th August 1690.
5. **James Lyon**. Born 14th July 1694. He died on 4th August 1700.
6. **William Lyon**. Born 25th July 1697. He died on 04th August 1700.

Frederick Lyon died on 4th August 1700 of phthisis (tuberculosis) in Airlie.

George Lyon of Ogil, Baron (6th Generation) was born in 1658 in of Wester Ogle. He married JEAN NISBET in 1673. She was born in 1650 in Craigentinnie. Sir George and Jean had the following children;

1. **John Lyon** was born on 12th August 1674.
2. **William Lyon** was born on 9th October 1675 in Ogil, Angus. He was ordained as a Reverend in the Presbyterian Church. He died on 4th January 1743 in Airlie, Angus.
3. **Patrick Lyon**s born on 11th December 1676.
4. **Margaret Lyon** was born on 30th May 1681 in Ogil, Angus.
5. **Robert Lyon** was born in 1685 in Ogil, Angus. He died on 1st August 1730 in Kinfauns, Perthshire.
6. **Katherine Lyon** was born in 1686.
7. **George Lyon** was born on 28th July 1688. He died in 1748.
8. **Elizabeth Lyon** was born on 4th January 1689.
9. **Jean Lyon** was born on 29th January 1691.
10. **James Lyon** was born in 1694 in Ogil, Angus. He died on 22nd December 1768.

Baron George died on 2st January 1703. Jean died on 6th October 1704.

CHAPTER 5

REFORMATION, REVOLUTION AND EMIGRATION,

—•◈•—

Oliver Cromwell and the death of a King
– Leaving for the new world

King Charles I

In the first five years, (1625-1630) of his reign King Charles 1ˢᵗ (1625-1649) summoned and dissolved Parliament three times. He tried to rule England without Parliament and for the next eleven years no Parliaments were held. The King's main adviser was William Laud, the Archbishop of Canterbury. Laud argued that the King ruled by Divine Right. He claimed that the King had been appointed by God and people who disagreed with him were bad Christians. When Laud gave instructions that the wooden communion tables in churches should be replaced by stone altars, Puritans accused Laud of trying to reintroduce Catholicism. Archbishop Laud also upset the Presbyterians in Scotland when he insisted they had to use the English Prayer Book. Scottish Presbyterians were furious and made it clear they were willing to fight to protect their religion.

In 1639 the Scottish army marched on England. Charles was unable to raise a strong army and was forced to agree not to interfere with religion in Scotland. He also agreed to pay the Scottish war expenses. Charles did not have the money to pay the Scots and so he had to ask Parliament for help. The Parliament summoned in 1640 lasted for twenty years and is therefore usually known as The Long Parliament. This time Parliament was determined to restrict the powers of the King.

The King's two senior advisers, William Laud and Thomas Wentworth were arrested and sent to the Tower of London. They were charged with treason, Thomas Wentworth, Earl of Strafford, was executed on 12ᵗʰ May 1641. Charles eventually fled from London and was aware that Civil War was inevitable, he began to form an army. Religion was an important factor in deciding which side the people supported. The King's persecution of Puritans meant that most members of this religious group supported Parliament, whereas most Anglicans and Catholics

83

tended to favour the Royalists. Large landowners often persuaded their workers to join their army. Landowners living in the north and south-west of England and Wales tended to side with the King, the latter group became known as Cavaliers, as opposed to Roundheads who were the people living in London and the counties in the south-east of England who mainly supported Parliament.

After three years of bitter fighting the war effectively came to an end with the defeat of the Royalist forces at Naseby. The battle was a disaster for Charles. About 1,000 of his men were killed and another 4,500 of his most experienced troops were taken prisoner. After Naseby, Charles was never able to raise another army strong enough to defeat the parliamentary army in a major battle. The Scottish invasion and simultaneous Royalist uprisings in England and Wales resulted in the short but bitterly-fought Second Civil War, culminating in Cromwell's victory over the Scots at the battle of Preston in August 1648.

Charles was in deep trouble because his officers had lost faith in him. It was now their belief that God was on the side of the Parliamentarian cause. Tired of his deceptions and intrigues, the Army denounced King Charles as the 'Man of Blood'. Many moderates were thrown out of Parliament in December 1648 by Cromwell, what was left was a small core group of MPs totally dependent on the Army for their survival. In January 1649 this core of MPs appointed a High Court of Justice and Charles was charged with high treason against the people of England.

Lyon family involvement

The Lyon father and sons had originally been supporters of the King and were Covenanters but had grown weary of the King's duplicity and scheming. They aligned themselves with Oliver Cromwell. The three young men had fought against the King in the Civil War, for Cromwell and his Model Army. *(To read more about the Civil War go to http://www.british-civil-wars.co.uk/)*

They were all in their twenties and had been allegedly born in Scotland from whence came their forebears the Lyon's of Glamis Castle with their Royal connections in Scotland. The Lyon brothers had all been involved in the religious uprisings with the Covenanters and the Puritans, being opposed to Charles who had more sympathy with the Roman Catholic Church and its teachings.

The King James Bible of 1611 had opened up a fervent new interest in the teachings of the Bible involving such denominations as the Presbyterians, Congregationalists, later the Quakers and many others in the United Kingdom.

The Church of England was split between the traditionalists and the Puritans. Cromwell, a Puritan by birth, defended the Puritan beliefs and caused much hatred amongst those who held to the traditions of the Church, especially the Roman Catholic influences of vestments and Communion practices such as the Mass.

During the Reformation in the previous century, the Book of Common Prayer, Calvin's teachings and the printing of the Tyndale and other Bibles helped to lead the monarchy, Henry VIII and Queen Elizabeth and others to follow Protestant teachings. At this time the Lyon males were it seems religious men; their forbears had fought for their covenanter beliefs and had defended James VI of Scotland and had come to England with him, when he came to take over the throne of England.

Oliver Cromwell

Cromwell history can be briefly summed up by a few dates and references. He was born 1599 in Huntingdon and his father was a Gentleman. In 1616 Oliver attended Cambridge University for only a year. In 1620 he married ELIZABETH BOURCHIER and they produced 9 children. He was elected to Parliament to represent Huntingdon in 1628. He became a committed Puritan at this time. He inherited a substantial inheritance; he became a freeman of Cambridge and its MP in 1640. He took up arms in the First Civil War in 1642 and he held Cambridge with a troop of 60 horsemen.

He attained the rank of Lieutenant General in 1644. The next year he helped to found the New Model Army led by Sir Thomas Fairfax. In June 1647 he fully supported the army against King Charles I. In 1648 they defeated the Royalists at Preston. It is important to note that the Lyon sons were quite likely in the Model army at the Battle of Preston in August 1648. Cromwell's signature was third on the death warrant. In June 1650 he was appointed Captain-General of the Commonwealth. *(http://www.british-civil-wars.co.uk/military/1648-preston.htm)*

In 1653 he was appointed Lord Protector of the Commonwealth. He refused the crown in 1657 and died suddenly in 1658 and had a State Funeral that year, mourned by many but jeered by his many enemies. England was still a country divided. The monarchy was not restored until 1660.

The Trial

On 20th January, the King's trial opened. He refused to answer the charges, saying that he did not recognise the authority of the High Court. In fact only 68 judges turned up for the trial. Those that did not appear were concerned about being associated with the trial of the King. In fact, there were plenty of MP's in Parliament who did not want to see the King put on trial. In December 1648, these MP's had been prevented from going into Parliament by a Colonel Pride who was helped and protected by some soldiers of Oliver Cromwell's Model Army. The only people allowed into Parliament were those whom Cromwell thought supported the trial of the King. This Parliament was known as the "Rump Parliament" and of the 46 men allowed in, only 26 voted to try the King. Therefore even among those

MPs, considered loyal to Cromwell, there was no clear support to put Charles on trial.

The Chief Judge was a man called John Bradshaw, who sat as head of the High Court of Justice. He was not one of the original 135 judges but none of the 68 that did turn up wanted to be Chief Judge and the job was given to Bradshaw, who was a lawyer. He knew that putting Charles on trial was not popular and he actually feared for his own life. But he was a man of strong principles with the determination to see 'justice' carried out. He had a special hat made for himself reinforced with metal to protect his head against attack. It was Bradshaw who read out the charge against Charles. It alleged that his tyrannical rule had wickedly overthrown the rights and liberties of the people of England. The hall where the King was tried was packed with soldiers to keep order. The public was not allowed into the hall until after the charge had been read out because there was a strong fear that the public might riot. At the trial Charles refused to defend himself as he said he did not recognise the legality of the court. His attitude was seen as arrogant and further proof of his lack of respect for parliament and his people.

Bradshaw announced the judgment of the court: that 'he, the said Charles Stuart, as a tyrant, traitor, murderer and public enemy to the good of this nation, shall be put to death by severing of his head from his body'. When the judgment of the court was announced, Charles, obviously now realising that he was in mortal danger, finally started to defend himself. He was told that his chance had gone and the King of England was bundled out of the court by the Parliamentary soldiers. His date of execution was set for January 30th 1649.

Before his execution Charles in his impassioned speech said that he never intended to divide the two Houses of Parliament and that he desired the liberty and freedom of the people as much as anyone else but he still maintained that a 'subject and a sovereign are different people' and he defiantly proclaimed that he was 'a martyr and that he had God on his side'. The judgement to execute the King shocked almost everyone who heard it, even Charles' enemies. To kill, by public execution, a King in England was without precedent. Cromwell himself was said to have 'hid his face' at the announcement of the execution order. He, nevertheless, was prepared to carry out the sentence. His Christian beliefs, as a Puritan, made him question whether the decision was right, in the light of the teachings of the New Testament, with its emphasises on forgiveness.

The King was beheaded on a scaffold outside the Banqueting House at Whitehall on 30th January 1649. The Reformation had affected many people in Scotland, Ireland, Wales and England. This was the start of a great change in history for the monarchy and the common people of the British Isles. At the trial of Charles I before the judges who were present, he was accused of being a 'tyrant, traitor and murderer; and a public and implacable enemy to the Commonwealth of England'.

It is claimed in Lyon history that three brothers were present as soldiers of Oliver Cromwell's Model Army at the execution of King Charles I. The anonymous executioner severed the head of the King at Whitehall on a cold day on the 30th January 1649. The crowd had very mixed emotions about the regicide but Oliver Cromwell's troops kept order and eventually the crowd dispersed, stunned by this great event in British history.

"Amongst the crowd that day were a father of 59 years of age and his three sons. Their life and family history would be changed for ever and so would the history of America. "Thomas, Henry and Richard Lyon were interestingly on guard before the Banqueting House and witnessed the execution of Charles I. A tremendous reaction followed the regicide and many a Puritan and Covenanter patriot of the insurgent army disappeared from London in the confusion of the horror of the execution."
(Chapter: Some New World Lyons – The Lyon Memorial - Vol. 2 p

After the execution of Charles I the English established a Commonwealth until 1653. This operated in Parliament to rule the country with Members of Parliament, one being Oliver Cromwell who represented Cambridge. Oliver Cromwell became the Lord Protector from 1653 until his death in 1658. His son Richard took over until 1659 when King Charles II was given the throne for the next 25 years. The Royalists who had always supported the King were still smarting from their losses during the previous Civil War battles and as a result the Kingdom was not safe for followers of Cromwell.

The Lyon family were in potential danger, as were many hundreds of those who had served the Roundhead cause. The country was very politically and religiously divided and it was not easy to distinguish who followed which cause apart from attendance at church on Sundays. The Lyon family members must have been weary of war. The climate at this time was one of extreme instability and unrest.

Richard Lyon senior lived at Heston, a small village ten miles west of London, with his three sons; **Thomas, Henry** and **Richard**. In those days the village had a population of about 300 souls. A 1650 map of London shows that London was a much smaller city than the present day. Westminster and the Houses of Parliament were next to open fields to the west. People were crammed into the central area above and below the river to the east of Parliament. To see maps of London at this time go to: *http://www.thelyonfamily.org.uk/lyon%20photos.html*

The Great Plague

The Great Plague in 1665 killed about 60,000 citizens out of a population of over 250,000. The City was monstrously overcrowded, filthy and no place for gentlemen to live. Heston lost 160 lives in the plague and this number might well have included the Lyon family had they not emigrated. It is not known for certain what happened to them in the days following the execution of the King but snippets of information tend to suggest that they rode to hide with friends in Essex.

Migration to the New World

American immigration records show Richard's three sons sailed for America in 1649. The reason why they decided to leave England could have been that they were very unhappy at the execution of King Charles; many people were repulsed by the action of Cromwell and his followers. Ships were frequently leaving England for the American continent at this time; thousands had been emigrating for over twenty years. Some voyages were horrendous because of the weather and disease but these were quite wealthy travellers and no doubt would be able to pay for whatever comforts were available. The wind and tides often dictated where they landed but there were well-established settlements all over New England

The three young men fled to America in 1649; **Thomas** (1621), **Henry** (1623) and **Richard** (1624), all born, according to records, at Glen Lyon in Scotland. Many genealogists refute this claim of their birthplace as this branch of the family had moved from Scotland many generations before. It is most likely that they were born at Heston in Middlesex, London.

Just before this time **Patrick Lyon**, 1st Earl of Kinghorne (1575–1615) and the 9th Lord of Glamis had died. His son **John Lyon** (1596) became the 2nd Earl of Kinghorne (1596–1646). His son, **Patrick Lyon**, the 3rd Earl of Kinghorne (1643–1695) became Earl of Strathmore and Kinghorne. These members of the family had been the clan chiefs in every way and still based themselves at Glamis Castle in Angus.

"In Scotland every clan was an independent force that withdrew at the discretion of its chieftain. The three Lyon brothers from Glen Lyon or Glamis took advantage of a particular national privilege. They had kinsmen in Middlesex and Norfolk counties who may have kept them in concealment during the departure of a ship for Colonies across the sea. It is a rational supposition that the young men landed at New Haven, Connecticut.

There lived a John Lyon of Badby of Northamptonshire England, one of the opulent company of 250 persons who came from London on the ship "Hector" on January 12th 1638, eleven years earlier, with Theophilus Eaton and Edward Hopkins as their directors. There was also the Puritan divine, John Davenport, their spiritual guide whose shared intention was to plant an independent colony on the Connecticut Coast.

When the Plantation Covenant was signed on June 4th 1638, John Lyne (Lyon) (We cannot find evidence that he was a member of the same Lyon family), affixed his signature among names that became historic when the story of New England was subsequently told. They were all anti-monarchists strongly in sympathy with the Parliamentarian Party. To their hospitable protection came the Regicides, Goffe and Whalley, in later troublous times". *(See Lyon Memorial book)*

"William Goffe was a leading supporter of Oliver Cromwell with his father-in-law and fellow-regicide Edward Whalley. Goffe fled to New England at the Restoration (after Cromwell's death) and hid in the frontier town of Hadley, Massachusetts. With the help of sympathetic colonists, Whalley and Goffe evaded capture by Royalist agents sent to seek them out. Goffe entered colonial folklore as the "Angel of Hadley", reportedly emerging from the forest to lead the settlers in repelling an attack by hostile redskins in 1675." *http://bcw-project.org/biography/william-goffe*

The three brothers took their beliefs with them to the New World. **Thomas** was a member of the newly formed Quaker movement and therefore would have probably been a pacifist. **Henry** was a Congregationalist. **Richard Jr.** has no record of church membership in the New World but his children and their wives were Congregationalist members. We know little about the religious beliefs of **Richard senior** but we believe that he was a serious Bible scholar as he had gone to Massachusetts in America to translate part of the Book of Psalms in 1640 and he had returned to England by this time and was living at Heston, Middlesex.

The Lyon family was a powerful organisation of which they were, no doubt, proud. They realised that it would be wise to join thousands of Puritans who had led the way to New England and they had heard wonderful things about their future homeland. Above all there was a Lyon tradition of over hundreds of years, they loved to own land and farm it. Most members of their family were farmers big and small.

They would have known that one of their cousins, orphaned **William Lyon,** who was born in Heston in 1620, had been living near Boston Massachusetts since

1635 – the first known Lyon to settle in America. By 1649 he had done well for himself in Roxbury and was settled with a Christian wife and two young children. He was to become the founder of an enormous dynasty still surviving today from New England to the West coast of America and south to Texas and Florida. Actually the distance from Fairfield, Connecticut, to their cousin William near Boston was about 160 miles over land. These distances were no greater than they had experienced travelling in the United Kingdom, for example, the distance between Glamis in Scotland to Heston is over 480 miles.

Part 2

CHAPTER 6
SETTLING IN THE NEW WORLD

·•❀•·

The early settlers in New England, William Lyon - First four generations

Under the reign of Charles I in early 1600s Charles tried to return 'Protestant' England to Roman Catholicism, reversing the Reformation. Puritans who had grown in strength now faced harassment and prosecution. Many of them decided to emigrate and start new lives in North America where they could practise their religion freely. These Puritans migrated to New England and established Plymouth Colony in Massachusetts Bay in 1620.

Virginia had been settled early in the 1600s and had immediately come under the rule of the King as a colony. Many of the early settlers starved to death like the settlers in Virginia at the beginning of the 17th century. In fact Jamestown became a burial ground for many immigrants for a variety of reasons including hostilities from the Indians, the bad weather and also crop failures.

(For those of you interested this story is available in both films and books but a summary is available on Wikipedia;
http://en.wikipedia.org/wiki/Jamestown,Virginia#Arrival_and_early_years_.281607 -1610.29)

Records indicate that the pilgrims in Massachusetts and New England seemed to have coped much better and there was a higher survival rate. Some of the members of the Lyon family settled near Boston, Massachusetts (MA) and later in Connecticut (CT), all in what is now known as New England. Later, that also came to include Maine, Rhode Island, Vermont, New Hampshire, New York State and also New Jersey. For more information on the original settlers visit the Winthrop Society website.

(http://www.winthropsociety.com/home.php)

Wikipedia gives a colourful account of the journey of the first settlers to New England in the Mayflower in 1620.

"Aboard the Mayflower, were many stores that supplied the pilgrims with the essentials needed for their journey and future lives. It is assumed that among these stores, they would have carried tools and weapons, including cannon, shot, and gunpowder, as well as some live animals, including dogs, sheep, goats, and poultry. Horses and cattle would come later. The Mayflower would also carry two boats: a long boat and a 'shallop', a sort of twenty-one foot dinghy.

She also carried twelve artillery pieces, as the Pilgrims feared they might need to defend themselves against the Spaniards, Frenchmen, or the Dutch, as well as the Natives.

It had been a miserable passage with a huge wave crashing against the ship's topside until a structural support timber fractured. So far the passengers had suffered agonizing delays, cold and the scorn and ridicule of the sailors, but had done everything they could to help the carpenter repair the fractured ship's beam. A mechanical device called a screw-jack was loaded on board to help them in the construction of homes in the New World. The beam was loaded into place with the screw-jack making the Mayflower secure enough to continue the voyage. There were two deaths, but this was only a precursor of what happened after their arrival in Cape Cod, where almost half the company would die in the first winter. On November 19th 1620, they sighted land, which was present-day Cape Cod. After several days of trying to sail south to their planned destination of the Colony of Virginia where they had already obtained permission from the Company of Merchant Adventurers to settle, strong winter seas forced them to return to the harbour at Cape Cod Hook, well north of the intended area where they anchored on November 2nd.

To establish legal order and to quell increasing strife within the ranks, the settlers wrote and signed the Mayflower Compact after the ship dropped anchor at the tip of Cape Cod on November 21st, in what is now Provincetown Harbour. The Mayflower Compact was signed that day. (This was an agreement about behaviour and expectations over land distribution and other legal matters).

On Monday, November 27th, an exploring expedition was launched to search for a settlement site under the direction of Christopher Jones. As master of the Mayflower, Jones was not required to assist in the search, but he apparently thought it in his best interest to do so. There were thirty-four persons in an open shallop – twenty-four passengers and ten sailors. On their patrol they were obviously not prepared for the bitter winter weather that they encountered. Due to the bad weather they were forced to spend the night ashore ill-clad in below freezing temperatures with wet shoes and stockings that became frozen. 'Some of our people that are dead,' Bradford wrote, 'took the origin of their death here'. The settlers explored the snow-covered area and discovered an empty native village. The curious settlers dug up some artificially made mounds, some of which stored corn, while others were burial sites. A Nathaniel Philbrick claims that the settlers stole the corn and looted and desecrated the graves, sparking friction with the locals. Philbrick goes on to say that, as they moved down the coast to what is now Eastham, they explored the area of Cape Cod for several weeks, looting and stealing native stores as they went. He then writes about how they decided to relocate to Plymouth after a difficult encounter with the local natives, the Nausets, at First Encounter Beach, in December 1620.

Bradford's *History of Plymouth Plantation* records that 'they took' some of the corn to show the others back at the boat, leaving the rest. Then, later, they took what they needed from another store of grain, paying the locals back in six months, and it was gladly received. During the winter, the passengers remained on board the Mayflower, suffering an outbreak of a contagious disease described as a mixture of scurvy, pneumonia and tuberculosis. When it ended, there were only 53 passengers, just over half, still alive. Likewise, half of the crew died as well. In the spring, they built huts ashore, and on March 31st 1621, the surviving passengers disembarked from the Mayflower. The Mayflower lay in New Plymouth harbour through the winter of 1620-1.

Due to the fear of Indian attack, in late February 1621, the settlers decided to mount 'our great ordnances' on the hill overlooking the settlement. Christopher Jones supervised the transportation of the 'great guns' – about six iron cannons that ranged between four and eight feet in length and weighed almost half a ton. The cannon were able to hurl iron balls as big as 3 ½ inches in diameter as far as 1,700 yards. This action made what was no more than a ramshackle village into a well-defended fortress. Jones had originally planned to return to England as soon as the Pilgrims found a settlement site. But after his crew members began to be ravaged by the same diseases that were felling the Pilgrims, he realized he had to remain in Plymouth Harbour till he saw his men began to recover.

On April 15th, the Mayflower, her empty hold ballasted with stones from the Plymouth Harbour shore, set sail for England. As with the Pilgrims, her sailors had been decimated by disease. Jones had lost his boatswain, his gunner, three quartermasters, the cook, and more than a dozen sailors. The Mayflower made excellent time on her voyage back to England. The Westerlies that had buffeted her coming out pushed her along going home and she arrived at the home port of Rotherhithe in London on May 16th, 1621 – less than half the time it had taken her to sail to America.

Jones died after coming back from a voyage to France on March 5th 1622, at about age 52. It is suggested that his journey to the New World may have taken its toll on him. For the next two years, the Mayflower lay at her berth in Rotherhithe, not far from the grave of Captain Jones at St. Mary's church there. By 1624, the Mayflower was no longer useful as a ship and although her subsequent fate is unknown, she was probably broken up about that time. The Mayflower was the final casualty of a voyage that had cost her master,

Christopher Jones, everything he could give."

(http://en.wikipedia.org/wiki/Mayflower)

The Pilgrim's migration was mainly for religious reasons because they were Puritans by faith and practice and they considered that Britain had become an ungodly place. They were not usually members of the Church of England but were mostly Presbyterians, Baptists and Congregationalists. They also established a Commonwealth in and around Boston, MA.

(http://en.wikipedia.org/wiki/Commonwealth_of_Massachusetts),

(http://en.wikipedia.org/wiki/Puritan)

The following decade from 1630 to 1640 marked the period of time known as the Great Migration. During this time, Massachusetts's population rocketed with the exodus of approximately 21,000 immigrants to New England, about a third of them being British. However, by 1660 (under the rule of Charles II), large-scale migration from Britain to New England rapidly decreased and was officially discouraged. Much status and income was gained by owning land, even though the soil in large parts of New England was poor and the forests had to be frequently cleared so that produce could be grown. There were also wild animals to trap and plenty of fish to catch. The native Indians knew how to enrich the sandy soil by burying fish into the poor soil which acted as fertilizer and improved the harvest.

Christian religion played a big part in the lives of the settlers and they nearly all attended church at this time as a result of which they were soon organised into God-fearing communities. The leading church ministers brought discipline and order to bear on their congregations. The influence of the Protestant churches and Puritan teachings was reflected in the choice of first names given to their children. There were unusual names like; *Deliverance and Thankful* as well as other pious names. Names were also taken from the Bible.

We will be following the history of early settlers in America of the Lyon family in the next chapters of the book. William will be traced through to about the time of the War of Independence in 1776. The stories of Thomas, Henry and Richard will follow in the next chapter through to the fourth generation in the mid - 1700s.

Later in the book we will move through to the American Civil War and then west and south as the family moved to new territories after living in New England. The first is William:-

WILLIAM LYON III (1620) OF ROXBURY, MASSACHUSETTS

Father: William II 1580-1634 Heston, Middlesex
Grandfather: William I -1555 -1624 Little Stanmore, Middlesex **Great Grandfather**: John Lyon 1521-1592 – the 7th Earl of Glamis.
Great Great Grandfather: John Lyon 1491-1528 born Glamis Castle – 6th Earl of Glamis

William Lyon was born in 1620. He was the youngest son of William Lyon II (1580) of Heston, Middlesex and ANNE CARTER. His father died aged 54 at Heston. His mother Anne, born in 1580 also died young in 1634. Smallpox epidemics were quite common in those days and it is possible that smallpox killed many of William's family. William had a sister Elizabeth born in 1616 at Heston, it is claimed that she died in 1710 in France. He also had two brothers both named John who, unfortunately, died at birth in 1617 and 1619 and possibly an older brother Thomas Lyon who was born in 1600 to another mother. William is sometimes referred to as the youngest son of William Lyon (1580). There is evidence that William III was baptised at Heston on December 23rd 1620.

William sailed on the 'Hopewell' which plied its trade to America with frequent trips. The 'Hopewell' on this occasion sailed on September 11th, 1635 and William is listed as being 'fourteen yeres' (sic). He made the journey with sponsors after he had been left an orphan at Heston near London. He travelled with Isack Heath aged 50 from Amwell, Little Hertfordshire, who had been a close friend of his parents. They had all attended the same church. Fifty of the fifty-eight passengers were under 30 years of age and most were single. Journeys across the Atlantic could be pleasant or horrendous depending entirely on the weather. Mr Babb, the captain knew the difficulties well and they landed at Roxbury Bay, just south of Boston, Massachusetts, in 1635.

William had descended from the Scottish nobility through the Lyon family relationship with King Robert the Bruce of Scotland. Scots are always very proud of their heritage and he would have been mindful of his family history. Life in this new country was very different from Heston, London and its surroundings. As a young man William would have very quickly become aware of the sufferings of the early immigrants. He settled in Roxbury which was an established village near Boston where he was among friends but no close family. 'The name is further registered in Rolls Office, Chancery Lane, London, as having sailed for New England 9/11/1635 and settled on Roxbury, Mass'.

It is an important distinction to make that at this time the settlers saw Massachusetts as an independent colony but Charles I did not recognise the state's independence from England. He saw it as British territory and stationed troops there. These new settlers had left their homeland for strong reasons of principle and integrity and were, for the most part, early pioneers desiring to form a new world.

Nearly all William's neighbours were from England and Scotland and they would have centred their social life on the church. Heston was approximately the same size as Roxbury but quite different in appearance. New England and later American towns were laid out in neat rows, grids, which usually comprised of eight blocks to the mile.

William Lyon is said to have been placed in the care of Isack Heath. There appears to be no reason to question the conclusion reached by Albert Welles in *American Family Antiquity*, 'that this was the William Lyon who was baptized at Heston, now part of the city of London, 12/23/1629, the youngest son of William and Anne (Carter) Lyon of Heston'.

William Lyon married 17th June 1646 (Roxbury Church records) to Sarah Ruggles, daughter of Thomas and Mary (Curtis) Ruggles of Nazing, England. She was born 19th April 1629 and came to America with her parents. The death of Sarah is not found in Roxbury town or church records and probably occurred in Rowley on 20th November 1677. William Lyon, now of Rowley, later married a Mrs. Martha Philbrick Casse (Cass), widow of John Casse.

> The Lyon Memorial tells us; "William Lyon in 1645 became a member of the Ancient and Honorable Artillery Co. of Roxbury. He received in 1648 a grant of six acres of land in Roxbury, and in 1652 another three acres 'upon the common, by John Polly's'. His name also appears as a grantee in deeds of land in Roxbury in 1651, 1658 and 1661, and as grantor in 1658 and 1672.
>
> When the new settlement at New Roxbury, now Woodstock, VERMONT, was determined upon in 1651 he was one of the 'goers', and he was assigned a lot there, although he did not actually occupy it. Several of his Grandsons (William, Thomas, John and Jacob), were prominent members however, of the new colony and a stepson, Ebenezer Cass, received a grant of land there. The Nazing Colony in Roxbury included brothers, John and Philip Eliot, William Curtis, uncle of Sarah Ruggles, and many familiar names.
>
> The Lyon homestead in Roxbury was on what is now Bellevue Avenue, formerly called Lyon Street. It was on the east side of the street, southwest of Atwood Street. William Lyon was admitted to full communion in John Eliot's Church in 1655 and became a freeman in 1666. He, with John Bowles signed Roxbury petition 25th October 1664 to the General Court, praying it to 'stand fast in our present libertys'. He lived to the age of 72 years. He was buried on the 21st May 1692 probably in West Roxbury

cemetery, although there is no stone there to mark the spot. His widow died about 4ᵗʰ August 1694. *(Roxbury town records)*

A recorded Deed dated 25ᵗʰ June 1651: "For valuable consideration in hand received' Captain Hugh Pritchard, late of Roxbury in New England, deeds unto James Morgan, Griffin Craft, Edward Bridge, **William Lyon**, John Mayes, Robert Seaber and JOHN RUGGLES and Isaac Johnson of Roxbury. My will is that my four sons, THOMAS AND SAMUEL, WILLIAM AND JOSEPH shall have 16 pounds apiece duly and truly paid unto them in current pay at current prices within 6 years after my death by my above mentioned executor. And for the better enabling my son JOHN LION to discharge these obligations, I the said William LION, SR give all my movables within and without doors excepting those things particularly given. And furthermore if in case that the salt marsh doesn't come to make Thomas and William 16 pounds apiece, then to be made up out of the estate.

The last will of William LION, witness my hand and seal -- Signed by William LION, Sr. and seal affixed. In presence of Jabez Tolman, John Grigs,

Francis Youngman; probated 27ᵗʰ October 1692." *(Lyon Memorial Massachusetts Family p.24-27)*

A Brief History of Roxbury, Massachusetts (MA)

For a map of the area at the time see Maps and Illustrations at the beginning of the book.

"Founded by English colonists in 1630, Roxbury began as an independent community, connected to Boston only by a narrow neck of land along Washington Street. Today, after massive landfill and annexation to Boston, Roxbury is at the city's geographical centre. It contains buildings and landmarks that tell the story of three centuries. Even with dense urban development, Roxbury has much open, green space, a legacy of its days as a farming town and as an early suburb.

The English settlers of the Massachusetts Bay Company established a group of six villages, including Boston, on the Shawmut Peninsula. Three miles south of Boston along the only land route to the peninsula, they founded Roxbury. The original boundaries of the town included the neighbourhoods of Mission Hill, West Roxbury, and Jamaica Plain as well as present-day Roxbury.

Roxbury had many resources the colonists were looking for: open farmland, timber and stone for building, and the Stony Brook for water power. Additionally, its location on the only road to Boston gave the town an advantage in transportation and trade and a strategic military position. The colonists soon began constructing buildings and roads that still define the neighbourhood today. Washington, Dudley, Centre, Roxbury, and Warren streets were all laid out in the first years of settlement.

The town centre was located at John Eliot Square, where the first meetinghouse was built in 1632, with its burying ground nearby at the corner of Eustis and Washington streets. Other landmarks that form early Roxbury are the three milestones that still mark Centre Street in Roxbury, Jamaica Plain, and West Roxbury, recording the distance to downtown Boston. An 18th-century marker, known as the parting stone, is still embedded at the fork of Roxbury and Centre streets, pointing the ways to Brookline and Dedham. Roxbury was defined by its rocky hills left by a prehistoric glacier. In the area of Roxbury Highlands are many outcroppings of native Roxbury puddingstone, a kind of composite rock used over the centuries in buildings throughout the Boston area."
(http://www.rcht.org/roxbury_history.htm)

On the map of the early Boston area, surrounding villages like Dorchester are now suburbs of Boston. Roxbury still has a Lyon Street showing on a more recent map. Several members of the Lyon family later moved to Dorchester and other towns in Massachusetts.

Summary of the history of the settlers

The earliest settlers left England and Scotland for various reasons; some for religious reasons, some because of their poverty, some were soldiers despatched to protect the people on behalf of the King at the time, some were criminals sent to make restitution for their crimes.

The educated and upper classes often became local leaders in their chosen settlements. Protestant churches were started in most places and organised their congregations with rules and laws to create peaceful and hard-working societies. The 'Protestant Work Ethic' is based upon the Calvinist emphasis on the necessity for hard work as a proof of a person's calling and worldly success. It is argued that Protestants beginning with Martin Luther had reconceptualised worldly work as a duty which benefits both the individual and society as a whole. The old 'work ethic' is still very much practiced in the USA and most likely the cause of its prosperity. Americans generally have fewer holidays than most countries and success is a mark of distinction more highly prized than titles. Everyone is a 'Mister or Missus' and no Lords and Ladies are tolerated.

The settlers needed property to provide for themselves and this meant depriving Indians of their properties, some land was pillaged from them, some was bought cheaply and in some cases intoxicating liquor became the currency to purchase the property. Some settlers traded weapons, spades and other tools to the local Indians. This invasion of Indian's lands was obviously not appreciated and continual wars took place for most of the first 100 years and beyond between the 'real' Americans and their invaders. There were cases of terrible cruelty on both sides but there were many cases of successful collaboration and mutual trust. The Indians had been at war with each other for generations and the usual cause was land or lack of it.

The plots were rich with trees but much of the soil was poor. It required farmers to provide for the settlers in this new country. Winters lasted from November until April some years and could be ferociously cold with temperatures 30 degrees below freezing, especially when the wind was blowing from Alaska and the West and from the North. Summers could be unbearably hot and the new settlers would take some time to acclimatise to these conditions.

Wherever settlers moved they would need farmers, cattlemen, shepherds, carpenters, plumbers, stone masons, foresters, wood mill operatives, hunters, doctors, dentists, lawyers, Ministers of religion, tradesmen and many more skills as they developed into larger communities. The local churches and citizens set up committees to decide legal matters and land distribution and in those early days agriculture was the big user of labour. Families often tended to be large and children were brought up to work the lands from an early age. Those who had owned property and farmed in the 'old country' certainly had an advantage over those who had little or no experience of such matters. As the communities grew they elected certain citizens as 'free men'.

The **Freemen** were the only colonists who were franchised to vote, and the franchise was not offered to all. One generally had to be a mature male church member, and must have experienced a 'transforming spiritual experience by God's grace, as attested by him and confirmed by church leaders'.

The Oath of Freeman agreed upon at the General Court, May 14th, 1634.

"I …being by God's providence an inhabitant and freeman within the jurisdiction of this common weal (commonwealth), do freely acknowledge myself to be subject to the government thereof, and therefore do hereby swear by the great and dreadful name of the ever-living God that I will be true and faithful to the same, and will accordingly yield assistance and support thereunto, with my person and estate, as in equity I am bound, and will also truly endeavor to maintain and preserve all the privileges and liberties thereunto, submitting myself to the wholesome laws made and established by the same. And further, that I will not plot nor practise any evil against it, nor consent to any that shall be so done, but will timely discover and reveal the same to lawful authority now here established for the speedy preventing thereof. Moreover, I do solemnly bind myself in the sight of God that when I shall be called to give my voice touching any such matter of this State, wherein Freemen are to deal, I will give my vote and suffrage as I shall in my own conscience judge best to produce and tend to the public weal of the body, without respect of persons or respect of any man. So help me God in the Lord Jesus Christ."

This oath did cause problems in Boston in the early days, only a small percentage of the people were given a vote and subsequently others were often denied their 'rights', whatever they saw as their rights. Already the leaders had made a rod for their own back and made evangelical or Puritan religion the prime mover in men's affairs. As we have already seen Quakers like Thomas Lyon in Connecticut years later saw much suffering for their faith, especially over the teachings of Quaker pacifism.

Another major problem was the loyalty of the early settlers and their descendants, whether to choose to support the King or Queen of England or to support the Commonwealth. Most people wanted freedom from tyranny and oppression by their past rulers. There were also immigrants from other countries, the Dutch, Germans and French who had been there for some time and they had their own political and social agenda.

There were constant wars between the French and British troops and problems with some Indian tribes. Life was not a 'bed of roses' for the settlers and the additional burden of being taxed and over-taxed by those in Britain was not conducive to peace and security. It was this over-taxation that eventually led to the War of Independence with the uprising in Boston, commonly known as the Boston Tea Party.

Another big problem was that of personal hygiene because of polluted water and food contamination, particularly during the very hot summers. Mosquitoes, flies and other insects were abundant in the forested area and people entering could easily become infected. There were doctors, but most cures were basic and ignorance caused mass outbreaks of cholera and typhoid fever. Thousands died regularly because of poor hygiene practices and sanitation.

Education was somewhat lacking at first but the churches soon organised schools, most using the Bible as the coursework book of preference. Children were taught mathematics, art and music and other subjects when they had teachers available to teach them. Harvard, Yale and Princeton Universities were founded; Harvard in 1636 in Cambridge, Massachusetts, Yale in 1701 in New Haven, Connecticut and Princeton in 1746 in Elizabethtown, New Jersey. These 'Ivy League' universities have continued to be great institutions of learning to the present day.

People settled in organised communities for the most part, for mutual protection. They set up legal systems and appointed what we now know as policemen to keep the streets safe and to keep crime to a minimum. Most towns provided taverns and drinking places for those who liked alcohol in moderation. These taverns were run by Christians under the aegis of the church to make sure that moderation in all things was the rule. Non-Christians could drink or buy drink from these places but were rationed and kept in order by the owner. Several Lyon family members ran these taverns as recorded in the public records available.

At one stage in the early days one of Henry Lyon's sons helped him to start a wood mill and he supplied prepared timber for the local area very successfully for many years. Capitalism soon reared its head and others in the growing community started up other timber mills to undercut the prime mover – the start of free enterprise! The same situation arose with the distribution of all food stuffs through local shops and area markets.

Breeding imported cattle became big business. Breeding hens and chickens, goats, sheep and other animals and exchanging them became another means of earning a living and competition was fierce at times. The Lyon families were in their element because land and real estate was generally their historical background. The purchase of further land became essential for all such agricultural families so people started moving further afield and families often split to acquire land elsewhere. Even today most people like to own their own property. As the saying goes 'an Englishman's home is his castle'.

The custom seemed to be that the size of families was often quite large. Some could afford to keep a large family because of their own financial success. They often believed that a large family was a blessing from God. They needed to make sure that enough children survived the sometimes awful conditions, especially in the winter also diseases were rampant and many children died as can be seen in the charts of the various families earlier in the book.

As families became too large to sustain themselves in their homesteads many of them moved to other states. From New England the settlers had a great deal of difficulty in negotiating the Appalachians to reach the temperate, agricultural and prairie states of Ohio, Kentucky and Indiana and the Mid-West. From New England this meant a trip by cart and horse or buffalo of at least 200 miles over the mountains. In winter these mountains were often inaccessible and dangerous. Land was offered very cheaply to those who had the wherewithal to purchase what was on offer in the west. Some states like New Jersey had already become 'garden states' and those living there were for the most part prospering as farmers.

Story of the family of William Lyon (1620) for 4 Generations

William Lyon married SARAH RUGGLES, daughter of Thomas Ruggles and Mary Curtis, on 17th March 1645/46 in Roxbury, Suffolk, MA. Sarah Ruggles was born on 17th February 1627/28 in Nazeing, Essex, England. They had the following children;

2nd Generation and 3rd Generation

1. **John** (1647-1703) went on to marry ABIGAIL POLLY (1654-1703) and their children were; John (1673-1725), William (1675-1741), Joseph (1678-1724), Benjamin (1679-1679), Abigail (1682-1782), Benjamin (1684-1704), Susanna (16871698), Bethia (1690-1724), Ebenezer (1691-1764), Nehemiah (1695-1725) and Hannah (1698-1737)

   John and Abigail were both church members at John Elliot's church. They both died of smallpox and were buried together in the same grave on January 15th 1703. Samuel Ruggles and Joseph Weld were appointed guardians of the minor children; Ebenezer, Nehemiah, Bethiah and Hannah.

2. **Thomas** (1648-1734) married ABIGAIL GOULD (1658-1748) their children were; Eliphalet (m) (1687-1747), Anna (1689-1693. (Because some of the names are strange to us from the Old Testament I have marked (f) female, (m) male)

3. **Samuel** (1650-1713) married DELIVERANCE (1655-1691) then SARAH GRANT (1671), and their children were; Sarah (1673-1724), then Samuel (1675-1682), Ebenezer (1676-1717, Abel (1680-1756), Henry (1682-), Margaret (1685-) and Johanna (1687-).
   Samuel was described as a 'mason' and was dismissed from the church. It is possible that he had been a member of a Masonic order which was prohibited by Puritan churches generally. There was a history in England and maybe among some settlers of Masonic membership. These rules against Masonry still apply with many Evangelical churches to this day. The record states that he returned to the church a few years later.

4. **William** (1652-1714) married SARAH DUNKIN (1665-1689) then DEBORAH FAIRBANKS (1654-1717). The Governor at the time of his death stated that 'William was non compus mentus' and therefore not fit to manage the estate; their children were; William (1677-1743), then Samuel (1679-1756), Hannah (1681-1720), Benjamin (1683-1683), Mehitable (f) (1684-1724) and Jacob (1696-1771).

5. **Joseph** (1654-1721) married MARY BRIDGE (1662-1710), and the children were; Mary (1682-1682), then Joseph (1684-1751), Mary

(1686-1687), Mary (1686?-1729), Rebecca (1685-1716), Eunice (1701-1738). Joseph was the first Lyon to serve his new country as a soldier achieving the rank of Captain. He took part in the war in 1676.

6.   **Sarah Lyon** married JONATHAN CURTIS (1672-1717).

Sarah Ruggles died on 30th September 1677 in Rowley, Essex, MA.

To see the full list of the William Lyon family to this day visit the website *www. thelyonfamily.org.uk/help/genealogy*

William Lyon 3rd and 4th Generation

To illustrate how families can be traced back to William III, the pioneer, father then grandfather is bracketed after the name.

Joseph Lyon (1684-1751) (Joseph, William). He married ELIZABETH PHILLIPS and they had the following children: Elizabeth, Mary, Anna, Zerviah (f), Joseph, Lucy, Susanna and <u>Theode</u>. (Names that are <u>underlined</u> refer to an early death under the age of five very common at this time.)

Joseph (John) Lyon (1678-1724) (John, William) married MARY ALDRICH, children: <u>Joseph</u>, Joseph, Benjamin, <u>Mary</u>, Hannah, Mary.

William Lyon (1675-1741) (John, William).   Married   (1)   DEBORAH COLBURN, children: William, Daniel, Ebenezer, Nehemiah, Jabez, Aaron, Moses, <u>Moses</u>, also married (2), MARTHA MORRIS child; Margaret.
William was appointed to a committee to build a schoolhouse in 1710 in Woodstock CT. In 1712 he was appointed to the position of gravedigger for the parish. For digging the graves of children under five he was paid two shillings. For the graves of children between six and twelve he was paid three shillings and for graves of over thirteen's, including adults, he was paid five shillings. For some years William served on many local committees and he was also a member of the local Congregational church.

John Lyon (1673-1725) (John, William). Married ELIZABETH NEWELL, children: Hannah, Bethiah, Caleb, John, Abigail, Elizabeth, Benjamin, Susanna, Joshua.

Thomas Lyon (1669-1717) (Thomas, William). Married ABIGAIL CLARK, children: <u>Thomas</u>, Seth, Gould, Abigail, Noah, Sarah, Esther.

Thomas settled in Woodstock Connecticut (CT) and was appointed the second Schoolmaster in 1704. He was later a Corporal in a Company in the French Indian War, chiefly engaged in 'scouting and ranging'. *(French and Indian War 1689- http://www.ushistory.org/declaration/related/frin.htm).* He died at age forty four in 1717. In his Will he commits his children to the care of his wife Abigail, to be brought up in the fear of God and industrious improvement of their time during their minority, expecting them and requiring them to be both dutiful and obedient unto her. He owned many hundreds of acres all of which he bequeathed to his wife and children.

Ephraim Lyon (1685-1727) (Thomas, William). Married ABIGAIL CROSBY, children: Thomas, Ephraim, Josiah, Amariah (m), Aaron.

Eliphalet Lyon (1687-1747) (Thomas, William). Married ELIZABETH JORDAN, children: Thankful (f), Abigail, Esther, Hannah, Elizabeth.

Jacob Lyon (1696-1771) (William, William). Married MEHITABLE BUGBEE, children: Philip, Elizabeth, Jacob, David, William, Nathaniel, Grace, Mehitable (f), Molly, Zubulon (m).

Samuel Lyon (1679-1756) (William, William). Married JOANNA WELD, children: Phebe, Jedediah (m), William, Jonathan, Hannah, *Sarah*, Edward, Eleazor (m), John.

They moved To Middleborough MA, he owned over seventy acres of land and lived to the age of seventy six.

Sarah Lyon (1673-1724) (Samuel, William). Married JONATHAN CURTIS, children summary – six girls not named Lyon.

Samuel Lyon (1675-1725?) (Samuel, William): Married (1) ELIZABETH CAPEN, children: Samuel, Samuel, Obadiah (m). Married (2) Mrs MARY ROBINS BATESON, no children.

Ebenezer Lyon (1676-1717) (Samuel, William): Married ELIZABETH TORBET, children: Jemima, Experience (f), Ebenezer, Henry, Josiah, Eleanor.

Abiel Lyon (1680-1756) (Samuel, William): Married JUDITH FERRINGTON, children: Experience (f), Abiel (m), Jonathan, Peletiah (m), Judith Ferrington, Obadiah, Mary, Samuel, Peter, Abigail.

Notes on Woodstock CT

"In the mid-17th century, John Eliot, a Puritan missionary to the American

Indians, established 'praying towns' where Native Americans followed Christianity and were therefore expected to renounce their religious ceremonies, traditional dress, and customs. One Praying town, called Wabaquasset, six miles west of the Quinebaug River in present-day Woodstock, was the largest of the three northeastern Connecticut praying towns.

In 1675, when King Philip's War broke out, some of the town's Indians, placed their allegiance with the Mohegans and the English while others supported the Indians led by Philip, rallying to arms on what is now Curtis Island in present Holland, Massachusetts and Brimfield, Massachusetts.

During the war, the Praying town became deserted, and the English with their Indian allies marched through Woodstock ....in the summer of 1676 burning any crops or stored corn they could find. In 1682, Massachusetts bought a tract of land, which included Woodstock, from the Mohegans. A group of 13 men from Roxbury, Massachusetts (home of the Pastorate of Woodstock's earlier visitor, John Eliot), settled the town in 1686 and named it New Roxbury. Judge Samuel Sewall suggested the town change its name to Woodstock in 1690, and in 1749 the town became part of Connecticut". *(http://en.wikipedia.org/wiki/Woodstock, Connecticut)*

The French and Indian War, as it was referred to in the colonies, was the beginning of open hostilities between the colonies and Great Britain. England and France had been building toward a conflict in America since 1689.

These efforts resulted in the remarkable growth of the colonies from a population of 250,000 in 1700, to 1.25 million in 1750. .

Life Expectancy of first four Generations of William Lyon family

Where a 'date of death' is unknown this death is included in the column headed '?'.

William Lyon	m/f	0-9	10-19	20-29	30-39	40-49	50-59	60-69	70-79	80-89	90-99	100+	?	Totals
Gen. 1	F							1						1
	M	1						4			1			6
Gen. 2	F		2		2	4	1					1	4	14
	M	3	2		1	5		4	4				1	20
Gen 3	F	2	3	6	1	2	4	6	5	2	1	1	12	45
	M	6	1	6	6	4	3	8	6	5			4	49
Gen 4	F	7	1	9	7	7	5	5	7	7	2		40	97
	M	18	2	8	5	7	6	9	11	10	3	1	25	105
	Totals	37	11	29	22	29	19	37	33	24	7	3	86	337
												Average age		47.45

There were substantial infant deaths in the fourth generation particularly in places like Woodstock and this could largely be blamed on the smallpox epidemic that was raging across America at the time. The average age is low at 47 years whereas other members of the family who came to America later in 1649 on the average seems to live longer. Another fact to note is that the early deaths in the 4th Generation for those aged between twenty and forty years is partly due to losses incurred in the War of Independence. The war continued from 1775 until 1782 and Massachusetts was heavily involved in the conflict.

According to the estimates of many historians approximately 40-45% of the Colonists actively supported the rebellion. Approximately 15-20% of the population from the thirteen colonies remained loyal to the British Crown and the remaining 35-45% was largely neutral.

The total loss of life throughout the war has not been quantified but it is believed that, disease claimed far more lives than battle. Between 1775 and 1782 a smallpox epidemic swept across North America, killing more than 130,000 people. Historian Joseph Ellis suggests that Washington's decision to have his troops inoculated against the smallpox epidemic was one of his most important decisions made.

More than 25,000 American Revolutionaries died during active military service and about 8,000 of these deaths occurred in battle. The other 17,000 recorded deaths were from disease, including about 8,000–12,000 who died of starvation or disease brought about by deplorable conditions whilst prisoners, when held in mostly decaying British prison ships in New York.

It is however likely that this tally of deaths from disease is far too low as, 2,500 Americans died whilst encamped at Valley Forge in the winter of 1777–78 alone. The number of Revolutionaries seriously wounded or disabled by the war has been estimated at between 8,500 and 25,000. The total American military casualty figure could therefore have been as high as 50,000.

(en.wikipedia.org/wiki/American Revolutionary War)

In the late 17th century leaflets and newspapers were busy trying to persuade people in Scotland and England to migrate to America and start a new life;

This Advertisement from a Scottish paper encouraged people to emigrate and start a new life. This is interesting for several reasons because it gives a flavour of the time in 1684 – after the second group of the Lyon family had emigrated to Connecticut and New Jersey. It is encouraging other Scots to join them in East New Jersey which would have been just south of New York City or New Amsterdam as it was then known. One tends to think that high pressure sales is a fairly recent innovation, not so, this seems to have been published in about 1684 selling the virtues of moving to America and particularly New Jersey. I will leave some of it in its original form, just remember that s's often look like the letter 'f'.

ADVERTISEMENT,

To all Trades-men, Husbandmen, Servants and others who are willing to Transport themselves unto the Province of New-East-Jerfy in America, a great part of which belongs to Scots-men, Proprietors thereof.[1]

WHereas feveral Noblemen, Gentlemen, and others, who (by undoubted Rights derived from His Majefty, and His Royal Highnefs) are Intereſted and concerned in the Province of *New-East-Jersie*, lying in the midſt of the *English* Plantations in *America*, do intend (God-willing) to fend feveral Ships thither, in *May, June*, and *July* enfuing, 1684, from *Leith, Montrosa, Aberdeen* and *Glasgow*. Thofe are to give notice to all Tradef-men, Huf-bandmen and others. who are willing and defirous to go there. and are able

ADVERTISEMENT

To all Trades-men, Husbandmen, servants and others who are willing to transport themselves unto the Province of New-East-Jersey in America, a great part of which belongs to Scots-men, Proprietors thereof.

Whereas several Noblemen, Gentlemen, and others, by undoubted Rights derived from His Majesty, and His Royal Highness, are Interested and concerned in the province of New-East-Jersey, lying in the midst of the English plantations in America, do intend, (God Willing) to send several ships thither, in May, June, and July, 1684 from Leith, Montrose, Aberdeen and Glasgow. These are to give notice to all tradesmen, husbandmen and others who are willing and desirous to go there, and are able to transport themselves and families thither, upon their own cost and charges, to a pleasant and profitable country, where they may live in great plenty and pleasure, upon far less stock, and with much less labour and trouble than in Scotland, that as soon as they arrive there, they shall have considerable quantities of land, set out heritably to themselves and their heirs for over, for which they shall pay nothing for the first four or five years, and afterwards pay only a small rent yearly to the owners and proprietors thereof, according as they can agree. And all tradesmen, servants and others, such as, wrights, coopers, smiths, masons, millers, shoemakers, &c. who are willing to go there, and are not able to transport themselves, that they shall be carried over free, and well maintained in meat and clothes the first four years, only for their service, and thereafter shall have considerable quantities of land, set out to themselves and their heirs for ever, upon which they may live at the rate of gentlemen all their lives, and their children after them: their ordinary service will be cutting down wood with axes and other easy husband-work, there being plenty of oxen and horses for plowing and harrowing &c. Let therefore all tradesmen, husbandmen, servants, and others who incline to go thither, and desire further information herein, repair themselves to any of the persons underwritten, who will fully inform them about the country, and everything necessary, and will answer and sattisfie (sic) their scruples and objections, and give them all other encouragements (I am leaving some spelling mistakes as in original source) according to their several abilities and capacities viz.

At Edinburgh let them apply themselves to the Lord Treasurer-Deput, the Lord Register, Sir John Gordon, **Mr Patrick Lyon** (see note below), Mr George Alexander, Advocates, George Drummond of Blair, John Swintoun, John Drummond, Thomas Gordon, David Falconer, Andrew Hamilton, Merchants; at Brunt Island, to William Robison, Doctor of Medicine; at Montross, to John Gordon, Doctor of Medicine, John Fullerton of Kinabar, and Robert and Thomas Fullertons his brothers etc. etc.. . And if any gentleman or other be desirous to buy or purchase any small shares or portions of land in the said province, they may repair to any of the foresaid persons, who will direct them how they shall be served, providing they do it timeously, because many more persons are daily offering to buy, then can be gotten well accommodated.

There is nothing more strange than to see our commons so besotted with the love of their own misery, that rather than quit their native country, they will live in much toil and penury so long as they have strength, being hardly able all their life to acquire so much riches as can save themselves from begging or starving when they grow old; mean time their children (as soon as they are able to walk) are exposed to the cruelties of fortune, and the charity of others, naked and hungry, begging food and raiment from those who cannot, or will not help them: and yet can hardly be persuaded to go to a most profitable, fertile and safe country where they may have everything that is either necessary, profitable or pleasant for the life of man, with very little pains and industry; the woods and plains are stored with infinite quantities of deer and roe, elks, beaver, hares and cunnies, wild swine, and horses, &c. and wild honey in great abundance: trees abound with several sorts of wine-grapes, peaches, apricots, chestnuts, walnuts, plums, mulberries, &c. The sea and rivers with fishes, the banks with oysters, clams &c. Yea, the soil is so excellent and fertile, that the meadows naturally produce plenty of strawberries, poppy (purpy), and many more tender plants, which hardly grow here in gardens: Wheat, Rye, Barley, Oats, Peas and Beans, etc. when sown yields 20 and sometimes 30 fold increase, and Indian Corn which is a grain most wholesome and pleasant, yields ordinarily 150, and sometimes 200 fold: sheep never miss to have two lambs at a time, and for the most part three, and these lambs have generally as many the next year. The winter lasts not ordinarily above two months; and one man's ordinary labour will with ease and plenty, maintain a family of ten or twelve persons; it is no wonder that Ogilvie in his New Atlas, calls this place the Garden of the World, and the Terrestrial Paradise: Why then should our countrymen, in spite of those and many other encouragements, be detained at home, either upon no ground at all, or upon such frivolous scruples and objections as these are.

First, they allege that it is a long and dangerous voyage thither! To which it is answered, that ordinarily it is not above 6 or 7 weeks sailing from Scotland, which in a good ship, well victualed, with good company in the summertime, is a rather pleasant divertissement than a trouble or toil, and it is certainly more dangerous to sail from Leith to London or Holland, than to New East Jersey.

Next, they say there is no company to be had there save Barbarians, woods and wilderness! To which is answered, that this is a great mistake, for this country has been peopled and planted these several years gone, so that horses, oxen, cows, sheep, Hogs etc. are to be sold almost as cheap there as in Scotland, and surely they are much better being of the English kind. Nor are the woods there anything as wild and inhospitable as the mountains here; savage beasts there are none save wolves, and they are the only enemy of the sheep. The natives are very few, and easily overcome, but these simple serviceable people creatures, are rather a help and encouragement, than any ways hurtful or troublesome; and can want of company, seeing there are many thousands of Scots, English, and others living there already, and many more constantly going over, and this summer there are many gentlemen going from Scotland, such as David Tochach of Monyvard, with his lady and family, etc. etc. ... and many others, who are persons of good quality and estates, and go not out of necessity but choice.

Lastly, they object that farfetched fowls have fair feathers, and they do not believe the truth of half what is written and spoken in commendation of these countries! To which is answered, they may as easily deny the truth of everything which they have not seen with their own eyes, for all these things are as verily true, as that there is such pleasant country as France, Italy, Spain etc. The things being matter of fact, are confirmed by letters from persons of undoubted credit, living on the place and by certain information of many eye-witnesses, who having once been there, can never be induced to live in Scotland, nor can be reasonably imagined that the persons above written are all fools, to be imposed upon by lies and fancies; on the contrary, there are none save those who are wise in their own eyes, but are really ignorant) that are not undeniably convinced of the excellency of the design. Let but such as condemn it be so just as first to hear it and know it, which they may easily do by applying to some of the foresaid persons, who can best inform them, and then if they think it not below them to be convinced, they will be forced to homologate. *(Confirm such)*

VIVAT REX

The list of contacts, in the advertisement, for would-be migrants contains the name of **'Mr Patrick Lyon'**. This is most likely the 3rd Earl of Strathmore and Kinghorne who was born in 1643 in Glamis Castle. He had resigned his title in favour of his eldest son John Lyon in 1682 and so had become plain Mr Patrick Lyon. What is remarkable is that his nephew Henry Lyon was already established as a leader in New Jersey.

Life was obviously tough in Scotland at the time and we know that thousands settled in New England and the records do not show many returning to the old country. No matter how much the advertisement exaggerates the case for emigrating this gives an amazing picture of the opportunities, with hard work and diligence, for those who 'chanced their arm'. America is still seen as a land of opportunity for the poor and needy and is to be praised for its generosity to those willing to take a chance.

There is so much interesting information in this advertisement it tells us a great deal about the Scottish people at this time. There had been migration from Scotland to America from the 1600s. Many in Glasgow and Edinburgh sought new opportunities for themselves and their families. We have up to now dealt mostly with the lives of wealthy landowners in Scotland who had served the Kings with distinction for hundreds of years. The new life in America must have appealed to both rich and poor, especially the hope of obtaining land and the escape from the politics in their home country. America offered new hope and many were willing to take the plunge across the Atlantic Ocean.

CHAPTER 7
THE FATHER AND HIS THREE SONS

————•⊛•————

RICHARD LYON (1590) – THE FATHER

Richard was born in 1590 in Heston son of William I (1555) from Little Stanmore, Middlesex who was the son of John the 7th Lord Glamis and was the younger brother of William II (1580). It is not known when he arrived in America but he married a MARGARET who was born 1602. A marriage was recorded in 1642 in Fairfield, Connecticut, when she would have been 40 and Richard 52 years old. The birthplace of Margaret was shown as England, so it is possible that she was the mother of Richard's sons, Thomas, Henry and Richard who were all born in England from 1621 onwards and the marriage of 1642 was a formality in America. Obviously all this is supposition and would mean that they had left their sons in England. Another point to make is that the information about this marriage is uncannily similar to a marriage attributed to Richard junior. What we do know is that Richard senior was in America between 1647 and 1651 to help revise the third edition of the Bay Book of Psalms

> "In a biographical sketch of Henry Dunster, first President of Harvard College, who came to America in 1640, there is mention of the publication of the Bay Psalm Book, which appeared in two editions, in 1640 and 1647. It was the first book printed in North America on the first printing press in North America, which was set up in President Dunster's house in Cambridge, MA. The translation of the psalms into English was done by Richard Mather of Dorchester and John Eliot and Thomas Weld of Roxbury. The new version was not entirely satisfactory, so it was given to President Dunster, a master of Greek and Hebrew, for further improvement. Associated with Dunster in that effort was **Richard Lyon.**" *(Sarah Elizabeth Titcomb. 1882. Early New England People. W.B. Clarke & Carruth, Boston (online at GenealogyLibrary.com)).*

Given the classical education required to edit a translation of the psalms, we can surmise that this Richard was of a social class that would allow for such an education.

113

History of the Bay Book of Psalms

"They hired 'thirty pious and learned Ministers', including Richard Mather and John Eliot, to undertake a new translation, which they presented here. The tunes to be sung to the new translations were the familiar ones from their existing psalters.

The first printing was the third product of the Stephen Day (sometimes spelled *Daye*) press, and consisted of a hundred and forty-eight small quarto leaves, including a twelve-page preface, 'The Psalmes in Metre', 'An Admonition to the Reader' and an extensive list of *errata* headed 'Faults escaped in printing'. As with subsequent editions of the book, Day printed the book for sale by the first bookseller in British America, Hezekia Usher, whose shop at that time was also located in Cambridge (MA).

The third edition (1651) was extensively revised by Henry Dunster and **Richard Lyon**. The revision was entitled

'The Psalms, hymns and spiritual songs of the Old and New Testament, faithfully translated into English meetre'. This revision was the basis for all subsequent editions, and was popularly known as the New England Psalter or New England Version. The ninth edition (1698), the first to contain music, included 13 tunes from John Plaiford's *'A Breefe Introduction to the Skill of Musick* '(London, 1654)." (*http://en.wikipedia.org/wiki/Bay_Psalm_Book*)

At the end of Part 1 we left three of our Lyon family Thomas, Henry and Richard Jr. at the foot of the scaffold watching as Charles I was beheaded on 30th January in 1649. The upheaval that followed this execution left the three brothers in turmoil as to their future in England. As Puritans the family would have supported Cromwell but many people felt it was entirely wrong to execute a King on any grounds – even a bad King. There was a lot of bad feeling, suspicion and animosity, which created a strong division of opinion in the country. The brothers decided to migrate to America to join their father Richard, and also to follow the example of their cousin William III who had arrived in 1635 and was living in Roxbury Massachusetts.

(*https://openlibrary.org/books/ia:lyonmemorial00lyon/Lyon_memorial.*)

THOMAS LYON (1621-1690)

The Lyon Memorial says Thomas Lyon was born at Glen Lyon but as previously noted Glen Lyon being the Ancestral home was often credited with births that actually took place elsewhere. It is more likely that Thomas was actually born in Heston, Middlesex, where the family are recorded to have been living at the time. After the decision to emigrate it would appear that the brothers set sail for American and landed in New Haven, Connecticut.

"There lived John Lyon of Badby, Northamptonshire England, one of the opulent company of 250 persons who came from London on the ship Hector on January 12th 1638, with Theophilus Eaton and Edward Hopkins as their directors and the Puritan divine, John Davenport, as their spiritual guide, to plant an independent colony on the Connecticut Coast. When the Plantation Covenant was signed on June 4th 1638, John Lyne (Lyon) affixed his signature among names that became historic when the story of New England was told.

They were all anti-monarchic people strongly in sympathy with the Parliamentarian Party." *(Lyon Memorial 2, p 34)*

American records show that Thomas settled in Greenwich, Fairfield County, Connecticut (CT). He married MARTHA JOANNA WINTHROP in June 1647, the daughter of Henry Winthrop and Elizabeth Fones. Martha was born in 1630 in Groton, Suffolk, England.

MARTHA WINTHROP was from a wealthy and titled family in England. Her father was Henry Winthrop and his father was Governor John Winthrop, one of three American colonial leaders, father, son and grandson, who was Martha's brother. The story of her grandfather John Winthrop, an aristocratic leader in Massachusetts and Connecticut, is worth reading for an example of outstanding clarity about the goals of many of the early settlers. Unfortunately Henry drowned in Salem Harbour within an hour of arriving in America. The rest of the information is taken from the Lyon Memorial books.

"The Winthrop family name in various spellings may be traced back more than seven centuries. It was during the reign of Queen Elizabeth I that John Winthrop was born on January 12th, 1588 * (this text is starred because it says...the dates given are in the Old Style of dating...for the New Style add 10 days. The above date of John Winthrop is the generally accepted one.) His father, Adam Winthrop, was Lord of Groton Manor in Suffolk, England as had been his father before him. This estate was to descend to John long before his decision to found a new home in America.

Little is known of John's boyhood except that he grew up amid the quiet beauty of Suffolk. His writings testify that he was well educated although there are no records of any schooling except the final stage when he entered Trinity College Cambridge at age fourteen, and remained there less than two years.

He wrote at age fourteen, 'About fourteen years of age, being in Cambridge, I fell into a lingering fever, which took away the comfort of my life. For being there neglected and despised, I went up and down, mourning with myself, and being deprived of my youthful joys, I betook myself to God, whom I did believe to be very good and merciful and would welcome any that would come to Him, especially such a young soul, and so well qualified as I took myself to be; so as I took pleasure in drawing near to Him.' He was admitted at Gray's Inn (1613) and practiced law in London, being admitted to the Inner Temple in 1628.

During these years in England, John Winthrop lived a quiet meditative life. A journal kept by him at this time and called 'Experiencia' is a revelation of his devout piety and earnest faith. Underneath a stern and rather rigid exterior, Winthrop possessed a delicate sensibility abounding in love and tenderness. In a letter to his wife from the ship which was to bear him away to the wilderness across the sea, he wrote, 'And now my sweet soul, I must again take my last farewell of Thee in Old England. It goeth very near to my heart to leave Thee.'"

To continue with the family of **Thomas Lyon** and MARTHA JOANNA WINTHROP, they are said to have had two children before she died in 1653. It is probable that **John Lyon** was actually the son of Thomas and MARY HOYT because many records give the birth of John as 1655, after the death of Martha Winthrop who died young.

1. **Mary Lyon** born August 1649 in Stamford, Fairfield County, Connecticut was the first of their children born after they had left England that year. She died in 1713 at their home in Rye, Fairfield, CT

2. **John Lyon** born 1655? He died in Greenwich, Fairfield, CT in 1736. He may well have been the son of Mary Hoyt or he could have been born earlier before Martha Winthrop died.

Thomas later married MARY HOYT, born about 1635 in Stamford, Lincolnshire, England. Thomas and Mary had the following children (possibly also the above John;

1   **Abigail Lyon** was born 1654 in Greenwich, CT and died there in 1713 in Greenwich, Fairfield, CT.

2   **Samuel Lyon** was born in 1661 in Greenwich, Fairfield, CT. He died in 1713 in Greenwich, Fairfield, CT.

3   **Deborah Lyon** was born in 1663 in or Rye, Fairfield, CT. She died in 1713 in Rye, Westchester, New York.

4   **Sarah Lyon** was born in 1665 in or Rye, Fairfield, CT. She died in 1687 in Greenwich CT.

5   **Thomas Lyon** was born in 1673 in Greenwich, Fairfield, CT. He married Abigail Ogden, daughter of John Ogden and Janet Bond in 1700 in Greenwich, Fairfield, Connecticut, USA. She was born in 1677 in Greenwich, Fairfield, CT. She died on 26th November 1760 in Rye, Westchester, New York. He died on 1st May 1739 in Byram Bridge, Greenwich County, CT.

6   **Joseph Lyon** was born in 1677 in or Rye, Fairfield, CT. He married Sarah Lyon in 1701 in Greenwich, Fairfield, CT. She was born in 1679 in Greenwich, Fairfield, CT. She died on 26th March 1769 in Rye, Westchester, New York. He died on 21st February 1761 in Rye, Westchester, New York.

7   **Elizabeth Lyon** was born in 1680 in Greenwich, Fairfield, CT. She died on 28th November 1713.

Thomas produced a large family but, unfortunately, at least four of them died in the same year. Although I have spent a great deal of time on research on this interesting fact I can find no definitive explanation. It may be that they all died of the same disease.

The leaders of the community seem to have been the Meads, the Husteds and the Pecks. Thomas Lyon was an important member of the Greenwich community, although records show that he was obviously not seen as a leader, there is probably a good reason for this as Thomas was at this time a Quaker. Greenwich community was run mostly on religious grounds, much of the early history of the town concerns the Protestant churches, particularly the Congregational church. Thomas and some of his family were Quakers as seen in the list of six members below; this is taken from a Quaker website.

(http://www.genealogy105.com/quaker.html)

Thomas LYON. Born circa 1621 in England. Thomas died in Byram Neck, Greenwich, Fairfield Co., CT circa 1690, he was 69. Buried in Lyon
Mary HOYT. Born circa 1630 in Charlestown, Suffolk Co., MA. Mary died in Byram Neck-Greenwich, CT. Buried in Lyon Cemetery, Byram Neck Greenwich, CT.

Simon HOYT.

Thomas LYON. Born circa 1673 in Stamford, CT. Thomas died in Byram Bridge-Greenwich, CT. before 1ˢᵗ May 1739, he was 66. Thomas married ABIGAIL OGDEN. Abigail died before 26ᵗʰ November 1760.

Susannah LYON. Born 1745 in NY. Susannah died 4ᵗʰ November 1809 in Otsego Co., NY

Joseph LYON. Born 1712 in Greenwich, CT. Joseph died in White Plains, NY on 23ʳᵈ December 1776, he was 64. Joseph married Mary DISBROW.

The above entries in the Quaker records are significant proof of the religious commitment of Thomas and at least one generation of his family. The Thomas Lyon family continued to live in Fairfield County, Connecticut for many years.

The Quakers (Friends) in America

"Friends made a most profound effect on the course of American history. The first Quaker missionaries arrived on America's shores in 1656, one hundred and twenty years before the signing of the Declaration of Independence. Mary Fisher and Ann Austin landed at Boston where the Puritan authorities had them seized and kept under close guard. A hundred of their books were burned in the marketplace and they were dispatched to Barbados on the next departing ship. Their bedding and even their Bibles were confiscated to pay the jailer's fee. The Pilgrim Fathers wanted religious freedom for themselves but offered it to no one else.

Friends were welcomed in Rhode Island which was founded as a haven from the intolerance of Puritan Massachusetts. So overwhelming was the response there that at one time half of the population were Friends, and the colony elected Quaker governors for thirty-six consecutive terms - more than a century. Friends were also well received in Maryland. Lord Baltimore established the colony as a refuge for persecuted English Catholics and was willing to give liberty of conscience to others in religious matters. Spokespersons for the Quaker faith made some deep inroads into Virginia as well.

In 1657, a boatload of Quaker missionaries from England landed on Long Island. One of them, Robert Hodgson, drew large crowds to his meetings. He was arrested, imprisoned, flogged and treated very severely. At last some of the Dutch colonists interceded on his behalf and secured his unconditional release. Many continued to respond to the Friends message in spite of a firm edict issued against it by Governor Peter Stuyvesant. Finally on December 27ᵗʰ, 1657, the citizens of Flushing drew up a magnificently worded protest reminding their Governor that their charter allowed them 'to have and enjoy Liberty of Conscience according to the Custom and manner of Holland, without molestation or disturbance.' This came to be known as the Flushing Remonstrance. It was the first time that a group of settlers in the New World petitioned the government for religious freedom. It was commemorated in a United States postage stamp issued three hundred years later.

Meanwhile the persecution of Friends in Puritan Massachusetts grew more intense. Friends were lashed behind carts and whipped from town to town.

They were branded with an 'H' for heretic; they had their tongues bored through with a hot iron; their ears were cut off; they were banished. Finally Governor John Endicott succeeded in having the death penalty invoked for any Friends who returned to the colony after being banished beyond its borders. Four Quakers were hung on Boston Common--William Robinson, Marmaduke Stephenson, William Leddra and Mary Dyer. She was the first woman to suffer death on these shores for her religious convictions. Today a statue of her stands on Boston Common, a reminder to all that our religious freedom was bought at a precious price.

In 1671, George Fox along with twelve others came to America and trekked up and down the Atlantic Seaboard. In 1672, he and a William Edmondson, who had already preached successfully in Ireland, became the first preachers who ever held any kind of Christian worship within the borders of the Carolinas. Later, John Archdale would become the Quaker Governor of the Carolinas and one-half of the representatives of the legislature were Friends. The outbreak of persecution of Friends back in England again led seventeen Quakers to purchase East Jersey to serve as a refuge where Friends could practice their faith without interference. Robert Barclay, the brilliant young Scottish Quaker theologian, served as Governor of the colony for a time.

Then, in 1681, William Penn accepted the grant of land which became Pennsylvania as the payment of a debt which King Charles II owed his father. The Duke of York, who later became King James II, threw in the territory of Delaware on the deal. Penn landed in his colony on the good ship 'Welcome' in 1682. He met with the Indians under the great elm at Shackamason, the ancient meeting place of the tribes and made friends with them. He purchased land from them at a fair price and concluded a treaty with them that was agreeable to all. A century later the humanistic French philosopher, Voltaire, would observe that his was the only treaty ever made between white men and the Indians that was never sworn to and never broken." *(http://thorn.pair.com/earlyq.htm)*

This has been a long excerpt but it helps to understand the religion and beliefs of **Thomas Lyon**. His family followed the teachings of George Fox for several generations; there is little mention of other churches until the 4th and 5th Generations. There are few who actually fought in the War of Independence and despite the suffering of many of their fellow Quakers throughout America the Lyon family seemed to survive persecution.

Life Expectancy of first four Generations of Thomas Lyon

Thomas Lyon	m/f	0-9	10-19	20-29	30-39	40-49	50-59	60-69	70-79	80-89	90-99	100+	?	Totals
Gen. 1	F			1	1		2	1						5
	M						1	1	2					4
Gen. 2	F			1	1		4	1		3		2	1	13
	M				1	2	3	2	1	1				10
Gen 3	F			2	2	3	2	3	3	2			3	20
	M			2	1	2	3	1	5	10	2		3	29
Gen 4	F		1		2	4	2		4	4	8		13	38
	M				1	2			8	5	9		4	29
	Totals	0	1	4	8	11	17	17	21	30	13	2	24	148
												Average age		67.78

In four generations there are no infant deaths recorded but note there were 24 unknown dates of death for various reasons. There were; 13 unknown female deaths recorded from age 10-39, 11 deaths from age 40-69, 21 deaths from age 70-99 and 2 females lived to over 100. The total of the Lyon family grew to 148 in four generations.

The average age of those known is 67.8 years, quite a remarkable lifespan in what must have been hard times. To see more details of the family of Thomas Lyon visit the website under American Family and Thomas Lyon. There are descendant charts and Ancestry lists available for printing in the form of PDF's.

(www.thelyonfamily.org.uk/help/genealogy)

There were no known deaths as the result of the 1776 War of Independence in this small survey. Possibly the cause of this latter fact is that Thomas was a Quaker whose teachings taught Pacifism and objected to war in any form. This made them very unpopular and many were persecuted for their faith by other Christians. There were some members of the family in later generations who joined the army and navy so they obviously did not all support the beliefs of their ancestor Thomas Lyon.

Thomas died in 1690, and Mary Hoyt died in 1692 at Simsbury, Hartford, CT. When Thomas died he left much land which would eventually become valuable but in 1694 it was only worth £57 and 12 shillings and his son Samuel was worth £88 out of a total for the town of £2,638. There certainly were some wealthier people but none admitted to be worth more than £200.

THE HENRY LYON STORY

Henry (1623) was a brother of Thomas (1621) and Richard Lyon (1624) and also settled in Connecticut (CT). He later moved to New Jersey where he became an early resident of Newark. Henry Lyon was the most enterprising and forceful of the three brothers. He settled first in Milford, CT, removed later to Fairfield, CT, and finally joined the Colony that established in New Jersey the town of Passaic to which the name Newark was afterwards given. The descendants of Henry Lyon were prominent in the early history of New Jersey and included several officers in the Revolutionary Army.

A branch of the family established itself at an early date in Rhode Island. Another branch removed to Ohio and aided in founding the city of Cincinnati. Still another, Reverend James Lyon, ardent patriot in the Revolutionary war, planted the family name in Maine. **Henry** married ELIZABETH BATEMAN who was born in 1631. They had several children;

1   **Thomas** was born in Fairfield CT in 1653– he married ELIZABETH, he died intestate and left about 100 acres of land in Elizabethtown, NY. They had 3 sons and 3 daughters. He died in 1694, her death is recorded as 1717

2   **Mary** born in Fairfield CT in 1654, she married JOHN WARD who was deeded '6 acres of valuable land' by grandfather Henry after the early death of his daughter. They had 1 son born John 1676. She died about 1684

3   **Samuel** 1655 - 1703 married SARAH BEACH 1654 of New Haven CT, they had 2 boys and 3 girls. He then married HANNAH PIERSON they had 2 boys and a girl.

4   **Joseph** 1658-1725 married MARY PIERSON, they had 4th girls and 1 boy. He then married SARAH BROWN 1652-1694, they had 1 boy.

5   **Nathaniel** 1662-1700 married MARY, they had 3 girls.

6   **John** 1665-1694 married HANNAH, no known descendants.

7   **Benjamin** 1666-1719 married BETHIA CONDIT they had 2 girls and 1 boy, he was a local Justice of the Peace.

8   **Ebenezer** 1670-1738 married ELIZABETH WINANS 1668- 1739, they had 7 girls and 1 boy. He was a Captain of 3 different ships and was a soldier in 1698, they lived in Elizabethtown.

Life Expectancy of the first Four Generations of the Henry Lyon family

Henry Lyon	m/f	0-9	10-19	20-29	30-39	40-49	50-59	60-69	70-79	80-89	90-99	100+	?	Totals
Gen. 1	F				1								2	3
	M			2	1	2	2							7
Gen. 2	F		1		5		1	5	1				8	21
	M				1		3	3	3				2	12
Gen 3	F	1	1	1	1	1			1				8	14
	M	3			3	1	5	10	6	2			10	40
Gen 4	F	4		1	1	2	2	5	1	2		2	25	45
	M	4		6	4	3	8	7	9	7	1		43	92
	Totals	12	2	8	18	8	21	32	21	11	1	2	98	234
													Average age	53.30

The average age was about 53.3 years. There are two centenarians and a large number of unknown dates of deaths. On the left of the table, 12 infant deaths in the last two generations and 26 others dying before they were 40 years of age. The total list of descendants of Henry Lyon can be found on the website under his name. Also available is the list of his ancestors back to King Robert the Bruce and before.

Founding of Newark, New Jersey

I have included another long quotation about the involvement of Henry in his community after moving to New Jersey. He was obviously a capable man who seems to have inherited an ability to organize and lead others becoming a landowner like his ancestors before him. He had followed Puritan practices in his new homeland and was proud to be a settler and an American citizen. For a map of the area see Maps & Illustrations at the beginning of the book.

"The New Haven Colony founders were Puritans who had fled England to establish a strict theocracy and were displeased by the imposed merger with their liberal neighbours. The New Haven colonists believed that only members of the Puritan church should be allowed to vote, and that only the children of church members could be baptized, strictures that did not appear in the new colony's constitution.

Determined to pursue their theocracy elsewhere, the New Haven Puritans sent Robert Treat and John Gregory to meet with Philip Carteret, the new Royal Governor of New Jersey. They chose a site to settle near Elizabethtown, up the bay and along the Passaic River. In the May of 1666, Puritan settlers led by Treat purchased the land directly from the

Hackensack Indians for goods - including gunpowder, one hundred bars of lead, twenty axes, twenty coats, guns, pistols, swords, kettles, blankets, knives, beer, and ten pairs of breeches -- valued at $750, a percentage of which was assessed upon every family that arrived in the new colony within the first year of its settlement."

(http://www.thirteen.org/newark/history.html)

"In 1670, the first hotel opened on the corner of Broad and Walnut Streets (now the location of Grace Episcopal Church) in the home of Thomas Johnson, Newark's first constable. Newark's first shoemaker, Samuel Whitehead, arrived in 1680 by which time the population had reached 500, and Azariah Crane opened the first leather tannery in 1698. Under the direction of its second President, Reverend Aaron Burr, the College of New Jersey (later Princeton University) moved from Elizabethtown to Newark in 1747, before finally settling in Princeton in 1756. While in Newark, Burr's wife Esther gave birth to Aaron Burr, Jr., who would later become the third Vice President of the United States.

In 1662, the King (Charles II) made New Haven Colony part of the more liberal Connecticut Colony, much against the will of the New Haven colonists. In response, many ardent Puritans began making plans to leave Connecticut. In 1667, a contingent of families from Milford, CT, including **Henry Lyon** and his family, arrived at and founded a town on the Passaic River in the Province of New Jersey, which town they named New Milford. The name was shortly changed to New Ark (now Newark). Henry Lyon was first Treasurer of the city of Newark, NJ, and thus one of its founders."

(http://dgmweb.net/Resources/GenLin/Gen-LyonHenry.html)

An extract from the Lyon Memorial gives some idea of the problems the settlers faced in New Jersey:-

"Property was in abundance and childhood was sadly abbreviated in a place where there was no school. In winter the children were mother-taught or father-taught to read the Bible. It was the only book possessed by most families, and to be familiar with the Laws and the Prophets, the Gospels and the Epistles was a liberal education. Play-time was a sinful waste of daylight to these religion-awed, task-weary boys and girls.

Some of the planters were college-bred men (their minister, Reverend Abraham Pierson, was a graduate of Trinity College, Cambridge) and but a few of them were untaught. They realized the importance of having their children, their sons especially, instructed in the rudiments. But after the stipend of eighty pounds was collected for the pastor there was no money to pay a schoolmaster, if these work-tired lads could be spared from farm labour.

A sense of insecurity stayed with the planters, with their wives and children. The meeting-house was fortified against a sudden attack, and the men in the fields and the clearing went armed, and the 'look-out' was a child that kept watch through the sowing and tilling and reaping, and while the fuel was cut for winter. They meant to keep faith with the tribes, and by fair dealing earned themselves the after title of 'The Doors of Justice'. But constant nerve-trying, heart-trying vigilance went with their kindness to the savages. Intrusion could not be repulsed nor trespass punished."

(Lyon Memorial Families of Connecticut & New Jersey — p54 — Sidney Elizabeth Lyon)

Henry Lyon was Newark's first Treasurer from 1668 until 1673, looking after the public funds. We know little about Henry before he left England but it is obvious that he had some business acumen before arriving in New Jersey. Henry and Thomas Johnson, the first town constable, were responsible for taking in the wheat tax and moving the grain to Elizabethtown for the Governor to store or administer when demanded. Henry had to raise the money for the minister and local town rates.

The minister Reverend Pierson received $80 per annum, quite an amount in America with plenty of cheap land available at 1 penny per acre in places. **Henry** was also Newark's first inn-keeper with the help of the constable, and provided board and lodging for any visitors. The hostel was built to stop visitors pestering the townsfolk for food and lodgings and provided food and shelter for strangers to the town and regular visitors who might be there on business. His wife, Elizabeth Bateman Lyon, must have been tired of providing for strangers when the sanctity of her home was invaded and her young children were deprived of her care.

Two years later Henry Lyon opened a public house and the constable was appointed to make sure that strong drinks were sold wisely and were licenced by the Magistrate to limit sales to persons who wanted the liquor. At that time he held the only licence to supply alcohol in Newark. Wine may have been served at home, but it is doubtful if brandy-drinking and rum-drinking went on in Henry Lyon's house. However, total abstinence was not necessary and there were no laws against drinking intoxicating drinks. Nothing was said in regard to selling in small quantities to be drunk on the premises. It is to be presumed that the planters were temperate people, and the 'dram-drinking stranger was brought to decent moderation by the moral discrimination of Henry Lyon, Thomas Johnson and Mr Jasper Crane the next licensee'.

A licence to build a new church was given in 1668 but it was not built until 1670 when it was limited to 36 feet x 36 feet square with doors and wooden floors. The congregation had to stand, listening to three hour long sermons, before seating was provided in 1678. In 1676 it was decided that a school should be built, up until then it was the custom to teach the children at home, mostly from the Bible. John Catlin, probably a lawyer by profession was town attorney for two years and he may have taught the three R's to pupils of various ages, in day classes and night classes, till he and his wife, Mary, in 1684, sold their home, lot Number 11, of the Branford allotment, to Henry Lyon. They moved to Deerfield, where Mrs Catlin and her sons, Joseph and Jonathan, were killed in the assault of the French and Indians, February 29th, 1704. Before the first term at the school in 1684 began the Lyon family had moved to Elizabeth Town and Henry Lyon took the oath there, and rapidly became one of the leading men in political and commercial affairs.

It was recorded on November 8th 1675 that Henry was a member of the General Assembly. On February 4th 1681, he was made one of the Judges of Small Causes. On February 28th 1681 he became a member of the Governor's Council and on August 1st 1681 he was appointed Justice of the Peace which during the Colonial period was equivalent to that of Judge of the Supreme Court. In December 1682, Henry was appointed Commissioner to lay out and appoint all necessary highways, bridges, passages, landings and ferries for the County of Essex, on November 26th 1684 he was a Representative in the Council of the Governor and on May 1st 1686 he received his commission as a Judge. Furthermore he was one of the Town Associates.

"Scotch (Scottish) thrift, integrity and foresight had made him a fortune. Besides having 306 acres of land within, the limits of Newark, he owned 306 acres at Elizabeth Town. The ancestral habit of accumulating property was strong in him. Life must have been easier for Elizabeth Bateman Lyon than when she was mistress of Newark's first inn. Servants were to be had, seventeenth century luxuries, and perhaps the London fashions.

At an early date various hamlets and clusters of farm houses gradually sprang up in different localities. The facilities for navigation and the attraction of water privileges drew quite a number of early settlers to the banks of the Rahway River. Another group of planters, mostly of one family, gave the name to the neighbourhood known as **Lyons Farms**. Elizabeth's older sons married early - courtships, weddings and grandchildren were happy family happenings before Elizabeth died in 1703."

However this date is probably incorrect as Henry is recorded as having married Mary in 1689, who was the mother of their daughters Mary Lyon born 1690 and Dorcas Lyon born 1692. Henry mentions Mary as being his wife in his will made in 1702. *(The Lyon Memorial by Sidney Elizabeth Lyon page 62)*. His second marriage must have occurred in 1689 or 1690, for Mary and Dorcas, the second wife's daughters, were minors when their father wrote his will in 1702. No doubt Mary was a Newark woman and influenced her husband's return to the town he had helped to found.

Henry had given a large subscription for the support of the pastor Reverend Harriman at Elizabethtown. However he still retained his church privileges at Newark. On July 24th 1680, some years after he left, it was voted;

> "That Henry Lyon hath a right to, and shall have a seat in the meeting house, paying proportionally with his neighbours. He had fought the good fight and his time was running out. His first-born, Thomas, had died in 1694, and John had followed his elder brother. Nathaniel passed on in 1696. His fellow pilgrims, one by one, put out the candle of life to go to sleep, till but few were left of the comrades that climbed the hill of hope together. New friends are but favourite acquaintances. 'Loving wife Mary' was in his will. At Newark there were others of the long-gone who had New Haven, Branford and Milford recollections in common, and who could exchange memories of Scotland and England."

He is described as a man of physical and mental vigour, and one of physical and moral bravery. He was of 'good understanding and memory' when he wrote his will — here given in full, that posterity may know him through his own words:

> "Whereas I, **Henry Lyon**, Senior of Newark, in ye province of East New Jersey being weak in body yet of good understanding and memory — Do make this my Last Will & Testament (hereby making all other wills and testaments at any time by me made void and null) in manner and form following:
>
> **First**, I bequeath my Soul into ye hands of Almighty God hoping for Salvation from ye Riches of his grace by ye atonement of Jesus Christ & through faith in his blood. Also I commit my body to the Earth Decently to be buried & there to Rest until the Resurrection of ye just. And for my Worldly Estate both Real & personal I dispose of as followeth- 'Imprimis: I will & bequeath to my Loving Wife Mary Lyon Eighty pounds & I give unto my two Daughters Dorcas & Mary Lyon to each of them Eighty pounds & also my will is yet my house & other buildings & Land & Meadow in Newark shall be kept for ye bringing up of my Daughters

Dorcas & Mary Lyon until they be eighteen years of age & Also my will is yet my wife Mary Lyon & my Daughters Dorcas & Mary Lyon shall pay unto my four sons (viz.) Samll Lyon, Joseph Lyon, Benjamin Lyon and Ebenezer Lyon twenty pounds out of my living in Newark when my Daughters Dorcas & Mary Lyon shall be eighteen years of age, & if my wife Mary Lyon do leave this house then my two Daughters afore'sd shall repay unto my wife what she payd of ye said twenty pounds unto my four sons afore'sd. **2ndly**, my will is & I do will & bequeath unto my two Daughters Dorcas & Mary Lyon to them their heirs & assigns for Ever my house Land & Meadow in Newark after my wife's deceased."

Henry Lyon lived for 84 years (1623-1707).

The 'Lyon Memorial' books will be a lasting monument to Henry Lyon of Milford, Thomas and Richard Lyon of Fairfield, and their kindred: William Lyon of Roxbury, Peter Lyon and George Lyon of Dorchester and of every descendant of these "first-comers" enrolled in this book.

The effects of the War of Independence on the Henry Lyon Family

The following are some of the Henry Lyon family who took part in the war against the British between 1775 and 1783. This data is taken from the Lyon Memorial book about Henry Lyon.

Moses Lyon [Benjamin, Benjamin, Henry] was born at Lyons Farms, N. J., in 1731. He married MARY HARRIS, who was born in 1732. They were lifelong members of the First Presbyterian Church of Elizabethtown, N. J., and are buried in the old churchyard. Moses Lyon was a revolutionary soldier and served as a private in Captain Abraham Lyon's Company, second Regiment, Essex County, New Jersey Militia, during the revolutionary war. His sons, **James, Henry** and **Nathaniel**, aided the cause of American Independence, the first two as artificers, and the third as private in the second Regiment, Essex County Militia and Continental Line. His son **Moses** was a drummer boy in the same regiment. Moses died March 27th, 1813, Mary died June 2, 1809.

Captain Matthias Lyon [Benjamin, Benjamin, Esq, Henry] was born at Lyons Farms in 1738. He is buried in the churchyard of the First Presbyterian Church at Elizabethtown. Matthias Lyon was an officer in the revolutionary war being Captain in Colonel Philip Van Courtland's Battalion, Brigadier General Nathaniel Heard's Brigade, State troops, June 4th, 1776, engaged in the Long Island campaign; discharged December 1st, 1776; also Captain in Second Regiment, Essex County

Militia, by return dated October 25th, 1777, to June 2nd, 1778. He participated in the battle of Monmouth June 28th, 1778. He died November 11th, 1797.

Moses Lyon [Mattaniah, Isaac, Thomas, Henry] was born in 1757. He married ESTHER, born 1759, daughter of John and Sarah WARREN; he was a soldier in the Revolutionary war, and served as an artificer in Captain Joseph Lindsley's Company of Artificers, Continental army; enlisted at Morris, Morris Co., March 17th, 1776, for one year, aged 19; reenlisted in Morris County, New Jersey, December 26th, 1776; he was present at the battle of Trenton, Princeton, January 3rd, 1777; discharged at Morristown, March 17th, 1777; re-enlisted June 1777 for the war as an express rider in Captain Jeremiah Dunn's Troop of Express Riders, Continental army (afterwards commanded by Captain John Asgill, and by Captain Robert Dunn); discharged at the close of the war. Moses Lyon made an application for a pension on September 25th, 1832, at which time he was 75 years of age, and residing at Aurelius, N.Y., and his pension was allowed for two years for his actual service as Express Rider, Revolutionary War, 'enlisted at Morris, Morris Co., N. J., and served under General Thomas Mifflin'. He died on 18th September 1832.

Enos Lyon [Thomas, Thomas, Thomas, Henry] was born in 1748. He was a soldier in the Revolutionary war, and was granted a pension May 13th, 1818, for service as a private in the New Jersey line. He married NAOMI, daughter of Cornelius and Joanna (Harrison) JONES, who was born 1769, and was baptized at the First Presbyterian Church at Orange, N. J. in November 1774. Naomi Lyon was granted a widow's pension in 1841, at which time she was living at Manchester, Passaic Co., N. J.

Moses Lyon [Thomas, Thomas, Thomas, Henry) was born in 1762 and lived at Short Hill, N. J. He was a soldier of the Revolutionary war, and was granted a pension in 1840 for military service. At this time he was living at Madison, Delaware Co., N. Y.

Captain Abraham Lyon (Abraham, Joseph, Samuel, Henry) was born in Newark in 1760, and lived there. He was an officer in the Revolutionary war; Captain in Fourth Battalion, New Jersey Continental Line, first establishment, November 28th, 1776. He was in the battle of Short Hills, N. J. June 26th, 1776; the battle of Brandywine, Del., September 7th, 1777; the battle of Germantown, PA., October 4th, 1777, the battle of Monmouth, N. J., June 28th, 1778; retired as a supernumerary officer February 11th, 1779. Abraham Lyon, of Newark; was no doubt of the same branch of the family as the foregoing, though possibly of the sixth generation. He married HANNAH, daughter of Elihu and Elizabeth (Price) OGDEN, but no further record has been found. Abraham died March 2st 1799.

"On the 7th of December, 1774, the planters at Newark held a town meeting at the Court House to state their loyalty to the Colonies. A committee of observation was appointed from among them whose duty it was 'to see how the people acted on the question of the General Congress,' to publicly advocate active opposition to the mother country, and to see that certain sons of Belial, the Tories in their midst, were duly ostracized.

The men of influence in this committee were; Joseph Allen, Garrabrant, Caleb Camp, Bethuel Pierson. Solomon Davis, John Range, Samuel Pennington, Joseph Hidden, Jr., Samuel Condit, John Peck. **Joseph Lyon**, Thomas Cadmus, Jr., James Wheeler, **Abraham Lyon**, Ichabod Harrison. Jonathan

Sayre, Robert Johnson and Robert Nell Jr. Two of these patriots in the cause of American Independence, **Joseph Lyon** and **Abraham Lyon** were descendants of **Henry Lyon of Newark**". *The Lyon Memorial, I have highlighted the members of the family involved.*

Husbands of the Lyon daughters were often involved in the war, here is a case in point:

General Benjamin Ludlow (MARTHA LYON), was born in 1763. Benjamin Ludlow was Major General of the New Jersey militia. He was Judge of Morris County Court, and several times member of the Legislative Council of the General Assembly of New Jersey. He died January 27th 1817.

Israel Ludlow (MARTHA LYON), was born at Long Hill, N. J. He came to the Northwest Territory after the Revolutionary war, with the emigrants from Elizabethtown, Newark, Trenton and Morristown, and settled near Fort Washington [Cincinnati]. He was one of the surveyors of Symmes' Purchase between the Miami Rivers; was one of the founders of Cincinnati, Ohio and one of the original proprietors of Dayton. Ludlow Street in the latter city is named for him. He later married CHARLOTTE CHAMBERS of Chambersburg, PA., and lived in Cincinnati, Ohio, and in Rising Sun, Indiana.

James Lyon [Moses, Benjamin, Benjamin, Henry] was born at Lyons Farms, N. J., August 3st, 1755; As New Jersey was the battle ground of the American Revolution, and the Lyons were of democratic principles, James Lyon inevitably took up arms against King George. A certificate of service shows that he served as an artificer, Captain Jeremiah Bruen's Company, Colonel Jonathan Baldwin's artillery artificers Regiment, Continental army; enlisted July 7th, 1777, for three years, age 23, residence Elizabeth, NJ; discharged at Morristown, NJ, July 7th, 1780; expiration of term of service — during the Revolutionary war. James Lyon made an application for pension on August 20th, 1832, at which time he was 77 years of age and residing in Hamilton Co., Ohio. A pension was allowed 'for three years' actual service as an artificer in the New Jersey State Troops. A part of the time he served under Captain Bruen and Colonel Baldwin" Bureau of Pensions, Washington, D. C. He died at Woodburn, near Cincinnati, Ohio, September 20th, 1841, 'full of years.'

Henry Lyon [Moses, Benjamin, Benjamin, Henry] was born at Lyons Farms in 1756. He married JOANNA, born 1766; Four years previous to her death she was bereft of the last of her nine children, six of whom were victims of consumption, and died unmarried. Henry Lyon, a soldier of the Revolutionary war, served as an artificer in Captain Caleb Bruen's Company of Artificers, Essex County, New Jersey Militia; enlisted at Long Island, March 1776 for one year; discharged March 1777 at expiration of term of service; re-enlisted as an artificer in Captain Jeremiah Bruen's Company, in Colonel Jonathan Baldwin's Regiment of Artillery Artificers, Continental Army, for three years; discharged at Morristown, N. J., expiration of term of service, during the Revolutionary war. In 1840 his widow was granted a pension, at which time she was living at Newark, aged 74 years. Henry and JOANNA LYON and their nine children are buried at Connecticut Farms, N. J. Henry died May 19th 1824. Joanna died October 1st 1859, at the advanced age of 91 years and nine months, having survived her husband by 33 years.

Nathaniel Lyon [Moses, Benjamin, Benjamin, Henry] was born at Lyons Farms, July 3rd, 1759, he was a soldier of the Revolutionary war, a private in Captain Daniel Wood's Company, First Regiment, Essex County Militia; enlisted in fall of 1776, and served two weeks, age 18; private Captain Jacob Crane's Company, Eastern Battalion, Morris County Militia; enlisted December 1776 for three months; at battle of Springfield, NJ, December 17th, 1776; private in Captain Abraham Lyon's Company, Fourth Battalion, New Jersey Continental Line, Colonel Ephraim Martin; enlisted May 30th, 1778 for nine months; at battle of Monmouth, N. J., June 28th, 1778; discharged Elizabeth, NJ, February 1779; afterwards served in Militia to close of the revolutionary war. He applied for a pension September 11th, 1832, at which time he resided in Montgomery County, Ohio. He died in Marion County, Indiana in September 1833.

Richard Lyon [Moses, Benjamin, Benjamin, Henry] was born at Lyons Farms, near Elizabethtown, N. J., about 1766, the youngest child of Moses and Mary (Harris) Lyon. At the time of the opening of the Northwest territory, Richard Lyon, with his wife and their three children, Abby, Sarah and Richard, emigrated from New Jersey and settled at Osage, Illinois., a town planted by New Jersey men, among them several of the Lyons. He died in New York City, December 1821.

Joseph Lyon Captain [Matthias, Benjamin, Benjamin, Henry] of the town of Jersey, Bergen Co., N. J. was born in 1762, and was living in 1816. He was a soldier of the Revolutionary war, a private in Captain Isaac Reeves' Company, Second Regiment, Essex Co. Militia, spring of 1779; served one month, age 17 years a private in Captain John Ogden's Company, Second Regiment, Essex Co. Militia, 1779, served one month; private Captain John Edward's Company, Second Regiment, Essex Co. Militia, summer of 1779, served six weeks; private Captain Squire's Company, Second Regiment, Essex Co.- Militia, April 1780, served one month; private Captain Jarolomon's Company, Second Regiment, Essex Co. Militia, July 1780, served one month; private Captain Robert Nichol's Company, Second Regiment Essex Co. Militia, September 1780, served one month; private Captain Isaac Reeves' Company, Second Regiment, Essex Co. Militia, October 1780; served one month; private Captain Thomas William's Company, Second Regiment, Essex Co. Militia, November 1780; served 26 days; private Captain Isaac Gillman's Company, State Troops, December 18th, 1780; discharged December 19th, 1781- during the Revolutionary war. Date of death unknown.

There are no doubt many others of Henry Lyon's family who served in the war. Some paid the ultimate price with their lives.

Deaths in the war

Samuel Lyon, Jr. [Samuel, Benjamin, Benjamin, Henry] was born Sept. 1753, and died Dec. 3, 1776. Samuel and his brother **Tappan** were soldiers in the American Revolution. Samuel and Tappan were captured by the British and died in the horrible Sugar House prison in New York. The following letter written by this Samuel who was a witness of the public demonstration in New York City at the time of the declaration of American Independence is of historic interest. The beginning of the letter is torn off:

"... immediately in that I wrote for some things to be left at Daniel Sayres for John Stewart to fetch over on Friday, but I do not know whether he will come before Saturday. The things I wrote for was a thick jaccoot, woosted stocking and woolen ones, a knife, fork and spoon, and the reasons for my wanting them are in some measure removed, yet I want them still and if we shall go anywhere to encamp (as I expect we shall) I should want them as much as ever. If you receive this or the other letter in time, I should be glad if you would send the things to Sayre's as it is uncertain weather, I shall have another opportunity to get them. Our sick are all removed except two, who, I believe, will be sent home. You desired I should write how I get washing done. My washing is done very well at the following prices, for a shirt 6d, jaccoot or breeches 6d., stocking 2d per pair; sock 1d., handkerchief 1d. It costs me for washing 1/9 per week, and board, if I get it at the tavern as some do, is 20s per week and however I have not learned to be so extravagant, & God grant I never may.

Soon after our arrival today Independence was proclaimed in this City by the Inhabitants at the City Hall, when the King's coat of arms engraved in a stone about five feet square was tumbled from the top of the hall and broken to pieces on the pavement, upon which a large crowd of people gave three cheers. Then they gathered the pieces and placed them on a fire prepared for the purpose & gave three cheers more and after which they soon dispersed. They likewise resolved that all the pictures of the King's coat of arms in all the Churches should be taken out and burned.

Friday morning at 6 o'clock. Jonathan Pierson this morning obtained liberty of the General to go home so that if you send the things to his house he can fetch them over, and if you will send me a small cheese it will not be amiss, as there is neither butter nor cheese to be got here unless for very extravagant prices. I have been to Holt's and the year is up for news and they want the money. If you will send the money over I will pay him. My love to all Relations and inquiring Friends. Mr. Pierson is just going, no more at present but remain.

Your loving brother,

Sam. Lyon, Jun."

Prison Memorials of NYC (New York City):

Untold Story of America's First POWs by James Renner. From the Archives (July & August 1999) of the Washington Heights & Inwood Report

"British Provost Marshal William Cunningham, who ruled POW prisons in NYC, personally presided at and took pleasure in the execution of American patriots, including Nathan Hale whose statue in City Hall Park is near the Sugar House Prison window memorial. Many of those executions took place on Barracks St., now called Chambers St. also near it.

One of the least known and least spoken about subjects of the American Revolution were rebel Prisoners of War who were jailed in New York City. . . . New York City had become the main site for the prisoners because it was the only city to be held by the British for the duration of the war. Many of the prisoners were from the Battle of Long Island on

August 26th, 1776 (1,300) and from the Battle of Fort Washington on November 16th, 1776 (3,000).

During the occupation of New York by the Royalist forces many prisons had been filled. The British commandeered barns, churches, taverns, private homes and sugar houses for trials and incarcerations. The lack of space in New York City was compounded by the filling of the jails with rebels and by two great fires during the autumn of 1776 thus forcing the occupation forces to use converted ships. The man responsible for the prisons on land and in the water was Provost Marshal William Cunningham. In lower Manhattan one of the most famous prisoners was the Rhinelander Sugar Warehouse located near Liberty Street. The warehouse was built in 1763 and was demolished in 1875. The only remnant of this building is a window salvaged from the factory and set into a memorial behind the Municipal Building located at Centre and Chambers

Streets.

Noted examples of private homes in northern Manhattan used as temporary prisons were the Morris-Jumel and the Dyckman Farmhouse . . . . . during the occupation of New York City by the British, it was estimated that 11,000 prisoners perished on the ships. The brutality on these ships had inflicted untold suffering in an unprecedented scale. Flogging and other acts of violence had run rampant on the ships. Overcrowding, starvation, and disease (smallpox, dysentery, typhus and yellow fever) were of epidemic proportions. Many of the prisoners dared their guards to kill them. . . .

On the average there had been 11 ships used as prisoners in the waters of the Hudson and East Rivers. By the end of the war a total of 25 ships had been used as prisons. . . . The most famous and notorious prison ship was the H.M.S. Jersey, a 64 gun veteran British warship that was unfit for naval service was partially dismantled and converted to house the rebel prisoners. The JERSEY, located in Wallabout Bay (now the Brooklyn Navy Yard), held about 1,100 men and gave up about 6 to 8 bodies per day. The chances of survival on board the JERSEY were less than 1 out of 5.

The Prison Ship Martyr's Monument was erected in Fort Greene Park Brooklyn. The park and surrounding area was named for General Nathaniel Greene who was instrumental in the design and construction of Fort Washington in Manhattan and Fort Lee in New Jersey. The locale was the site of Fort Putnam, one of a chain of forts used by the Rebel Army in the battle of Long Island. . . . The Martyr's Monument, designed by Stanford White . . . is the most austere and moving of the war memorials in New York City. It was dedicated on November 18th,

1908 with President William Howard Taft in attendance. . . Lower Manhattan boasts another monument to honor the American prisoners. In Trinity Churchyard and cemetery on Broadway and Wall Streets is a memorial where American soldiers of the Revolution are remembered. This monument was erected by the Vestry of the Church in 1852 and is located in the north-east corner of the cemetery. It is a sandstone tower designed in the Gothic-Revival style. This monument honors the unknown American soldiers and sailors of the Revolutionary War who were imprisoned and died and were buried in unmarked graves during the occupation of New York by the British."

THE RICHARD LYON JR. STORY

Richard (1624) first settled in Fairfield County, Connecticut. He was the youngest of the three brothers who escaped from England after the execution of Charles I. It is said that they were more than just witnesses of the execution as they were soldiers in Oliver Cromwell's Model Army. It is also said that Richard brought his sword with him to America. Richard married MARGARET (no maiden name known), they had 7 sons and 4 daughters. All records state that Margaret was born in 1624 in Fairfield CT, which was mainly occupied by Belgians, Dutch and Germans at that time. The records also state that they were married in 1642 but as this Richard was in England at that time this was unlikely. It is possible that Margaret was born and married in England and came with Richard to Fairfield, CT. Apart from information in his will, little is known about Richard but that he fathered a large family and started a dynasty, with hundreds of descendants still living today all over America and Canada.

He settled in Fairfield, Fairfield County, CT in 1649 after fleeing from England and was made a Freeman there in 1664, he was Commissioner for Fairfield in 1669 and at his death in 1678 left an estate valued at £632 (a considerable amount at that time).

His descendants settled in Fairfield, Redding and neighbouring towns, extending gradually northward into Massachusetts and Vermont. During the Revolution they were mostly loyal to the cause of Independence. From Vermont some of them moved to Michigan – among these the Honourable Lucius Lyon who represented the new state of Michigan as a Senator in the Congress of 1837-39. Richard and Margaret had the following children;

1. **Moses Lyon** (son of Richard Lyon and Margaret) was born about 1651 in Fairfield County, Fairfield, Connecticut (CT). He married MARY MEEKER about 1680 in Fairfield, CT. She was born on 6th October

1656 in Fairfield, Fairfield. She died on 28th March 1718 in Canterbury, Windham, CT. He died on 2nd March 1698 in Fairfield, Fairfield, CT.

2.   **Richard Lyon** was born about 1653 in Fairfield, Fairfield, Connecticut. He married MARY FRYE in 1687 in Redding, Fairfield, CT. She was born on 9th February 1668 in Fairfield, Fairfield, CT. She died in 1708 in Fairfield, Fairfield, CT. He died in January 1740 in Redding, Fairfield, CT.

3.   **Esther Lyon** was born about 1657 in Fairfield, Fairfield, CT. She died date unknown.

4.   **Hannah Lyon** was born about 1659 in Fairfield, Fairfield, CT. She died in November 1743 in Westport, Fairfield, CT.

5.   **William Lyon** was born about 1659 in Fairfield, Fairfield, CT. He married PHEBE in 1693 in Newtown, Fairfield, CT. She was born in 1663 in Fairfield, Fairfield, CT. He died on 4th November 1699 in Fairfield, Fairfield, CT. She died in 1715 in Fairfield, Fairfield, CT.

6.   **Elizabeth Lyon** was born in 1660 in Fairfield, Fairfield, CT. She died in 1695 in CT.

7.   **Abigail Lyon** was born about 1667 in Fairfield, CT. She died on 6th March 1698 in Fairfield, Fairfield, CT.

8.   **Samuel Lyon** was born in 1670 in Fairfield, Fairfield, CT. He married SUSANNA JACKSON on 10th September 1697 in Fairfield, Fairfield, CT. She was born on 10th September 1670 in Fairfield, Fairfield, CT. She died on 19th October 1718 in Fairfield, Fairfield, CT. He died in 1733 in Fairfield, Fairfield, CT.

9.   **Joseph Lyon** (son of Richard Lyon and Margaret) was born in 1673 in Fairfield, Fairfield, CT. in 1695 he married MARY JACKSON. He died March 16th, 1698.

Here are a few extracts from The Lyon Memorial:

"Richard Lyon had a house and lot recorded in the Land Records of Fairfield ('Fayrefeild') in January, 1653, and was made a freeman there in 1664. In 1673 he had recorded five acres of land at Barlow's Plains, and 18 acres 'on the Rocks'. He was chosen Commissioner for Fairfield, May 1669. It is related that on the occasion of a witchcraft trial 'the prisoner was sharply rebuked by **Richard Lyon**, one of the keepers, for bold language'. From the abusive reply which is recorded one may gather that the rebuke was well deserved.

The will of Richard Lyon, dated April 12th 1678, probated October 17th 1678, is almost the only source of information about his family. It reads: —

'The Last Will and Testament of Richard Lyon of Fairfield weak in body, but perfect in mind and memory do make this my last will and testament. Imprimis: I give my body to a comely burial and my soul unto the hands of God from whom I received it and my temporal estate that God hath given me I dispose of as followeth;

My will is that first after my decease my funeral charges and just debts shall be payd (sic). I give and bequeath to my son Moses Lyon one-third part of my land in Pequaneck [Bridgeport] lying on the eastward side and to run the whole length of that land. Also I give him the fifth part of my long lot to run the whole length to bound it the Southwest side. Also I give him two acres of meadow below the new bridge as the way goeth into Sascoeneck. Also my two acres of land in the old field I do give him, also a gun and a Razer and my biggest pewter platter. It is to be minded one hundred acres of the long lot is already given by deed of gift to him which is part of it above said where it lie and if there be any room on the old field land when I do decease it is to be as my estate but otherwise he is to possess it at my decease and the remaining part of the long lot that Moses is to have beside the hundred acres Moses is to possess at my decease.

It is my will that Moses shall pay to my cosen (cousin) Mary Fitch seven pounds within two years after my decease. I give to my son Richard Lyon the third part of my land in Pequaneck lying on the farther side next Benjamin Turney and to run the whole length. Also I give him one hundred and fifty acres of my long lot next Moses' part running through the whole length, and fifty acres of it he is to possess at my decease. I give him two acres of meadow in Sascoeneck running the whole length of it lying on the side by that which was Mihil Fryes.

I give unto my son William Lyon a third part of my land in Pequaneck also I give him one-fifth part of my long lot to run the whole length, and to lye next Richard's land, and also I give him two acres of meadow in Sascoeneck lying next the beach, and what is left above these Two acres and six more of that piece of meadow if any: William shall have it by his two acres. Also I give him my long gun and my back sword and my belt I give him; he to have his portion at nineteen years of age.

I give unto my sons Samuel and Joseph Lyon my lot and house and barn I live on. Also I give them that lot I had of Thomas Morhouse called his home lot the whole lot to lie on the northwest side; Joseph to have the Northwest. Also I give them four acres of meadow in Sascoeneck beside Richard's and William's above said. If it fall short of four acres then they must take up with what is: all these several parcels with house and barn is

136

equally to be divided between Samuel and Joseph. I give unto my daughter Hester Perry four pounds fully to her dispose and I give unto my son-in-law Nathaniel Perry his son Joseph Perry my grandchild three pounds, and unto my son-in-law Nathaniel Perry I give three pounds in carting and plowing as he have occasion. I give unto my wife **Margaret Lyon** whom I do hereby make my Executrix of this my last will, I say I give her three score pounds out of my estate and the use of the house I now live in and the barn and the home lot and the rest of Samuel and Joseph's portion above mentioned to use and improve while she remains a widow, or until the said Samuel and Joseph have attained the age of twenty-one years when they are to have their portions.

I give unto my daughters Betty Hanna and Abigail, when my wife hath paid her two score pound out of the movables, the rest of the moveable estate I give them equally to be divided provided it exceeds not forty pounds which if it do the over plus is to be divided between my three youngest sons and my three youngest daughters equally. I will my three youngest daughters Betty, Hanna and Abigail shall have their portions paid them at nineteen years of age unless they marry before that age if they do then to receive their portions. And if either Samuel or Joseph dye before they come to age to receive their portions the other son to have the whole, he paying a third part of the value of the said portion equally unto William and the three youngest daughters, and if any of my three youngest daughters dye before they come of age to receive their portions then the portion shall be divided equally unto the survivors of the three youngest sons. And if William dye before he come of age to receive his portion then Samuel and Joseph shall have his land, and they shall pay to my three youngest daughters a third part of the value of his land equally to be divided among them.

And it is my will that if the movables fall short of my wife's three score pound and my daughters' forty pound a piece as above then my land In Sascoeneck lying between Goodman Cobbes and Thomas Shornington shall go in to make it up to that. This is my last will I have here-unto set to my hand this 12th April, 1678.

Richard Lyon - his mark.'"

As we can see in this Will Richard remembered all his family and showed concern for their well-being until his last breath. This will shows a farmer and landowner and a fulfilment of the family trait of the Lyon family to own land and rely on it to make a living.

Life Expectancy of first four Generations of Richard Lyon family

Richard Lyon	m/f	0-9	10-19	20-29	30-39	40-49	50-59	60-69	70-79	80-89	90-99	100+	?	Totals
Gen. 1	F				2					1			1	4
	M			1		2		1		2			1	7
Gen. 2	F			1			2						6	9
	M			2	1	3	2	2	4	1			1	16
Gen 3	F	1		1	2	2	2	1	1	4	1	2	22	39
	M	6	1		3	5	2	1	10	4	2	1	13	48
Gen 4	F	3		1	1			6	5	8	1		29	54
	M	6	1	3	1	10	8	6	8	5	5	2	23	78
	Totals	16	2	9	10	22	16	17	28	25	9	5	96	255
													Average age	57.70

Note the table shows 9 deaths of children under the age of 9 in 4th Generation. There were at that time frequent smallpox and other fatal illnesses from disease and from various wars between the settlers and native Indians and against British rule. The next generation produced 25 children, the 3rd Generation 87 children and the 4th Generation 132 children. Richard's family and descendants can be found on the website.

Richard Lyon Families in Redding, Connecticut

There were multiple Lyon (sometimes spelled Lion) families in Redding, CT. Some were Congregationalists, others Anglican. Among the original members of the Congregational church at its organization appear the names of **Daniel Lyon** and wife, and **Benjamin Lyon** and wife. They were enrolled by Rev Mr Gay and **Richard Lyon**. All settled in the south-eastern part of the town, near what is now the Easton line, presently known as Lyon's Plain.

"When Revolutionary opinions were being debated in 1775, **John Lyon;** was one of the signers of the Redding Loyalist Association's position statement featured in the New York Gazetteer. When the names of the signers were made public he was taken up and ill-treated by a mob and robbed. Next his property was seized and Lyon left Redding for New York, joining British forces in Long Island. John Lyon's property was quite expansive as he purchased adjoining properties over the course of the 18 years he lived on Redding Ridge: orchards, two barns, two houses (one of which he rented out), a 20 acre farm a half mile from the homestead, 30 acres of woodland a mile and half away. He held a yolk of oxen, three milking cows, three heifers, two horses, and twenty-three sheep at the time of his departure."

(http://mybrothersamisdead.historyofredding.com/my-brother-sam-isdead_ characters.htm).

This is the only known case of a member of the Lyon family being loyal to the Crown of England at this time, there may have been others but this case is recorded.

Some members of Richard's family who took part in the War of Independence against the British

The following extracts are from the Lyon Memorial:

"**Nathan Lyon** [Richard, Richard] was born in Fairfield, Conn., November 28th, 1703. From Land Records of Redding it is learned that the name of his wife (widow) was ABIGAIL. In 1729 at a meeting of the (Presbyterian) society of Redding, Nathan Lyon, Moses Knapp and Daniel Crofoot made strenuous objections to the 'hiering' (hearing) of any other than a minister of the Church of England in 1738 these same names appear in a list of seven parishioners of Mr Beach. He died in Redding, November 2st, 1757 and was buried in Redding Ridge Episcopal Church Cemetery.

Lieutenant Daniel Lyon [Daniel, Richard, Richard] was born in Fairfield, Conn., August 11th, 1719. He settled in Redding and married first "ANNAH" who died soon after the birth of her only son, Jacob. He married second RUTH (KNAPP) WHEELER, widow of Seth Wheeler, and daughter of Moses Knapp. He appears to have served in the Revolutionary war with the rank of Sergeant. The date of his death and place of his burial has not been ascertained.

Captain Henry Lyon [Nathan, Richard, Richard] was born in Redding, Conn., in 1730. His wife's name was REBECCA. She was born in 1732. Both were buried in the Episcopal Church cemetery at Redding. In May 1762, he was appointed Ensign to the 'Train Band' in the Eastern Division of Redding, 4th Regiment. In May 1765, he was appointed Lieutenant in the same Company. In May 1769 he was appointed deputy from Redding, being at that time called Captain Henry Lyon. In May, 1771 he was appointed by the Connecticut Assembly Justice of Peace in Fairfield County. He was reappointed in 1772, and again in 1773. No record has been found of any children. He died in that place December 24th, 1773. Rebecca died March 7th 1775.

Ephraim Lyon [Ephraim, Samuel, Richard] was born in Fairfield, Conn.; baptised June 15th 1740. He married according to Redding Land Records, ANN ADAMS. He took an active part In the Revolutionary War. He was one of the Committee of Safety appointed in Fairfield, December 29th, 1774. In May 1774 he was appointed Lieutenant in a company of militia in the western part of North Fairfield, belonging to the 4th Regiment. He was among those called out for active service in March 1777, 'operating at Fairfield and Stratford,' and again at the alarm at New Haven in July, 1779.

Doctor John Lyon [John, John, Samuel, Richard] was born in Fairfield, Conn, (according to one record in Danbury, Conn.), April 19th, 1756. He went with his brother to Massachusetts, making his home in Lanesboro. In his father's will in 1793, he is said to be 'of New Milford.' He served, as his brothers Jabez and Kimberley did, in the Revolutionary war. According to the report of the Bureau of Pensions, dated April 29th, 1805, he was in the Battle of Bunker Hill. He was probably twice married, but no record has been found of the first marriage. According to the aforesaid Report of the Bureau of Pensions, he married January 1st 1786, at Lanesboro, Mass., SARAH LOCKWOOD, who, as his widow, applied for a pension August 19th 1843, being then 73 years of age, and living in Moriah, Essex Co., N. Y. According to the same Report, John Lyon died at Moriah, N. Y., February 7th 1817. This does not agree with the statement above, which is believed to be correct. No record has been found of the descendants of Doctor John Lyon. He died before December 1799.

Kimberley Lyon [John, John, Samuel, Richard] was born, probably in Fairfield, Conn., date not ascertained. He was living in Lanesboro, Mass. during the Revolutionary war, in which he took an active part. He enlisted July 22nd 1779 as private in Captain Samuel Clark's Company, and served 1 month and 12 days at New Haven, Conn. His name appears in a list of men raised for six months service in July 1780, and he served again in October 1781 in Timothy Read's Company; marched from Lanesboro to Stillwater; service 10 days.

Nehemiah Webb Lyon [Stephen, Ebenezer, Richard, Richard] was born in Weston, Conn. August 16th, 1759 He married, August 26th 1778, SARAH TREADWELL (Weston T. R.). He was a revolutionary soldier, having enlisted in Najah Rennet's Company in 1781. He was recorded as a pensioner in Fairfield Co. in 1832 and in Weston in 1832, and remained on the pension roll until his death in 1860. His children nearly all lived to a good old age and he died there in his one hundred and first year in 1860.

Jabez Lyon [John, John, Samuel, Richard] was born in Fairfield, Conn., March 18th 1747. He removed to Lauesboro, Mass. Nothing has been learned about him except that he served in the revolutionary war. He enlisted first, April 26th 1777, in Captain Joseph Barnes' Company; in Colonel Symond's Berkshire Co. Regiment; he provided service 24 days. He was called out on alarms repeatedly, serving in various companies, viz., to Manchester, July 9th 1777; at Claverack forty days, in October and November, 1779; twice on alarms in October 1780.

Thomas Lyon [John, John, Samuel, Richard] was born in Fairfield, CT., October 9th 1749 He settled at New Ashford, Berkshire Co., Mass., about 1770, and lived there until 1801, when he went to join his son-in-law, **Seth Lyon**, in Lima, N. Y. In 1812 he moved to Avon, Livingstone Co., N. Y., where he spent the remaining years of his life. The following items are found in the New Ashford Record.

Thomas Lyon, et al. appointed to 'take notis of all Breaches of the peace Either of God or man, and make information to the Committee of Safety'. March 22nd 1779, Thomas Lyon was nominated assessor; September 24th 1781, chosen constable; March 24th 1783, chosen selectman, assessor and highway surveyor; March 15th 1784, 'Lieutenant Lyon' chosen on a 'Grand jury'. He was a soldier in the Revolution. He enlisted in 1776 at New Ashford, and served at Ticonderoga; afterwards fought at Bennington under General Stark, August 16th 1777, and was at the surrender of Burgoyne, October 17th 1777. This he recites in an application for a pension August 11th 1832. The pension was granted but he was then advanced in years and did not live long to benefit by it. He married May 10th 1769, THANKFUL RUSSICA. She was born in 1752, and died at Lima, N. Y. in August, 1809. She was of a Huguenot family of De Russica, which came over from France to escape religious persecutions. Thomas Lyon married a second wife whose maiden name was GREEN. There were no children by this marriage. He died in Avon, N. Y., on March 4th 1835."

Others are listed on the website www.thelyonfamily.org.uk/help/genealogy

Members of the Lyon family involved in the war of Independence.

The table below shows the number of descendants of the Lyon families engaged in the War of Independence as recorded in the three Memorial Books in 1905. To see all their names please go to; *www.the lyonfamily.org.uk/help/statistics*

The members of the family are in alphabetical order; Henry Lyon, Richard and William Lyon families, some were officers and some unknown rank.

	Henry	Richard	Thomas	William	Officers	Unknown	Total
CT		20	9	25	5	18	79
MA		5		26	2	51	102
NH				3	2		5
NJ	39				3		42
NY	5		66		3		74
RI	2						2
VT				1			1
Total	46	25	75	55	15	69	305

CT = Connecticut, MA = Massachusetts, NH = New Hampshire, NJ = New Jersey, NY = New York state, RI = Rhode Island, VT = Vermont

Some members of the family were opposed to the revolution and supported England's claim to rule the New England states. Some of these were told to move from their homes, some went to Canada, some moved to other states such as Pennsylvania. The Quaker members of the family were often opposed to war but Thomas Lyon's family, who were Quakers, seem to have sent more to war than his brothers Henry and Richard.

William's family seemed to contribute most soldiers in Massachusetts, maybe because the troubles started in Boston and much of the early fighting was in that state. Another fact worth noting is that by tradition Lyon family members were farmers and leaving their land was tantamount to creating poverty for their families. It was not easy to forgo ploughing and reaping for an ideal when there were other townsfolk who were willing to take up arms. England was not the only enemy; there were still troubles with some Indian tribes and long standing feuds over land ownership.

The Lyon family members were at that time Protestants and church goers and depending on the preachers they obeyed, would sometimes be pacifists who were taught to love their neighbours and their enemies. Puritan preachers still held sway in the new colonies and they were divided about the practical issues regarding their basic beliefs.

PETER LYON OF DORCHESTER, MASSACHUSETTS

Peter is not related to William, Thomas, Henry or Richard. He was a weaver in England. His family is very interesting in that, from humble beginnings, he built a dynasty of one of the largest families to populate New England with the Lyon name. It does appear that Peter was in America before 1640 as can be seen from the text below.

(These words are taken from Lyon Memorial - Massachusetts families, page 320, by Albert Brown Lyons) and is a description of the life of Peter Lyon in America.

"Somewhat more than two and a half centuries ago, there walked the lanes of Good Old Dorchester a young man in whose breast were struggling conflicting emotions: the weaker, perhaps, a yearning for the dear ones whom he should never see again; the stronger, the comforting assurance that, in the disturbed condition of England, the Test and Conventicle Acts were little likely to cross a thousand leagues of sea.

The Religion Act 1592 was an Act of the Parliament of England. The Act imprisoned without bail those over the age of sixteen who failed to attend Church; persuaded others to do the same; who denied Her Majesty's authority in matters ecclesiastical; and who attended unlawful religious conventicles. If after offending they did not conform in the next three months they would be exiled forever from England. The Act fined those who harboured recusants £10 for every month hidden. The Act stated that the Act would continue no longer than the end of the next session of Parliament.

This young man was known to genealogists as Peter Lyon the First. Of his antecedents and of his age nothing is known with certainty. As to his English home, all data points to London of either Essex or Middlesex stock. That he was made freeman in 1649, and that his first recorded child was born in 1650 indicate that he was born between 1620 and 1630. It is possible, indeed, that he was twice married, and that SUSANNA, member of the First Church in 1639, was his first wife. This supposition might account for some of Lyon name who appear at an early date, but who have no apparent connection with those whose position in the colony is definitely known.

The short and simple annals of Peter's life are meagre enough. By occupation he was a weaver. He was made freeman in 1649 of Dorchester. In 1657 he received £1 bounty for killing a wolf. In 1664 he signed a petition to the General Court as inhabitant of Dorchester, MA. In 1665 he granted a strip of ground for a highway. He was given permission to entertain Peter Green, of Concord, into his family for one month, an event that may have some connection with the marriage of his son Nathaniel, who had a son born in Concord in 1680. In 1672 he appears to have been much concerned about his sons, for in answer to a summons from the Selectmen, he reported that they follow their employment, and that he would look diligently after them. He served on the jury in cases of appeal, life, limb and banishment, 1675-1685, and in 1681-2 held what would now be considered the very undesirable office of tithing man. He sold a house and lot on Green St. to the Davenports in 1693.

His wife Ann died November 26th 1689. He died 1693-4th. Administration on the estate of Peter Lyon, weaver, late of Dorchester, was granted to his son in-law, Daniel Morey, carter, of Boston, January 8th 1694. Inventory presented by Daniel Morey; amount, £35 8s. 6d.There is no record of his death, and the place of his burial no man knoweth to this day."

The family records for Peter is available on the website. *www.thelyonfamily.org.uk/help/genealogy*

GEORGE LYON

George is another Lyon not related to William, Thomas, Henry and Richard. George Lyon was born in England and married, October 14th, 1661, HANNAH, daughter of Thomas and Sarah TOLMAN. Little is known of the birth or the ancestry of George, or of the date of his arrival in America. The history of the Lyons of England indicates that he might have been of Essex origin, and this supposition is supported in some degree by the fact that his friend, William Blake, who subsequently married George's widow, was from Little Baddow, Essex, near the home of the Essex Lyons.

George and Hannah were admitted to Dorchester Church 1668, and they joined the Milton church 1681. They lived on the Milton side of the Neponset River. In 1666 George bought the 19th lot, 32 acres, 'beyond Neponset mill on Neponset River,' and in the deed he is styled 'husbandman.' He added to this property by buying the 18th lot, 33 acres east of his lot between the highway on the south and the Neponset on the north' in 1674, with his brother-in-law, James Tucker,

He is recorded as having been paid at Milton, August 23rd 1676, for services at Punkapoag during King Philip's War, and his sons had subsequently some military experience against the French and the Indians. The children of George and Hannah (Tolman) Lyon, recorded in Milton, MA were:

1. **George** born 16th October 1662; married 14th February, 1687-8, Thankful Badcock; died 26th October, 1694.
2. **Thomas** born 1666; married October 28th 1680, Joanna Payson; died February 9th 1750.
3. **Henry**, born June 6th 1670; died December 28th 1696.
4. **Hannah**, born November 14th 1678; baptised 1674; married February 26th 1690, Abijah Baker; she and her husband dismissed to Dorchester January 8th 1718; later removed to Medfield.
5. **Edward**, born September 22nd 1678. 'Edward, aged about 17, son of George Lyon, late of Milton, chooses his brother Thomas as his guardian.' (*This extract from Lyon Memorial - Massachusetts by Albert Brown Lyons 1905 page 369*) George died October 6th 1690.

George's widow Hannah re-married in 1698, a William Blake and died August 4th 1729 (*Blake's Annals*). The expenses of her funeral are noted in the Bible of her son Thomas. Her will states that 'for the parental love and affection I bear to my well beloved son, Thomas Lion', she conveys to him 'all my right and interest in the 10th lot on the 12 divisions in Dorchester, and other parcels of land which was the estate of my father, Thomas Tolman, of said Dorchester.

Hannah died August 4th 1729 [*Bible Record*].

To see the rest of the family tree, visit the website under George Lyon, where his known descendants are listed.

America became the United States of America with its own democratic constitution in 1776. Hopefully the new country would have learned from the mistakes of the past in Britain and other European countries.

"The Declaration of Independence IN CONGRESS, July 4th 1776. The unanimous Declaration of the Thirteen United States of America.

"...... We hold these truths to be self-evident, that all men are created equal, that they are endowed by their Creator with certain unalienable Rights, that among these are Life, Liberty and the pursuit of Happiness.--That to secure these rights, Governments are instituted among Men, deriving their just powers from the consent of the governed, --That whenever any Form of Government becomes destructive of these ends, it is the Right of the People to alter or to abolish it, and to institute new Government, laying its foundation on such principles and organizing its powers in such form, as to them shall seem most likely to affect their Safety and Happiness. Prudence, indeed, will dictate that Governments long established should not be changed for light and transient causes; and accordingly all experience hath shown, that mankind are more disposed to suffer, while evils are sufferable, than to right themselves by abolishing the forms to which they are accustomed.

"*(http://www.archives.gov/exhibits/charters/declaration.html)*

CHAPTER 8
ANOTHER VIEW UP TO THE WAR OF INDEPENDENCE BY JOHN BOGIN

•◉•

We all like to see ourselves in the best light. We play down our bad side and promote our good side. The same is true about countries at war; if we are defeated it was because of the terrible odds against us, we were betrayed, and our enemies used prohibited weapons that no God fearing man would ever use. The winners often claim that God was on their side and the heroism of their cause was sufficient to overcome all odds. With those thoughts in mind here are my comments on the American War of Independence from an English perspective. For ease I will refer to the Colonists at all times as Americans. The term British will cover Britain and her allies.

The roots of the American War of Independence can be found in a war that is called by many names. In Europe it is known as the Seven Years War 1754-1763 (but it actually lasted nine years). In North America this is referred to as the 'French and Indian wars' or the 'Great War of Empire'; by the French as the 'Guerre de la Conquete'. It could be that one incident that occurred in Ohio Country on 28th May 1754 started the Seven Years war, which is thought to have cost the lives of a million people across four continents.

Ohio Country itself was an area west of the Appalachian Mountains and South of Lake Erie. For hundreds of years this had been the hunting ground of the Haudenosaunee League of Nations commonly known as the Iroquois. The Iroquois had moved westwards away from the more numerous Europeans who were now living in the Thirteen British colonies. In doing so the Iroquois in their turn had pressured other smaller tribes into moving further west. By the middle of the 18th century the eastern part of North America (America and Canada) was divided as follows on the map.

The British Colonists from New England, on the East coast were probing westwards. The French had used the major rivers of the continent to further their explorations. The French had called the northern part of their territory New France. This was a much larger geographical area than New England but with fewer people. New France extended from the Saint Lawrence and included the Great Lakes and curved down to New Orleans on the Gulf of Mexico. They called the southern part of this area Louisiana.

To the north and west was another much larger but sparsely populated British area around Hudson Bay. Between the French and British areas which we would now call 'No Man's Land' but which were patrolled and claimed by both countries. Despite the French and British claiming these areas, the land was still very much inhabited by the American Indians. It would have been foolish for either side to attempt to ride rough shod over them but, the settlers tried it on occasions and suffered accordingly.

On one occasion, the French kidnapped fifty members of the Iroquois parliament and sent them to France as galley slaves. In the end the French were scouring the galleys to find and repatriate the survivors in an attempt to placate the Iroquois. Only thirteen survived to return home.

In May 1754 the French had been building Fort Le Boeuf very close to the undisputed line of British territory which annoyed both the British and the Iroquois. (This site is near Uniontown, Pennsylvania). The Lieutenant Governor sent a message, via a Major in the Virginia Militia, politely, requesting that the French commandant stop building and leave the area. The French commandant, politely, refused. The Major reported back to headquarters and was told to return to the area and protect Fort Prince George that was being built by the British. In the meantime the French had destroyed Fort Prince George and were building the much larger Fort Marquis Duquesne. On the 28th May 1754 the Major ambushed a French unit killing and wounding some and capturing the rest. It was reported that the French commander Joseph Coulon de Jumonville died either during the action or when in the captivity of the British.

Many sources regard this as the start of the Seven Years war. The name of this Major who committed this atrocity was Major George Washington, who later became the first President of the United States of America. The war continued and ended with a victory for Britain and her allies. The resulting peace treaty was signed in Paris on the 10th October 1763. During the discussions prior to the signing of this treaty the French were offered a number of options one of which was the return of their old territories (New France) east of the Mississippi. If they accepted that offer they would renounce their claims for the islands of Guadeloupe and Martinique; they decided to keep the islands.

One great mistake was made by the British General Amherst. His handling of the distribution of the lands previously owned by the French and the Indians resulted in the Pontiac Rebellion in 1763. To assuage the feelings of the various tribes, including his allies, the Iroquois, George III issued the Royal Proclamation of 1763. This was to thank the Iroquois and other tribes who had helped Britain to defend the Americans against the French and their native allies and to help calm the situation by providing a homeland for them.

Although Britain 'won' the war the cost in men and materials was high and by the end Britain was almost bankrupt and was looking to put its finances on a firmer footing. One way any government does this is by raising taxes. In 1764 in an attempt to raise money, a Stamp Duty Tax was imposed. A government stamp was to be purchased for use on all official documents and paper goods. This, the first direct tax that Britain had imposed was withdrawn because of American complaints.

British merchants were experiencing a 'credit crunch' and wanted to be paid for the goods that they had supplied to the Americans during the war and they wanted pounds sterling rather than Continental currency. The Americans did on occasion use Tobacco notes, literally a note promising to pay the bearer a stated amount of tobacco. The British merchants also started to refuse credit. This upset the Americans even more. The British Government actually reduced taxes on sugar and molasses but did still demand that the taxes were paid; previously the higher taxation had not always been enforced.

The Royal Proclamation of 1763 now came in a new light. The Americans did not see why their westward progress should be stopped and certainly not because of the indigenous tribes. The Proclamation became another reason for the War of Independence. The relations between Britain and the Americans rapidly deteriorated and eventually the War of American Independence started. The final straw was when British troops tried to remove illegal arms stored by the Americans at Lexington and Concorde. If you subscribe to the Mel Gibson version you will know that Britain was kicked out in six weeks by good wholesome American boys carrying hickory sticks in one hand and apple pies in the other. Well; not quite.

The British problem was suffered by many Empires; too much land to be defended by too few soldiers. It would have been hard for the British to defend all the territory they claimed without the American Revolution; the added strain was too much. This was one reason that they employed German mercenaries or as the Americans called them Hessians.

It has been estimated that the American opinion at the time could be divide into three; one third being Patriots, one third Loyalist and the other third being Neutral. Some of the neutrals were said to have two flags in their farms. The appropriate flag was to be flown whenever that particular army was marching past. This was also a good time to make money if you were not worried about where the money came from. The problem with being neutral is that both the Patriots and the Loyalists will have a grievance with you.

Particular comment should be made about The Society of Friends, the Quakers. The great majority of the Quakers believed in Non-Violence although some, including Nathanael Greene, (spelling correct) actually rose to the rank of Major General in the American Army. The average Quaker was figuratively 'on a hiding to nothing.' They may be regarded as the first religious martyrs of the new country. If they did not support the Revolution they would suffer for it and were regarded as Tories and Loyalists. They could not pay taxes to the Patriots, if those taxes were to aid the revolution or they would be expelled from the Society. All this despite the statement that; "Quaker thought played a crucial role in the formation of the American ideal." In passing; two of the ships carrying tea which were 'attacked' in the Boston Tea Party were owned by Quakers.

One thing that the American Revolution did for the American Colonies was to unite them. At this time a colonist could describe himself as a British American or even give the name of his state as his nationality. Colonists would say that their country was Maryland etc. When George Washington asked the men of New Jersey to swear allegiance to the United States they refused saying that their country was New Jersey. Conversely one thing that the American Revolution did was to split opinion in Britain. The Tories and the Whigs, separate political parties at the time, took opposing views. The Tories supported the Loyalists and the King, the Whigs supported the Patriots.

Many people regarded the British soldier of the time as a fierce fighting machine pitted against American civilians. Although it is true that soldiers were fighting civilians, many of these soldiers had never been in battle before coming to America.

We make mistakes if we try to put people into categories The British thought of the Americans as 'backwoods men' who could shoot the eye out of a squirrel at 200 yards. George Washington used this idea of the sharp shooting backwoodsman by suggesting that his men should wear buckskin clothes with fringes dyed in natural colours. An American veteran would still stay there, it was his country. A British veteran would probably be shipped home. Many Americans were of course town dwellers who would never have needed to handle a firearm until they joined the militia. There is a third group, those British soldiers who had retired and stayed in America and now sided with their adopted country. Another myth is of the iron discipline that the British soldier was subject to. Many instances of indiscipline including actual assaulting an officer were almost overlooked.

The Declaration of Independence was signed on 2 July 1776.

– end of John Bogin article

CHAPTER 9

THE AMERICAN CIVIL WAR—1861-1865

The American Civil War between the Union states of the north and the southern Confederate states was one of the most terrible occurrences in the history of the 230 year old Commonwealth of America.

"In the spring of 1861, decades of simmering tensions between the northern and southern United States over issues including States rights versus Federal authority, westward expansion and slavery exploded into the American Civil War (1861-65). The election of the anti-slavery Republican Abraham Lincoln as president in 1860 caused seven southern states to secede from the Union to form the Confederate States of America; four more joined them after the first shots of the Civil War were fired.

Four years of brutal conflict were marked by historic battles at Bull Run (Manassas), Antietam, Chancellorsville, Gettysburg and Vicksburg, among others. The War Between the States, as the Civil War was also known, pitted neighbour against neighbour and in some cases, brother against brother. By the time it ended in Confederate surrender in 1865, the Civil War proved to be the costliest war ever fought on American soil, with some 620,000 of 2.4 million soldiers killed, millions more injured and the population and territory of the South devastated".

(http://www.history.com/topics/american-civil-war)

What is so sad is the needless deaths of many young men and the dividing lines that are still there between the north and south even though slavery is officially a thing of the past.

Statistics are notoriously unreliable and historians often quibble about statistics that exist regarding the Civil War, and it's no wonder – while records were kept during the war much of the information has been gathered from personal documents such as letters and diaries. Record-keeping as we know it today did not exist during the Civil War era; exact enumeration of men who served, casualties, and other factors was simply not possible with the limitations of the technology at that time. When one considers that most of the statistics gathered by record keepers during the war travelled along with military camps, it is amazing that any records survived at all. Another point to remember is that most participants enlisted for 90 days and many re-enlisted later in the war in other regiments and have sometimes been listed many times.

The Lyon and Lyons family involvement

Unionist and Confederate armies.

State	Lyon	Lyons	Lyon	Lyons	State	Lyon	Lyons	Lyon	Lyons
	Unionist		Confederate			Unionist		Confederate	
Alabama			37	24	Mississippi				41
Arkansas	3		6	9	Missouri	42	19		
California		6			New Hampshire	5	10		
Connecticut	49	24			New Jersey	21	40		
Delaware		2			New Mexico	2			
Florida		1	1	8	New York	175	244		
Georgia			36	46	North Carolina	1		3	22
Illinois	61	108			Ohio	76	157		
Indiana	41	75			Pennsylvania	94	145		
Iowa	50	34			Rhode Island	10	14		
Kansas	7	6			South Carolina			11	21
Kentucky	23	31			Tennessee			145	76
Louisana			11	65	Texas			118	51
Maine	19	29			Vermont	12	8		
Maryland	4	13	3	2	Virginia			169	32
Massachusetts	26	72			West Virginia	6	40		
Michigan	74	30			Wisconsin	46	27		
Minnesota	4	20			Totals	851	1155	540	397
					Totals	Lyon	1391		
						Lyons	1552		

The table shows the number of participants in that war by state whether they were a Lyon or a Lyons.

In total I can trace Lyon 1391 members and Lyons 1552 members. Some members of the Lyon (s) family served for a short time some for long periods. The occasional deaths of the families have been recorded but the total of fatalities is unknown at present.

The numbers who participated as recorded on the Ancestry websites for the Lyon Civil War Service records are as in the chart below. There is a difference between the two charts because the Memorial books are not a totally accurate record of participants and, as been stated before, some soldiers enlisted more than once. This is only a rough guide but hopefully interesting. The number of deaths is probably correct.

	Confederate	Unionist	Total	Deaths
Lyon	461	1,215	1,676	98
Lyons	426	1,790	2,216	146

These are official numbers for US Civil War Soldiers 1861-65 records. The number of deaths includes death by enemy weapons, accidents, diseases and other causes.

Some soldiers only enlisted for a specific number of days i.e. 90 and later reenlisted with the same company or another company so the above figures are not totally reliable. It should be noted that Civil War records are constantly changing as new information is received from families and research.

Famous members of the Lyon family in the Civil War.

NATHANIEL LYON (July 14th, 1818 – August 10th, 1861) was the first Union General to be killed in the American Civil War and is noted for his actions in the state of Missouri at the beginning of the conflict.

Nathaniel Lyon is a controversial figure in American history. Some credit his quick action and hard line Unionism for stopping the Missouri secession movement.

"Lyon was born on a farm in Ashford, Connecticut. As a boy he hated farming. His relatives had fought in the American Revolution and he was determined to follow in their footsteps. Lyon entered West Point on July 1st 1837. He hardly looked the part of a soldier:

William T. Sherman, who was a year ahead of him, described Lyon as a 'lymphatic boy, who didn't seem to have energy enough to make a man'. But his four years at the academy hardened Lyon into a driven soldier. Lyon thrived as a cadet, and in 1841 he graduated from West Point ranked 11th in a class of 52.

He was assigned to the Second Infantry after graduation and served with them in the Seminole Wars and the Mexican-American War. Promoted to First Lieutenant for "conspicuous bravery in capturing enemy artillery" at the Battle for Mexico City, he was then posted to the frontier where he participated in the massacre of Native Americans at Clear Lake, California. After being reassigned to Fort Riley, Kansas, Lyon became a staunch abolitionist while serving in the border wars known as 'Bleeding Kansas.

On December 24th 1861, the United States Congress passed a resolution of thanks for the eminent and patriotic services of the late Brigadier General Nathaniel Lyon. The country to whose service he devoted his life will guard and preserve his fame as a part of its own glory. The Thanks of Congress are hereby given to the brave officers who, under the command of the late general Lyon sustained the honour of the flag and achieved victory against overwhelming numbers at the battle of Springfield, Missouri.

The 24th Missouri Volunteer Infantry was recruited as 'The Lyon Legion' in honour of the General, and carried a unique regimental colour, depicting a Lion beneath a constellation of six stars. Lyon County, Iowa, Lyon County, Kansas, Lyon County, Minnesota, Lyons Valley, Jamul, California and Lyon County, Nevada, are named in Nathaniel Lyon's honour. Two forts were also named in his honour: Fort Lyon in Colorado and Fort Lyon (Virginia), which defended Washington, D.C., during the American Civil War in Virginia. Lyon Park in St. Louis, Lyon Street in San Francisco and Lyon Lane in Carson City, Nevada are also named for him.

The Civil War, America's bloodiest conflict, cost nearly 1,100,000 casualties and claimed more than 620,000 lives. The campaigning armies left destruction in their wake, particularly in the Southern states that bore the brunt of the fighting. Best estimates place the total number of war-time clashes in excess of 10,000, many of them large scale encounters that resulted in staggering losses for both sides. Engagements such as Gettysburg, Shiloh, the Wilderness and Chickamauga are ranked among the great battles of history; they bear witness to the courage and tenacity with which the Federal and

Confederate soldiers fought for their beliefs."

(http://www.thelatinlibrary.com/chron/civilwarnotes/lyon.html)

CHAPTER 10

LEAVING NEW ENGLAND—A NEW ADVENTURE

—•❂•—

Moving west and south across the USA and finding new land and businesses. Some outstanding Lyons in the USA.

The steady move westwards and southwards started before 1840. Lyon(s) were mostly farmers and land-owners and large families were becoming difficult to support in New England because of the shortage of farming land for their growing families. Traditionally the sons and sometimes the daughters acquired land from their parents on their death. This caused problems, as after about four generations of large families, what was originally 200 acres could have been sub-divided many times and the other available land could often have been bought by other families. A complete table of statistics of the Lyon families' locations is at the front of the book in Maps and Illustrations.

1840 Census

To obtain these numbers I went through the records of the census returns and could have saved myself a lot of work by finding the website where this had been done before. The Census produced a total of 1404 families. Of about 1360 Lyon families recorded there were; Massachusetts (64), New Jersey (89), New York (433), Connecticut (150) and Ohio (113) at the time.

USA 1840

Some of these families had 14 children or more while some were single inhabitants at a particular address when the census was taken. The census only recorded the family as one unit and did not take into consideration the size of the family.

The records give a breakdown by enumerating the ages of the members of the family and whether they were white or black and whether they were slaves or not. Slaves were often listed in census reports – this can cause confusion. Without going into great detail it would be impossible to be certain how many members of the homestead were named Lyon.

Before 1840 the first big move was of 113 families to Ohio. More moves west were; 50 families to Michigan and 19 to Illinois. Other families moved south; 41 to Kentucky, 25 to Virginia and 25 to Tennessee. They had to travel by foot or in most cases with wagons and horses, exploring new territory with all its hazards and expectations. Normally one or two members of the family would have gone ahead, found land and sent for the rest of the family once they had settled their claims. These were intrepid explorers, the west had not yet been opened up to large numbers of American citizens. Generally everything west of the Mississippi was known as the 'Wild West'. Its heroes were strong individuals who risked their lives for their adventures. Other states west of the River Mississippi and in the south had very few families venturing there initially.

This Mississippi river was a deterrent to many potential explorers because of its size and the need to travel so far north with wagons and cattle and livestock into what is now Wisconsin and Minnisota. The lands up to this point were fairly flat and trekking was tedious through Ohio, Indiana and Illinois. The migrants had not yet seen the mountains to the west, later known as the Rockies. There were also a large number of Indian tribes to encounter, some friendly, some rather unwelcoming to these strangers.

The chart summarizes the move away from the Eastern states with census counts for 1880 and 1920 – there has been a more recent census published for 1940. In 1880 there were 93,584 Lyon family members and in 1920 there were 166,822.

1880 Census

By 1880 the move west and south was enormous. Alabama (376), Connecticut (746), Georgia (387), Illinois (808), Iowa (665), Kansas (405), Kentucky (628), Michigan (890), Missouri (487), Ohio (648) – the list goes on. Then there was the enormous growth of families in the New England States like New York.

The Lyon families can be found in the countryside in California, especially the now famous Napa Valley. The end of the trail or the railway was now California with 200 families, mostly setting up farms in the wonderful climate after freezing winters in the eastern and northern states they had passed through. For some here was a paradise that could only be dreamed of. Some no doubt tried to find gold but most were genuinely looking for good land. The Lyon families were now all over California but not very often in cities, except recently, as seen by the 1940 census. Of course by then long treks were no longer necessary because of cars, trucks and especially aeroplanes, which are now the standard mode of transport in such a large country.

1920 Census

By 1920 the members of Lyon families were growing in many states i.e. California (385), Illinois (302), Michigan (270), New York (846), Texas (145) but many were still living in their original states.

The government had encouraged the movement of its citizens to farm the large areas of land and create new townships. The land had been owned by the native 'Red Indians' whose tribes had owned the land for many centuries. This move west was an invasion and wars and feuds were a hazard to be faced daily.

Moving south

It is almost impossible to evaluate what happened to the members of the Lyon family in the south after the Civil War — the numbers of families did reduce, sometimes dramatically. In some southern states the war over slavery may have had some adverse effect on these families. They were, no doubt, for the most part still farmers, hardly any living in towns or cities.

Land was also available in the **south** so we see more movement between the 1880 and 1920 census returns. Virginia (370), West Virginia (150), Kentucky (900), North Carolina (1,000), Tennessee (450), Arkansas (130), Georgia (490), Florida (46), Alabama (450), Mississippi (240), Louisiana (110), Texas (350), Oklahoma (87).

The Railways and their effect on travel

Several big changes had occurred after the war, the railways had become the main means of transport so settlers could have moved almost anywhere in the USA. We know that there was a growth in numbers in California and that several members of the family did move there.

From the mid-1980s the growth of the railways was relentless. Those from the Southern States had used different track gauges but all went back to standard gauge in 1886. The building of railways was immense and the west coast was reached in 1869 after years of hard work and often loss of life.

As factories grew they needed more workers and people moved from the country to the centres of manufacture. Cities like New York and Chicago grew enormously as centres of finance and white collar employment. The Midwest states became the main manufacturers of cars and trucks. Food was often canned and could be stored for longer. People wanted all the 'mod cons' so manufacturers set up wherever there was enough population to hire. Farmers could now send their produce by rail and air to all parts of the USA so they usually prospered, although those who had moved to mid-western states could still be wiped out by natural catastrophes and adverse weather conditions.

Census year	1840	1880	1920
Lyon families	1,360	14,500	18,628
Individuals *	7,533	93,584	166,822
US population - Millions	17.019	50.189	106.021

We must remember that the number of individuals in a household may well be accurate but this number could include slaves and others not necessarily with the name Lyon. Statistics are not always accurate because there are so many sources. It is claimed that that there are now over 1 million members of the family in the USA alone.

Outstanding Lyons – Henry Lyon

The family tree is shown after the name.

John Bacon Lyon (Robert B., Moses, Moses, Benjamin, Benjamin, **Henry**) John was born April 15th 1829 at Canandaigua, N.Y. He married at Conneaut, Ohio, February 9th 1852, EMILY WRIGHT, born October 9th 1832. He settled in Chicago, where he was one of the founders of the Board of Trade. He was widely known in the commercial world, a man of great business sagacity and one whose name stood for the highest ideals of integrity and fair dealing. John died at Chicago, Illinois. December 20th 1904.

Clarissa Lyon (Wade) (Robert B., Moses, Moses, Benjamin, Benjamin, **Henry**) Clarissa was born at Conneaut, OH, October 26th 1843. She married, February, 27th 1866, JAMES P. WADE (Benjamin F, James, Samuel, Captain Samuel, Major Nathaniel, Jonathan). MAJOR GENERAL U.S.A. JAMES F. WADE was commissioned 1st Lieutenant 6th Ohio Cavalry 1861. He had the rank of Captain in 1866, and rose by successive grades to the rank of Major General in 1903, commanding the Philippines. He was appointed Brigadier General of Volunteers in February 1865, and honourably mustered out April 15th 1865, at the breaking out of the Cuban war, he was made Major General of Volunteers and rendered valuable service in directing the evacuation of the Spanish troops from Cuba. To his son, Lieutenant John P. Wade, a member of his staff was granted the privilege of raising the stars and stripes over Moro Castle.

Hanford Lyon (Nehemiah Webb Stephen (?), Ebenezer (?), Richard, **Richard**)
Hanford was born in Easton, Conn., Rock House District, July 27th 1795. Until the age of 14 years, he lived on his father's farm. He was then apprenticed in Danbury to Elijah Sanford, and six years later established a saddlery business in Bridgeport. He became a member of the firm of Fairchild, Lyon & Co. in the same line of business, and later was principal in the firm, Lyon, Wright & Co. He was one of the most prominent citizens in Bridgeport, occupying many positions of responsibility and honour. He was a director in the Connecticut Bank, director and President of the old Bridgeport Bank, director in the Pequonnock Bank, first President of the City Savings Bank and director and President of the City Light Company. He was a member of the first Congregational Church in Bridgeport, in politics a Whig, and later an ardent Republican and an active supporter of the Union Cause in the Civil War. Hanford died December 21st 1879.

Walter Lyon (Walter, Jacob, Daniel, Daniel, Richard, **Richard**)
Walter was born at Herrick, PA., July 9th 1812. He was married April 5th 1838, by Reverend Adam Miller, a Presbyterian minister of Hartford, Susquehanna Co., PA, to MARIA ANTOINETTE GIDDINGS, of Herrick, PA., who was born February 28th 1819. She was daughter of Captain James and Lucy (Deming) Giddings, and grand-daughter of Captain Jabez Deming, who served in the Connecticut Militia during the Revolution as a Captain.
Walter Lyon was one of nature's noblemen. 'His word was as good as his bond'. He was quartermaster, 8th Division Pennsylvania Volunteer Battalion, Third Brigade of the Washington Guards, Adjutant General's Office, Harrisburg, PA. He was School Commissioner for a number of years. He died suddenly of cerebral-spinal meningitis. It was found after his death that he did not owe a person a dollar. Walter died at Herrick, PA. May 8th 1872.

William H. Lyon (Wakeman, Thomas, John, John, Samuel, **Richard**)
William was born at Lima, NY, August 19th 1814 and he was reputed to have visited every state and territory in the Union. He was married at Saginaw, Michigan in the old log Fort, to ESTHER W. RIGGS, daughter of Jeremiah and Grace (Bishop) Riggs. She was born in West Avon, New York. Jeremiah Riggs came to Michigan in 1828, and was appointed Superintendent of Indian affairs by General Lewis Cass, then Governor of the Territory of Michigan. Esther died In Flint, Mich., January 16th 1855. William died at Griflin, GA., February 6th 1891.

Theodatus Timothy Lyon (Timothy, Thomas John, John, Samuel, **Richard**)
Theodatus was born in Lima, NY, January 23rd 1813. He came with his parents while yet a schoolboy to Plymouth, Michigan. After teaching School, and helping to construct and manage a railroad he became interested in experimental horticulture, and this became his life work.

"His first experiments were made at Monroe, Michigan, but later he located in the fruit belt of Western Michigan, and there, on a ten acre tract of handy land, he carried on for more than a quarter of a century his studies in pomology, becoming one of the highest authorities in America in this specialty.

In 1892 the state of Michigan rented and made a sub-station of Mr Lyon's plot, and the citizens of South Haven bought and donated to the state five acres adjoining it. Mr Lyon was able thus to pursue his studies to better advantage, the State providing for the publication of his valuable annual reports. He had under observation more than 1500 varieties of fruits, and his reports as to the vigour, productiveness, hardiness, etc. of each, are invaluable to the fruit grower.

Mr Lyon was employed also by the United States Department of Agriculture to make a complete list of the names and synonyms of every variety of fruit cultivated in America - a work for which his wide practical knowledge of the subject pre-eminently fitted him".

He married, December 6th 1838, MARILLA GREGORY, born April 9th 1819, daughter of William Sherwood and Lydia Perrin Gregory. They had no children. Theodatus died on February 6th 1900 in South Haven, Michigan.

James Walters Lyon (Walter, Walter, Jacob, Daniel, Daniel, Richard, Richard)
James was born at Herrick, Susquehanna Co., PA, April 24th 1848. As a young man he entered the employ of a large publishing house, becoming a member of the firm at the age of twenty-four. In 1872 he opened a branch at Guelph in Canada, and that place became his home. In 1873 he sold out his interests in the United States, and secured full control of the business in Canada, which he pushed with characteristic energy and with most gratifying success. He soon became the largest individual publisher in Canada.

In 1884, according to official reports, forty per cent, of the total manufactured goods exported from Toronto, where his publishing plant was located, were his publications. He established branches of his business in Australia, South Africa and South America and in the East and the West Indies, and Port Arthur, Fort William and Manitoba. The large fortune he has acquired was the legitimate reward of untiring energy, directed by rare business sagacity, with no suggestion of the taint of unfair dealing or sharp practices.

"James Lyon has now practically retired from active business, and aside from looking after his real estate investments, devotes his time largely to municipal and other public matters. He is President of the Guelph Radial Railway Company, Director of the Guelph Junction Railway, Vice-President of the Board of Trade, Director of the Home Life Insurance Company of Toronto, etc. He is also an Alderman of the City of Guelph". *This was written in 1905 in the Lyon Memorial books.*

Colonel Leander Delos Lyon (Lyman J., Miles Samuel, Thomas, John, John, Samuel P, Richard)]

Leander was born at Hillsdale, Mich., November 9th 1847. At an early age he moved with his parents to Hudson, Mich. As a youth, he assisted in the commissary department of the regiment to which his father belonged during the latter part of the civil war. In August 1866 he was married to Miss ANNIE R. BAKER, at Detroit, Michigan. Shortly after he removed to Buffalo where he was employed on the 'Express,' one of his associates on the staff of that paper was the now famous **Mark Twain**. He remained in Buffalo seven years and afterwards engaged in newspaper work successively in Chicago (1873), Circleville, OH. (1875) and Watertown, SD. (1882), making his permanent home in the last named place.

Mary Mason Lyon February 28, 1797 – March 5, 1849 (Aaron, Aaron, Aaron, Seth, Thomas, Thomas, William III)

Mary was an American pioneer in women's education. She established the Wheaton Female Seminary in Norton, Massachusetts, (now Wheaton College) in 1834. She then established Mount Holyoke Female Seminary (now Mount Holyoke College) in South Hadley, Massachusetts in 1837 and served as its first president (or 'principal') for 12 years. Lyon's vision fused intellectual challenge and moral purpose. She valued socioeconomic diversity and endeavoured to make the seminary affordable for students of modest means.
http://en.wikipedia.org/wiki/Mary_Lyon#Religion

There are undoubtedly more names and stories of successful members of the Lyon family. If readers would contact me via Email I will gladly consider them for the future. The stories can be recent, as long those who are involved with living people will have their approval. The website www.thelyonfamily.org.uk can post these stories.

THE AMERICAN LYON FAMILY SUMMARY

The families began with William III in 1635 and Thomas, Henry and Richard in 1649. They all had a large numbers of descendants. They were not the only members of the Lyon family to emigrate from Scotland and England over the centuries but the number who joined them later may never be known.

The Lyon family in Britain were mostly land owners and farmers. When they arrived in America many continued their occupation on the land. There are records that a few were religious leaders, some carried on other businesses such as builders and builder's merchants. Some went to universities and became lawyers and administrators of local cities and towns. Many were semi-skilled labourers and many ran small businesses and inns. We have few records available from 1900 onwards because the sites like Ancestry.com often hide 'living people' from their lists.

The Lyon Memorial books state;

"There had been great changes in Great Britain since the three **Lyon** brothers left for the New World. Cromwell had ruled over the United Kingdom for nine years. He had broken the shackles of feudalism, and the emancipation of all humanity had begun its slow progression toward liberty of conscience and liberty of speech. Charles II had flittered away his reign through tyranny and profligacy. James II had ended in banishment and death and would be last of the Stuart dynasty.

William of Orange, invited to England by a Parliament displeased to have a Catholic King, invaded in 1688. King James fled the country on 23rd December and, in February 1689, the English Parliament declaring that, by fleeing, James II had abdicated. Parliament then offered the throne jointly to William and Mary, the Protestant daughter of James to whom William owed his claim to the throne.

Scotland was a divided country politically, culturally, and religiously. The Stuarts had ruled Scotland since the time of Robert II in late 14th century, and had also sat on the English throne since 1603. The Scottish Gaelic-speaking, mostly Catholic and Episcopalian Highlanders tended to stay loyal to the Stuart King James VII, while the English-speaking, mostly Presbyterian Lowlanders - who were the majority and held most of the political power in Scotland - tended to support William of Orange. The losses at the battle of Killikrankie had shaken all Scotland. In this battle the Scots were badly defeated.

(http://en.wikipedia.org/wiki/Battle_of_Killiecrankie). These times had left their imprint on progress since the day King Charles 1st was beheaded."

Killikrankie was a battle in 1689 between the forces supporting King James and those supporting the new king William of Orange. Even though the supporters of King James won they were weakened and scattered a month later at the battle of Dunkeld.

Wikipedia says. "the Battle of Killiecrankie was fought between Highland Scottish clans supporting King James VII of Scotland (also known as James II of England) and troops supporting King William of Orange on 27 July 1689, during the first Jacobite uprising. Although it was a stunning victory for the Jacobites, it had little overall effect on the outcome of the war and left their leader dead. Their forces were scattered at the Battle of Dunkeld the next month"

Lyon Memorial continues;

"The colonies had grown in numbers and riches and promise. There was easier breathing when William and Mary reigned, and since Anne was Queen, but there were still enemies of their rulers. These colonial yeomen, who had been Roundhead soldiers, were English subjects who became careful with their tongues. But in private they spoke about the battles of Naseby and Dunbar and what they knew of the secreting of Goffe and Whalley and their involvement in opposition to King Charles. It was not wise to talk about the Great Civil War and of the London and the trial and execution of Charles Stuart. But in the sanctuary of their home, Thomas and Richard and Henry Lyon told their children of how they had been soldiers in Cromwell's army; of how they were on guard before the scaffold at Whitehall and witnessed the regicide and of their flight to America.

The Connecticut, the New York and the New Jersey branches have preserved the knowledge of their English and Scottish origin. General Nathaniel Lyon and Major Sidney S. Lyon, men of broad intelligence and flawless integrity, accepted these traditions. Their ancestors were Lyons of Glen Lyon, and the presence of Thomas, Richard and Henry Lyon at the execution of Charles I was made authentic by oral transmission from father to son in the three direct lines, widely divided by time and place. General Nathaniel was the first Unionist General to die in the Civil War in the 1860's."

Part 3

CHAPTER 11
THE WARRINGTON LYON FAMILY

·•❀•·

The largest number of Lyon family members in the United Kingdom lived in Lancashire according to information available on ancestry.com website. The most famous of these families is the family of **Thomas Lyon** who moved to Warrington in Lancashire in the 1600s with his father **George**.

Thomas Lyon of Appleton Hall, Warrington, Lancashire

George Lyon and his son, Thomas, left Scotland in the early 1600s and moved to Warrington in Lancashire. Many members of the family moved to this area at about this time from Scotland and northern England. We can guess that the Civil Wars may have brought them to the area, many settled near Warrington and in the Liverpool area. They obviously had money and were most likely landowners in Scotland but George, born in 1586, being the youngest of four brothers was maybe looking for other new opportunities to prosper.

George produced another son Baron **John Lyon** of Ogil, Angus. He stayed in Scotland and had a large family. George had a wife CATHERINE WISHART (1592–1635). Her death may have been a reason to move to Warrington. Four generations earlier George was related to **John Lyon the 3rd Earl of Glamis** and before that to King Robert the Bruce of Scotland.

The family followed the pattern of life first developed in their home country. They prized the possession of land and farmed successfully. They eventually built a large mansion, Appleton Hall, in Warrington. They owned hundreds of acres of land in the area at Hulme, Winwick, Church Street Warrington, Burtonwood, Bold Colliery, Collins Green, parts of the Manchester Ship Canal and businesses too many to mention here. They served their community as Justices of the Peace and as financial founders and supporters of a bank and many businesses in the town. They started schools in the area and were trustees of several large charities. A later member of the family started a bank with other local businessmen. Some became ministers in the Church of England and were educated at leading public schools including Eton, Wellington and Harrow. There seems little evidence that they were involved in party politics although they may, however, have belonged to Masonic Lodges in the family tradition.

The family were also great contributors to their local area and served as Justices of the Peace and represented the monarch as Lieutenants.

The male members of the family often married wealthy wives which did not harm their chances of success.

The family Lyon also served their country well; dozens lost their lives or were injured in various wars, usually in the British army serving all over the world. Some moved to foreign lands where they grew various crops and created large farms in Africa, India and elsewhere. *(Furneux, 1996, see Bibliography)*. Appleton Hall was actually in Cheshire, and north of the River Mersey was Lancashire before the boundary changes. Appleton Hall was a large building in a beautiful setting looking up to the rolling hills south and west of the house. There were dozens of rooms and it was the most palatial home for many miles. There is nothing left of it now because it was demolished in the 1960's to make way for building large estates of new houses and bungalows. Lyons Lane which crosses the A49 provides land for some very large houses in wooded settings.

While they lived in Warrington the family always maintained houses in Mayfair and the more expensive parts of London. They mixed with Royalty and would have had close relations with the Bowes-Lyon branch of the family - the Earls of Strathmore.

Family genealogy

For those wishing to see the full list of families go the Lyon and Parr families in Appendix G.

Thomas Lyon, left Scotland and settled in Warrington, Lancashire, where he purchased property. He was the youngest son of **George Lyon** of Balmuchtie, Angus, youngest of Cossins. History does not tell us why Thomas left Scotland but we know that many members of the family moved to Lancashire where other Lyon family members settled at that time. He served in the Royal Scots Greys, and settled eventually at Warrington in Lancashire.

1st Generation

Thomas Lyon was born in 1626 in Scotland. He married DOROTHY who was born in 1630. Thomas Lyon and Dorothy 1630 had **Thomas Lyon** who was born in 1656. Thomas Senior died in 1694 in Warrington, Lancashire.

2nd Generation

Thomas Lyon (Thomas) was born in 1656. He married FRANS JONES. She was born about 1660. Thomas Lyon and Frans had **John Lyon** who was born in 1688. His father Thomas died in 1694 in Appleton, Warrington.

3rd Generation

John Lyon (Thomas, Thomas) was born in 1688 in Warrington. He bought land in Warrington and purchased estates in Appleton. He married MARGARET EDWARDSON. She was born about 1692 in Prescot, Lancashire. John Lyon and Margaret had the following children: Thomas, Matthew (1716) and Ellen.
John and his son Matthew were bequeathed land at Hulme, Winwick, Church Street and Bank Key (Quay) in Warrington by a Matthew Page. John bought land in Appleton and was succeeded by his eldest son Thomas. John died in July 1752 in Appleton, Warrington, Cheshire.

4th Generation

Thomas Lyon (John, Thomas, Thomas) we do not know his date of birth but it must have been before 1716 when his younger brother was born. Thomas was described as a merchant in July 1760 and was leasing land in nearby Wigan. He died in 1776 without issue. His property passed on to his brother Matthew.

Matthew Lyon (John, Thomas, Thomas) was born in 1716 in Warrington, Lancashire. He was involved in the banking business in the mid 1750's. He also bought Shaw Green, Appleton in 1755. He married ELLEN FAIRCLOUGH. She was born about 1720 in Lancashire. Matthew Lyon and Ellen had the following children: Thomas B (1756), James (1758), Ellen B (1762), Ellen died about 1770. Matthew died in 1782 in Warrington, Lancashire.

5th Generation

Thomas B Lyon (Matthew, John, Thomas, Thomas) born 1756 or 1759 was in partnership with Joseph Parr and Walter Kerfoot in setting up the Bank of Parr, Lyon and Kerfoot, see below. He never married and invited his nephew Thomas to live with him in Warrington as his sole heir. In 1786. Thomas Lyon also went into partnership with William Orrett and Thomas Greenall and, in the following year, established the brewery which first brewed at the Saracen's Head on Wilderspool Causeway. Thomas B died in 1818 in Warrington.

James Lyon, Reverend (Matthew, John, Thomas, Thomas) was born in 1758 in Lancashire. He was the Rector of Prestwich, Lancashire. He married MARY RADCLIFFE. She was born in 1760 in Manchester, Lancashire. James Lyon and Mary had the following children: James Radcliffe (1785), Thomas B (1786), Sarah Ann (1793), John (1797), Matthew Nathan (1800), George (1801).
James died on 13th August 1836 in Prestwich, Lancashire. Mary died in January 1841 in Lancashire.

Ellen Lyon (Matthew, John, Thomas, Thomas) was born in 1762. She married JOSEPH PARR. He was born on 29th December 1755 in Warrington, Lancashire. Joseph Parr and Ellen B Lyon had the following children: Joseph Parr, Thomas (1792), Isabella. Joseph died on 18th November 1820.

Changes of Ownership – the Parrs and the Lyons.

It is about 1780, in fact, when there appear to have been great changes in the sugar industry in Warrington, and indeed, there is substantial proof of changes in ownership in the Horsemarket Street businesses. In 1781 we find it recorded that sugar refiners in Warrington were Joseph Parr and Co. and Thomas Lyon and Co., good old Warrington names that we still have associated with the town or district in the persons of Mr. Roger C. Parr, of Grappenhall Heyes, and Lt.-Colonel C. Lyon, formerly of Appleton Hall. It is fairly certain that our 'Sugar Houses' were those where the Parrs carried on their business. They then lived at Appleton 'in a cottage with a vinery'. To see more about 'Sugar Houses' or refineries see the web address below.
(http://www.themeister.co.uk/hindley/warrington_parr_&_firth.htm)

"In 1782 the late Mr. William Turner, of the firm of Turner and Kerfoot, solicitors in the town, in conversation with the late Thomas Lyon, spoke of the want of a bank in Warrington, and said to him; 'You have the money, so has Walter Kerfoot, my partner. Now Joseph Parr (who was a sugar boiler in the town) has a trade which is leaving him, and doing him no good. He has business habits, and may manage the bank'. It was in consequence of this conversation that the present bank was established under the firm first by Parr, Lyon and Kerfoot, which has now been in operation for 76 years with increasing prosperity. Thus wrote Mrs. Lyon, and Colonel Lyon records that the Thomas Lyon referred to was his grandfather's uncle, and owner of Appleton, and that Joseph Parr lived at Fir Grove, West Derby, and was Thomas Lyon's brother-in-law, having married his sister Ellen. And so, if the sugar trade has gone from Warrington - even if only to Earlstown - Warrington may congratulate itself on another historical business, which has left its mark on the country as the forerunner of a great banking system."

The Parrs were sugar boilers who used their wealth to make an early entry into banking. Parr's bank was founded on 25th September 1788 on the current site used by the National Westminster business centre in Warrington. It was the first bank in the town. Joseph Parr, Walter Kerfoot and **Thomas Lyon** were involved in the business. Branches were opened in St. Helens in 1839 and in Runcorn in 1853. In 1865 the name was changed to Parrs Banking Company Ltd. when it was converted to a joint stock company by J. Charlton Parr, Thomas Parr, James Fenton Greenall and Richard Assheton Cross. It then acquired branches in Northwich, Macclesfield, Wigan, Leek, Chester and Liverpool. Warrington was the headquarters from 1788 to 1891. By 1891 there were 40 branches in the North West of England and Wrexham. The first office in London was opened that year in Lombard Street when Fuller, Banbury and Nix, founded in 1737, was acquired. In 1892 Parr's merged with the Alliance Bank and in 1896 Consolidated was also absorbed leading to further expansion in the Midlands, South West and Cumberland.

By 1918 Parrs had 300 branches. That year the bank merged with the London County and Westminster and in 1923 the name was changed to the Westminster Bank. This combined with the District Bank and the National Provincial in 1969 to form the National Westminster. Cecil Francis Parr of Grappenhall Heyes, who died in 1928, was the last member of the family to serve on the board.

(http://www.thornber.net/cheshire/htmlfiles/grappen.html)

6th Generation

James Radcliffe Lyon (Rev), (James Reverend, Matthew, John, Thomas,
Thomas). He was the Rector of Pulford, Cheshire born 11th July 1785. He married 18th May 1814, FRANCES 'FANNY' daughter of George CLAYTON. She was born about 1786 in Lostock Hall, Preston, Lancashire. James Radcliffe and 'Fanny' had the following children: John Radcliffe (1818), Sophia (1820), Samuel Edmund (18220, William Barrie (1823), Edward (1826).

Frances died on 11th January 1869 in Pulford, Cheshire. James died on 6th December 1869 in Pulford, Cheshire.

Thomas B. Lyon (James Reverend, Matthew, John, Thomas, Thomas) was born on 2nd December 1786 in Prestwich, Cheshire.

Thomas received a Commission in the Volunteer Corps and he qualified as a magistrate in 1819. He was elected a member of the first Town Council and was the Chairman of the Sanitary Committee, the Trustee Savings Bank and the Water Works.

He married ELIZABETH CLAYTON in June 1820. She was born on 15th October 1792 in Lostock Hall, Preston, Lancashire. Thomas Lyon Esq, of Appleton Hall, was a magistrate and Deputy Lieutenant for the counties of Chester and Lancaster.

He became the squire of his estate when he built Appleton Hall. He said that 'it looked well from the hill, surrounded with undulation woods, pleasure grounds and rich pasture land'. Appleton Hall was actually in Cheshire whereas Warrington was at that time in Lancashire. He gave large amounts of money to the restoration of the Warrington Parish Church and spent a great deal on various facilities for the people of the town.

> "Lostock's Hall was destroyed by a fire. Some of the main brick work not affected by the fire was reused in 1764, to form the structure of a new building on the original site, as part of a regeneration project by William Clayton Esq. William's son, George Clayton inherited the hall following the death of William Clayton. George went on to live in the hall for many years with his wife Dolly, until he died in 1829, at the age of 86. George's second son, William became the new inheritor of the property, until he relocated to the South of England in the late 1840s."
> *(http://en.wikipedia.org/wiki/Lostock_Hall)*

Thomas B Lyon and Elizabeth Clayton had the following children: Agnes (1821), Thomas (1820) he later left for Sweden and never returned, Thomas Henry (1825), Eliza M (1825), Georgiana (1828), Francis (1834).

> "Thomas died on 17th August 1859 in Warrington, Lancashire. On his death he left an estate of over £100,000. He was buried at Stretton in the family vault alongside the two children who had died before him. In his obituary he was praised for the interest he took in his tenants and their welfare, and was described as unpretentious and independent of the trammels of luxury and fashion. He was succeeded by his second son."
> *(See Furneaux page 10)*

Matthew Nathan Lyon (James Reverend, Matthew, John, Thomas, Thomas) was born on 12th July 1800 in Prestwich, Lancashire. He married FRANCES LYON. She was born about 1805 in Stafford, Staffordshire. Matthew Nathan Lyon and Frances Lyon had the following children: Mary (1835), Frances D (1836), Eliza (1838), Catherine (1839), Charlotte (1840), James L (1842), George (1845), Nathan (1847)

Matthew died in 1883 in Broughton, Manchester

7th Generation

Georgiana Lyon (Thomas B, James Reverend, Matthew, John, Thomas, Thomas) was born on 22nd January 1828 in Great Budworth, Cheshire. She married RICHARD ASSHETON CROSS 1st Viscount Cross, son of William Cross and Ellen Chaffers on 4th May 1852 in Stretton, Cheshire. He was born on 30th May 1823 in Preston, Lancashire. Richard Assheton Cross 1st Viscount Cross and Georgiana Lyon had 5 sons and 3 daughters. Georgiana died on 20th January 1907 in Ulverston, Lancashire. Richard died on 8th January 1914 in Ulverston, Lancashire.

For full details of these families from here onwards - see APPENDIX G.

Francis (Frank) Lyon, Colonel (Thomas B, James Reverend, Matthew, John, Thomas, Thomas) was born on 11th January 1834 in Stretton. Cheshire. He married FLORA MARY ANNESLEY on 23rd June 1863 in London. She was born about 1841 in Scotland. Francis Lyon Colonel and Flora Mary Annesley had 4 sons and 2 daughters.

> "Frank entered one of the Artillery Regiments in 1852 and served in Canada, Central America and the West Indies. In 1880 he was made Superintendent at the Royal Laboratory at Woolwich which led to his involvement with the explosives range at Shoeburyness on the Essex coast. During the 1860s there had been much talk about the new 'ironclads' - the latest ships made of iron.
>
> At Woolwich Frank, now a Lieutenant Colonel invented some especially sensitive fuses for nine inch shells. In 1885 a party consisting of Lt. Col. Lyon and members of the Ordnance Committee of the War Office, went to Shoeburyness to demonstrate the fuses. The results were disastrous. The party was gathered round a live shell when it exploded. Gunner Allen was killed instantly, those standing near were thrown off their feet and many were seriously injured. Extra surgeons were sent for from London. Frank had both his legs blown off and died the following day. Altogether six people died. Frank's body was taken to the railway station on a gun carriage followed by more than 200 non-commissioned officers while the Garrison Band played the Dead March. He was taken

to London by special train en route for Warrington. His grave is in Stretton churchyard. Frank left four sons and two daughters. His eldest son, Charles, inherited the Appleton Estates when Thomas Henry died in 1914."

Francis died on 26th February 1885 in Shoeburyness, Essex. Flora died on 4th August 1924 in Amersham, Buckinghamshire.

Thomas Henry Lyon (Thomas B, James Reverend, Matthew, John, Thomas, Thomas) was born on 28th February 1825 in Appleton Hall, Cheshire.
After leaving Eton, Thomas Henry joined the Navy. He served in the first China War (1839-41) while still in his mid-teens and was wounded in the neck. In 1846 he was made a Lieutenant. He left the Navy in 1853. He then entered the 1st Royal Cheshire Militia as part of the garrison at Chester Castle during the Crimean War (1854-6). During the three years before his father died he began to appear in public life in Warrington, often at the same events as his father.
He was already a vice president of the Daresbury and Frodsham Agriculture Show. He was also a magistrate (taking the oath in 1855) and a patron of the Warrington Parish Church Restoration Fund Bazaar. *(Furneaux page 11)*
On 24th July 1860, Thomas Henry married Vanda, third daughter of Colonel John Wilson-Patten MP (later 1st Lord Winmarleigh) at St. George's Church, Hanover Square, London. Her father was Equerry to Queen Victoria and they lived in London with at least 25 servants listed on a census at that time. Vanda Patten Wilson was born in 1834.

"On 24th July 1860, Thomas Henry married Vanda, third daughter of Colonel John Wilson-Patten M.P. (later 1st Lord Winmarleigh) at St. George's Church, Hanover Square, London. The Rt. Rev. Bishop of Sodor and Man officiated, assisted by Reverend Richard Greenall. The recherché (exotic) breakfast was held in the Wilson-Patten's family mansion at 24, Hill Street, Berkeley Square, London. The bride was greatly admired and loved, especially by her father. The happy couple left for their honeymoon at Leatherhood (Leatherhead) in a travelling chariot drawn by four, high-spirited greys. Sadly, Vanda died in childbirth at Appleton Hall just a year after their wedding. When the state of her condition was apparent they telegraphed her father in London but he arrived an hour too late 'to have even a parting word from the daughter he loved so dearly'. She was only 27 years old and much lamented".

Thomas Henry then married EDITH GRACE BRANKER at St. George's Church, Hanover Square, London, on 11th July 1872. She was born on 8th May 1849 in Billinge, Lancashire. They had a son and a daughter, Dorothy, born in 1876.

Thomas Henry died on 13th February 1914 in Appleton Hall, Cheshire. Edith died on 12th March 1929 in St George Hanover Square, London.

Samuel Edmund Lyon (James Radcliffe Rev, James Reverend, Matthew, John, Thomas, Thomas) was born on 18th February 1822 in Pulford, Cheshire. He married CAROLINE LYON. She was born about 1831 in Preston, Lancashire. They had a son and a daughter. Samuel died in October 1899 in Stratton, Dorset.

Edward Lyon (James Radcliffe Rev, James Reverend, Matthew, John, Thomas, Thomas) was born on 21st November 1826 in Pulford, Cheshire. He married ALICE H J LYON. She was born about 1828 in India. He later married EDITH LYON. She was born about 1832 in St Pancras, London. Edward and Edith had 2 sons and 1 daughter. Edward and Alice had 2 daughters. Edward died in December 1917 in Chertsey, Surrey.

George Lyon (Matthew Nathan, James Reverend, Matthew, John, Thomas, Thomas) was born about 1845 in Broughton, Manchester, Lancashire. He married LAURA HASLOPE. She was born about 1842 in Hateley Heath, West Bromwich, Staffordshire. George Lyon and Laura Haslope had 3 daughters.

8th Generation

Dorothy Lyon (Thomas Henry, Thomas B., James Reverend, Matthew, John, Thomas, Thomas) was born on 4th January 1876 in Mayfair, London. She married RICHARD MAXIMILIAN (2nd BARON ACTON OF ALDENHAM) LYON-DALBERG-ACTON, son of John Emerich Edward Dalberg-Acton Baron and Marie Anna Ludomilla Euphrosina von Arco auf Valley, Countess, on 7th June 1904 in Kensington, London. Richard Maximilian (2nd Baron Acton of Aldenham) Lyon-Dalberg-Acton and Dorothy Lyon had 2 sons and 7 daughters. See Appendix G for more details of the family.

In her booklet Clare Furneaux states; "On 7th June 1904, Dorothy married Richard Maximilian Dalberg-Acton MYO, second Lord Acton and ninth baronet, at Brompton Oratory. Her dress was Louis XVI style with a train borne by her small cousin, Margaret Lyon. The reception was at the Lyon's London address - Rutland Lodge, Rutland Gardens, London. The lengthy guest list included the Lord Chancellor and telegrams were received from foreign royalties.

The dazzling array of wedding presents included diamond jewellery, ornaments, books, umbrellas, a pair of silver asparagus tongs and a silver pig pin cushion.

Appleton (Warrington) rejoiced enthusiastically when the bridal couple visited the Hall about two weeks later. It was the first visit for Lord Acton. There were swing boats, a shooting saloon, a dolly stall, dancing on the lawn, and tea was supplied by the Winmarleigh Cafe Company in a large marquee.

An arch was erected over the lodge entrance. The trees along the drive were decorated with bunting and the gardens were looking their best, thanks to the skill of James Parkinson, head gardener.

On 7th July the couple left for Berne, where Lord Acton was a secretary in His Majesty's Diplomatic Service. Lord Acton was born in Bavaria in 1870. His father was Professor of Modern History at Cambridge. It was thought that Lord Acton met Dorothy in Cannes where the Lyon family sometimes spent the winter. Seven years after his marriage, he became a British subject and in 1919 he added Lyon to his name."

Dorothy died on 17th March 1923 in Bridgnorth, Shropshire. Richard Maximilian died on 16th June 1924 in St George Hanover Square, London.

9th Generation

John Emerich Henry (3rd Baron Acton of Aldenham) Lyon-Dalberg-Acton (Dorothy Lyon, Thomas Henry Lyon, Thomas B. Lyon, James Lyon Reverend, Matthew Lyon, John Lyon, Thomas Lyon, Thomas Lyon) was born on 15th December 1907. He married DAPHNE STRUTT on 25th November 1931. She was born on 5th November 1911 in Kensington, London.

John Emerich Henry Lyon-Dalberg-Acton and Daphne Strutt had a daughter, Charlotte. John died on 23rd January 1989. Daphne died in February 2003 in Warwickshire, England.

10th Generation onwards

The rest of the family details are available for those who are interested and will be posted on the *www.thelyonfamily.org.uk/help/genealogy* - website as a booklet by Clare Furneaux, a local historian in Warrington. There are 20 pages of research in this booklet which is out of print. I am grateful to her for the extensive quotes that I have used.

Other members of the Lyon Family in England who served in the armed forces

Thomas Henry Lyon, born 28th October 1825, of Appleton Hall, Cheshire, Deputy Lieutenant, Justice of the Peace. High Sheriff 1867, late Lieutenant Royal Navy, sometime Captain of Militia. Thomas married 24th July 1860 to Vanda who died 17th July 1861. He then married the 3rd daughter of John Wilson-Patten, later 1st Baron Winmarleigh. He later married, Edith Grace Branker 11th June 1872 who died 12th March 1929, the only daughter of William Hill Branker, of Bispham Hall, Lancashire.

Francis Lyon born 11th January 1834, Colonel Royal Horse Artillery). Francis married 23rd June 1863 to Flora who died 4th August 1924, the youngest daughter of Hon. Arthur Annesley and sister of 11th Viscount Valentia. Francis died 26th February 1885.

Charles Lyon born 7th April 1865, Lieutenant Colonel, of Appleton Hall. Cheshire, Justice of the Peace and Deputy Lieutenant for the County, High Sheriff 1924, Lieutenant Colonel (Retired) late RFA, educated at Wellington and RMA. Survived his uncle 1914. Charles married 17th July 1894 Rachel Mary Fearne who died 30th June 1926, the only child of the late Sir Arthur Havelock GCSL, GCMC, GCIE, Governor of Ceylon.

Francis Lyon born 10th July 1867, Companion of the Order of the Bath (1921), CMG.(1916), CVO.(1922), Distinguished Service Order (1900), Hon. Brigadier General, formerly Colonel RFA, Military Attaché, Brussels 1918, had Belgian Croix de Guerre. Francis married 18th August 1910 Winifred Janet who died 13th November 1961, elder daughter of Joseph Cooksey Berwick of 27 Prince's Gate, SW. Francis died 21st February 1953.

Arthur Lyon born 25th January 1869, Late Major South African Constabulary, Captain, Border Regiment, educated Wellington, married 6th February 1913 Gladys Anita who was born in 1870. Arthur died in March 1920 in Runcorn, Cheshire. Gladys died in 1954.

Henry Lyon born 10th August 1872, Formerly Assist Dist. Commissioner, Niger Coast Protectorate, served in South African War with 3rd South Lancs. Regiment and South African Infantry and in World War I educated at Wellington, married 17th January 1917 Laura daughter of Victor A Lagerwall, of Port Elizabeth, South Africa. Henry died 22nd November 1940.

Francis Lyon born 11th January 1834, Colonel. Francis married 23rd June 1863 Flora Mary, who died 4th August 1924, 2nd daughter of the Hon. A. Annesley and sister of Viscount Valentia. Francis died 26th February 1885 leaving issue

Francis Charles Lyon born 25th May 1895, Lieutenant, Grenadier Guards, educated at Eton, **killed in action** 13th April 1918.

Frank Lyon born 1st March 1921, served in World War II as Captain Royal Intelligence Corps., Trentham, Fresnaye, Cape Town, South Africa educated at Eton.

Ivan Lyon born 12th August 1915, Distinguished Service Order (1944), MEMBER OF THE BRITISH EMPIRE (1943), Lt Colonel in the Gordon Highlanders served in World War II, educated Harrow, and RMA, Woolwich. Ivan married 27th July 1939 Gabrielle Anna Georgina daughter of the late Claude Bouvier, Legion d'honneur, Croix de Guerre, Croix de la Liberation (posthumous). Ivan was **killed in action** on or shortly after 14th October 1944.

This family is not complete but demonstrates that one branch of a family can have a great impact on any area of a country where they choose to live. We notice how many members of this family served in the armed forces and many gave their lives in many wars in the last three centuries.

The more complete records are available in the Appendix G.

CHAPTER 12

THE LANCASHIRE LYON FAMILY

—•❀•—

Rank	County	No. of People	% of Region
1	Lancashire	1772	0.05
2	Middlesex	489	0.02
3	Lanarkshire	452	0.05
4	Yorkshire	426	0.01
5	Lincolnshire	313	0.7

We cannot discover why so many members of this branch of the family had moved from Scotland, Norfolk, Middlesex and Northamptonshire where they originated from 1066. Records were not always kept and preserved and apart from parish registers there is little evidence of family relationships. The family below is typical of some Lyon families and the fact that records seem to have been preserved is an indication of a relationship with the Scottish family line.

The Sylvia Dillon (Lyon) family of Lancashire

When I first mentioned Sylvia in this book, it was her family tree that inspired me to look more deeply into the Lyon family history. I traced the Lyon ancestry history back to 1066 and eventually the relationship with King Robert the Bruce and John Lyon born in in 1314 in Scotland. See the early chapters of the book in Part 1.

1st Generation

John Lyon 7th Earl of Glamis, son of John Lyon 6th Earl of Glamis and Lady Janet Douglas Baroness Glamis was born in 1521 in Glamis Castle, Angus. He married JANET KEITH BARONESS OF GLAMIS, daughter of Robert Lord Keith Master Marischal and Elizabeth Beatrice Keith Douglas, on 6th February 1542 in Glamis, Angus, Scotland. Janet was born in 1528 in St Fergus, Banffshire, Scotland. John and Janet Keith had several children;
1. John Lyon was born in 1544 in Middlesex.
2. William Lyon was born in 1555 in Middlesex.

John died on 13th October 1592 in Ryslippe, Middlesex.

2nd Generation

William Lyon, son of John Lyon 7th Earl of Glamis and Janet Keith Baroness of Glamis was born in 1555 in Little Stanmore, Middlesex, England. He married ISABELL WIGHTMAN on 17th June 1576 in London who was born in 1559 in Harrow on the Hill, Middlesex. Isabell Wightman and William Lyon had the following children:

1.   Isabelle Lyon was born in 1580 in Heston, Middlesex.
2.   William Lyon was born in 1580 in Heston, Middlesex.
3.   Richard Lyon was born in 1590 in Heston, Middlesex. He died on 17th October 1678 in Fairfield, Connecticut, America. His story is told in Chapter 7.

Isabelle died in 1593 in England. William died on 7th September 1624 in Little Stanmore, Middlesex.

3rd Generation

William Lyon, son of William Lyon and Isabell Wightman was born in 1580 in Heston, London. He married an UNKNOWN lady who was maybe born in 1580 in Middlesex. They had the following child:

1.   Thomas Lyon, son of William Lyon and unknown was born in 1600 in St Lawrence, Little Stanmore, Middlesex.

William later married **ANNE CARTER** of Harrow on the Hill, Middlesex who was born in 1594. They married on the 17th of July 1615 at Heston. William and Anne had the following children;

1.   Katherine Lyon who was born in 1616 in Heston, Middlesex. She died in 1720 in France.
2.   John Lyon born 1617, died 1617 at birth.
3.   John Lyon born 1619, died 1619 at birth.
4.   **William Lyon born 13th December 1620 in Heston, Middlesex. He died in Roxbury, Massachusetts, America on 16th May 1692. William was the first known Lyon who migrated to America in 1635 his full story is in** Chapter 6 of this book.

William died on 18th Feb 1634 in Heston, Middlesex. Anne also died in 1634.

4th Generation

Thomas Lyon, son of William Lyon and unknown person was born in 1600 in St. Lawrence, Little Stanmore, Middlesex. He married BARBARA TYLCOCKE on 3rd July 1634 in St Mary, Harrow, Middlesex, she was born about 1605. Barbara Tylcocke and Thomas Lyon had the following children:
1. John Lyon was born in 1659 in St Lawrence, Little Stanmore, Middlesex.
2. Mary Downer was born in 1660 in Little Stanmore, Middlesex.

Thomas died in 1678 in St Lawrence, Little Stanmore, Middlesex.

5th Generation

John Lyon was born in 1659 in St Lawrence, Little Stanmore, Middlesex. He married ELIZABETH COLLETT, daughter of Richard Collett and Elizabeth Hunt on 21st September 1691 in St James Duke's Place, London, she was born in 1663 in England. Elizabeth Collett and John Lyon had the following children:
1. Thomas Lyon was born in 1684 in Newcastle upon Tyne, Northumberland, England.
2. Catherine Lyon was born in 1686 in Newcastle upon Tyne, Northumberland.
3. Patrick Lyon was born in 1692. He died in September 1709.
4. Philip Lyon was born on 29th October 1693. He died on 18th March 1712 in London.
5. John Lyon was born on 27th April 1696. He died on 13th November 1715.
6. Charles Lyon was born on 12th July 1699. He died on 11th May 1728.
7. Hendrie Lyon was born on 1 July 1700.
8. James Lyon was born on 24th December 1702. He died on 4th January 1735 in Edinburgh, Midlothian, Scotland.
9. Thomas Lyon was born in 1704 in England. He died on 18th January 1753.
10. Mary Lyon was born in 1712. She died on 26th May 1780.

John Lyon died 10th May 1712 and Elizabeth died 24th April 1723.

6th Generation

Thomas Lyon, son of John Lyon and Elizabeth Collett was born in 1684 in Newcastle upon Tyne, Northumberland. He married ALICE LOWE who was born on 16th March 1678 in Huyton by Roby, Lancashire. Alice Lowe was the daughter of John Lowe and Ellin Smith. Alice Lowe and Thomas Lyon had the following children:

1. William Lyon was born in 1699 in Liverpool, Lancashire.
2. Thomas Lyon, was born in 1700 in West Derby, Lancashire.
3. James Lyon was born in 1703 in West Derby, Lancashire.
4. Ellen Lyon was born in 1704 in West Derby, Lancashire.

Thomas died about 1723 in Rainford, Lancashire. Alice died on 9th January 1766 in Whalley, Lancashire.

7th Generation

William Lyon was born in 1699 in Liverpool, Lancashire. He married HANNAH JACKSON on 21st September 1729 in Rostherne, Cheshire. She was born in 1701. William Lyon and Hannah Jackson had the following children:

1. Thomas Lyon was born in 1730.
2. Hannah Lyon was born in 1732 in Rostherne, Cheshire. She died in 1758 in Alderley, Cheshire.
3. Sarah Lyon was born in 1736 in Prestbury, Cheshire. She died in 1825 in Alderley, Cheshire.
4. Frances Lyon was born in 1737. She died in 1818.
5. William Lyon was born in 1739 in Alderley, Cheshire. He died in Church Wetzel, West Virginia, United States.

Hannah died on 8th September 1765. William died on 12th October 1783.

James Lyon was born in 1703 in West Derby, Lancashire. He married MARGARY COOK JOHNSON on 25th September 1733 in West Lancashire. She was born in 1703 in West Lancashire. James Lyon and Margary Cook Johnson had the following children:

1. Thomas Lyon was born in 1731 in West Derby, Lancashire.
2. Daniel Lyon was born in 1733 in Prescot, Lancashire.

James died in 1755 in Eccles Parish, Lancashire

8th Generation

Thomas Lyon, son of James Lyon and Margary Cook Johnson was born in 1731 in West Derby, Lancashire. He married CHARLOTTE who was born in 1735 in West Derby, Lancashire. Charlotte and Thomas Lyon had the following children: Robert Lyon, was born about 1757 in West Derby, Lancashire.

1. Ann Lyon was born in 1759 in West Derby.
2. James Lyon was born in 1761 in West Derby.
3. Thomas Lyon was born on 17th May 1763 in West Derby.

We do not know the dates of death for Thomas and Charlotte.

Daniel Lyon, son of James Lyon and Margary Cook, was born in 1733 in Prescot, Lancashire. He married ANN JOHNSON on 31st December 1754 in St Peter & St Paul, Ormskirk, Lancs. She was born in 1733 in Lathom, Lancashire, Daniel Lyon and Ann Johnson had the following children:

1 Betty Lyon was born in 1755 in Ormskirk, Lancashire. She married James Mather in Bolton, Lancashire. He was born in 1753 in Bolton, Lancashire. Betty and James had two children;
  James Mather born in 1797 in Bolton. He died in 1841.
  Betty Mather born in 1788 in Bolton, Lancashire.
2 James Lyon was born on 22 January 1757 in Ormskirk, Lancashire.
3 Thomas Lyon was born in 1760 in Ormskirk.

Daniel died in 1791 in Rainford, Lancashire.

9th Generation

Robert Lyon, son of Thomas Lyon and Charlotte was born about 1757 in West Derby, Lancashire. He married JANE LANCELOT on 29th January 1784 in St. Nicholas Liverpool. Jane Lancelot and Robert Lyon had the following child:
1. John Lyon was born on 20th June 1786 in West Derby, Liverpool.

Dates of death or Robert and Jane are unknown.

James Lyon, the son of Daniel Lyon and Ann Johnson, was born on 22nd January 1757 in England, He married MARY MELINDA POLLY PRESKOT on 29th August 1776. She was born on 4th April 1759 in England. James Lyon and Mary Melinda Polly Preskot had the following children:

1. William Lyon was born on 4th September 1777 in Goffstown, Hillsborough, New Hampshire. He died in 1862.
2. James Lyon was born on 25th January 1780 in Tunbridge, Orange, Vermont. He died on 26th February 1801 in Strafford, Orange, Vermont.
3. Benjamin Lyon was born on 1st May 1781 in Deering, Hillsborough, New Hampshire. He died in 1860 in Union City, Union, Ohio.

4. John Lyon was born on 4th July 1784 in Tunbridge, Orange, Vermont. He died on 19th July 1866 in Strafford, Orange.1820 in Leavenworth, Crawford, Indiana.

5. Joel Lyon was born on 21st January 1789. He died on 2nd November 1855 in Leavenworth, Crawford, Indiana.

6. Isaac Lyon was born on 1st November 1791 in Turnbridge, Orange, Vermont. He died in 1870 in Nebraska.

7. Mary Polly Lyon was born on 9th May 1794 in Tunbridge, Orange, Vermont. She died on 26 Aug 1875 in Jefferson, Ashtabula, Ohio.

8. Timothy Lyon was born on 31st January 1797.

9. Malinda Lyon was born on 20th February 1800 in Tunbridge, Orange, Vermont. She died on 31st July 1838 in Leavenworth, Crawford, Indiana.

10. Ira Lyon was born on 12th August 1803 in Tunbridge, Orange, Vermont

Mary died in 1827 in Leavenworth, Crawford, Indiana. James died in 1841 in Schoolcraft, Kalamazoo, Michigan.

10th Generation

John Lyon, son of Robert Lyon and Jane Lancelot was born on 20th June 1786 in West Derby, Liverpool. He married ELLEN ROGERSON the daughter of Edward Rogerson and Ann Ashcroft was born on 29th October 1792 in West Derby, Lancashire. Ellen Rogerson and John Lyon had the following children:

1. Nancy Lyon was born on 15th May 1812 in Walton-On-The-Hill.
2. Elizabeth Lyon was born on 14th June 1814 in Walton-On-The-Hill. She died in Liverpool.
3. Thomas Lyon was born on 2nd July 1816 in Old Swan, Lancashire.
4. Edward Lyon was born on 31st August 1818 in Old Swan.

Ellen had two brothers; William Rogerson was born on 12th December 1793 in West Derby, Lancashire. Edward Rogerson was born in 1797 in Fazakerley, Lancashire.

Ellen died in January 1884 in West Derby, Lancashire, (Age: 54).

11th Generation

Thomas Lyon, son of John Lyon and Ellen Rogerson was born on 2nd July1816 in Old Swan, Lancashire. He married ELLEN WRIGHT on 10th Sep 1848 in Edge Hill, Lancashire. Ellen was born in 1830 in Old Swan, Lancashire. Ellen Wright and Thomas Lyon had the following children:

1. Mary Jane Lyon was born about 1848 in Old Swan, Lancashire.

2.   Peter Lyon was born in September 1851 in Old Swan, West Derby.

3.   Thomas Lyon was born on 27th December 1853 in Old Swan.

4.   William Lyon was born in 1857 in Old Swan, Lancashire.

5.   Joseph Lyon was born in September 1861 in West Derby, Lancashire.

6.   Alice Lyon was born about 1864 in Old Swan, Lancashire.

Thomas Lyon died in 1882 in Lancashire. Ellen Wight died in 1884 in West Derby, Lancashire.

12th Generation

Peter Lyon, son of Thomas Lyon and Ellen Wright was born in September 1851 in Old Swan, West Derby, Lancashire. He married ELIZA SWINBURN, daughter of John Swinburn and Matilda Swinburn in June 1874 in West Derby, Lancashire. Eliza Swinburn was born in June 1846 in Old Swan, Lancashire. Eliza Swinburn and Peter Lyon had the following children:

1.   Sophia Clarinda Lyon was born in June 1875 in Lancashire. She married John Hayes and had a daughter Clarinda in about 1900 in Liverpool.

2.   Alexander Peter Lyon was born in December 1878 in Widnes, Lancashire.

3.   Maud Ellen Lyon was born in 6th June 1880 in Liverpool, Lancashire.

4.   **Walter John Lyon** was born on 15th December 1885 in West Derby, Lancashire.

Eliza died in March 1898 in Lancashire. Peter died in September 1925 in West Derby, Lancashire. There is a photograph of Peter in the Postscript at the end of the book.

Thomas Lyon, son of Thomas Lyon and Ellen Wright, was born on 27th December 1853 in Old Swan, Lancashire, England. He married MARY TERESA MCGRATH. She was born in April 1852 in Lancashire. Thomas Lyon and Mary McGrath had the following children;

1.   Martha Ann Lyon born 1889 in Liverpool, Lancashire.

2.   William Lyon born 1891 in Liverpool, Lancashire. He died in 1957 in Ohio, USA.

3.   Joseph Henry Lyon born 1893 in Liverpool, Lancashire.

Mary died in 1919 in Tacoma, Pierce, Washington, USA. Thomas died in 1928 in Tacoma, Pierce, Washington, USA.

13th Generation

Alexander Peter Lyon, son of Peter Lyon and Eliza Swinburn, was born in December 1878 in Widnes, Lancashire. He married FRANCES BIRCH from Everton who was born in January 1880. Frances and Alexander Peter Lyon had the following children:

1   Eliza Lyon was born in 1900 in Liverpool, Lancashire.
2   Alexander Peter Lyon was born in 1902 in Liverpool, Lancashire.
3   Frances Lyon was born in 1904.
4   Joseph Lyon was born on 15th August 1905 in West Derby, Lancashire. He married Lydia Kelsey in December 1929 in West Derby, Lancashire. She was born on 30th May 1908 in Liverpool. She died in March 1971 in Liverpool. He died in December 1972 in Liverpool.
5   Thomas Lyon was born in 1908 in Liverpool.
6   Mary Lyon was born in 1910 in Liverpool.
7   Henry Lyon was born in September 1912 in West Derby, Lancashire.

Maud Ellen Lyon, daughter of Peter Lyon and Eliza Swinburn, was born on 6th June 1880 in Liverpool, Lancashire. She married WALTER AUSTIN WESLEY HOGG on 13th November 1898 in Everton, St Saviour, Lancashire. He was born in March 1876 in Liverpool. Walter Austin Wesley Hogg and Maud Ellen Lyon had the following children:

1.   Ethel Maud Hogg was born on 9th November about 1899 in Liverpool.
2.   Alfred Austin Hogg was born on 20th January 1901 in Everton, St. Saviour, Lancashire.
3.   Walter Alexander Hogg was born on 2nd November 1902 in Liverpool.
4.   Edith May Hogg was born in December 1906 in Liverpool.
5.   Lilian Maud Hogg was born in March 1909 in Liverpool.

Walter John Lyon, son of Peter Lyon and Eliza Swinburn was born on 15th December 1885 in West Derby, Lancashire. He married (HESTER) ESTHER ALEXANDER BLACKBURN, who was born on 17th May 1884 in Liverpool, daughter of Thomas Blackburn and Mary Ellen Heyes in June 1902 in St Benedict, Everton, Liverpool. Walter and Esther had the following children:

1.   Esther (Hester) Lyon was born 21st October 1905 in Liverpool, Lancashire. She married Sydney Foster she had one daughter. She later

married Bill Rimmington and had no children. She died 27th February 1979.

2. Lilian May Lyon was born 1st August 1906 in West Derby, Lancashire. She married Frederick John Griffiths. He was born on 30th September 1907 in Liverpool. They had 3 sons. Lilian died in March 1955 in Liverpool, and her husband died on 23rd August 1981 in Wirral, Merseyside

3. Dorothy Clarinda Lyon (aka Dolly) was born in 29th August 1907 in Liverpool. She married Samuel Dorman Boyle, they had 1 daughter and 2 sons. She died 23rd March 2006.

4. Evelyn Anne Lyon (aka Eve) was born 14th January 1910 in West Derby, Lancashire. She married Wilfred Pierce Knight on the 26th November 1932 and had 1 son and 1 adopted daughter. Evelyn died in June 1992.

5. Walter John Lyon was born 28th October 1911 in West Derby, Liverpool. He married Mabel Lewis and they had 2 daughters. Walter died 29th October 1959.

6. Elsie Rose Lyon (aka Rose) was born 12th March 1913 in West Derby, Lancashire. She married Robert Kirkby. They had 1 daughter. Elsie Rose died in 1963.

7. William George Lyon (aka Bill) was born on 15th September 1914 in West Derby, Lancashire. He married Lilian Martha Knight on the 26th October 1936. They had 4 sons and 1 daughter. He died on 28th November 1991 in Bickerstaffe, Lancashire. Lilian died on 10th August 2000 in Bickerstaffe. This is Sylvia's father and mother.

8. Alexander Peter Lyon (aka Alec) was born 4th February 1914 in Liverpool Lancashire. He married Ruth Rodgers, they had no children.

9. Richard Thomas Lyon (aka Dick) was born on 29th October 1919 in West Derby, Lancashire. He married Norah Tibke. She was born on 26th May 1921 in West Derby, Lancashire. Richard and Norah had 6 sons. He died 15th January 1985 in Birkenhead, Cheshire. She died in February 1987 in Birkenhead, Cheshire.

This is the family above, on the far right is a boy, Richard Thomas, despite his dress which he wore because he had not been 'breeched.' (Toilet trained).

Martha Ann Lyon, daughter of Thomas Lyon and Mary McGrath was born in 1889 in Liverpool. She married LEWIS J NEWMAN who was born in 1886 in Kent. Martha and Lewis had the following children;

1. Maria Teresa Newman.
2. Lewis John Richard Newman, born 1909 in Tacoma, Pierce, Washington, USA. He died 2001 in Mesa, Mariposa, Arizona, USA.
3. James Newman, born 1913 in Tacoma, Washington. He died 1982 in Tacoma.
4. George Newman, born in 1915 in Tacoma.

Joseph Henry Lyon son of Thomas Lyon and Mary McGrath was born in December 1893 in Liverpool, Lancashire. He married ETHEL PEARL LYON. She was born on 29th November 1893 in Ontario, Canada. Joseph Henry Lyon and Ethel Pearl Lyon had the following child:

1. John Lyon was born about 1920 in Washington, USA.

The other side of the coin

Not all people bearing the name Lyon are famous for their connections, lands, wealth and other positive claims. There are always 'black sheep' in any family – here is one example.

George Lyon of Upholland

"George Lyon was 54 when he was executed. Sentence was passed on Saturday 8th April, 1815 along with Houghton and Bennett. The other accomplice, Edward Ford, who had been working at Walmsley House, where the last robbery took place, as a painter, and for which robbery Lyon and his accomplices were eventually indicted. It was Ford who had suggested robbing the house to Lyon, and had himself taken part in some 17 previous robberies, but because he turned King's evidence he was spared the capital sentence. The execution of Lyon, Houghton, and Bennett, took place just before noon on Saturday, 22nd April 1815 - the year of the Battle of Waterloo.

Just five years before in 1810 the House of Lords had thrown out a law passed by the Commons that would have prohibited the death penalty for theft offences. All other capital sentences passed that day were commuted, except for the Upholland trio of Lyon, Houghton and Bennett, and two others, Moses Owen for horse stealing, and John Warburton for 'highway robbery'.

John Higgins, Chief Gaoler of Lancaster Castle - known as the gentleman gaoler - allowed Lyon to wear his best black suit and 'topped' jockey boots for his execution as he had promised, and these items had duly been brought over from Upholland for him. On that Saturday morning just before noon the condemned men were marched from their cells in Lancaster Castle to the Drop Room, and through its doors and out on to the scaffold, and in front of the usual hanging day crowd, some 5000 people who crowded onto the grass bank of what had once been the castle moat, and is opposite that which is called Hanging Corner, the sentences were duly carried out.

Visitors to Lancaster Castle today can still visit the Drop Room, where the condemned had their arms pinioned before execution, and see the pitch-dark, windowless dungeons which had also been used to hold the dozen or so Lancashire witches over a century earlier. The sentences were duly carried out by Old Ned Barlow, who was hangman of Lancaster Castle and who in his career executed some 133 people. After his death Lyon's body was handed over to Simon Washington, landlord of The Old Dog Inn in Upholland, and a companion, for its return to Upholland for burial. The Old Dog Inn building still stands on the steep street called Alma Hill, in the village.

Lyon had not wanted his body left at Lancaster as it would have been handed over to surgeons for dissection as was the normal procedure with the bodies of executed criminals. In a poignant letter to his wife written on the 14th of April with the aid of the prison chaplain the Reverend Cowley, who had visited all the prisoners on death row, he implored her to arrange for his body to be returned home. That return journey home undertaken by Simon Washington and companion was horrendous, made during a raging thunder storm, so bad, with thunder and lightning all around the cart, that at one stage both men had to shelter under it from the torrential rain, Washington declared that the devil himself had followed them throughout the journey, and he swore he would never make such a journey again.

As the cart approached the final part of its journey, a huge crowd was observed moving off from Orrell Post near Upholland in the direction of Gathurst, to observe the return of George Lyon's body. When word came through that the cortege was instead passing through nearby Wrightington and heading for the road through Appley Bridge instead, the crowd rushed across the fields from the Gathurst Bridge which still spans the Leeds to Liverpool canal, to meet the cart at Dangerous Corner, and then followed it in procession through Appley Bridge, and up the long steep climb through Roby Mill, until it eventually reached Parliament Street in Upholland, and the last few hundred yards to The Old Dog Inn, where Lyon's body was laid out in the landlady's best parlour overnight.

Hundreds of people gathered outside the pub the next day, and even climbed onto the roofs of adjoining buildings, to see the coffin as it was taken for burial to St. Thomas's churchyard in Upholland on Sunday 23rd April 1815. George Lyon is buried in his mother's (some say his grandmother's) grave, the inscription simply reads 'Nanny Lyon, Died 17th April 1804'. His name is not recorded on the stone. Directly opposite the grave stood the famous haunted house, with violent poltergeist happenings over a long period in 1904. This drew thousands of sightseers to the village, and many locals thought that the ghost of George Lyon was responsible."

(http://www.lan-opc.org.uk/Upholland/highwaymen.html)

We can see that the family members moved to southern Lancashire before the Appleton Lyon family was established in Warrington. There was a Lyon family in Rainford circa 1574.

LYON of Rainford and Melling in Lancashire by Thomas Steel. Permission to reproduce has been given.

"The Lyon family in whom our interest lies seems to have originated in Rainford and Windle townships (Prescot parish) and in Bickerstaffe

(Ormskirk). Particular difficulties arise because Rainford Chapel passed out of Church of England control (and thus of proper recording of vital events) for a long period in the 1600s (returning only in 1700) and also because of the Quaker allegiance of the Bickerstaffe Lyons. A link between the Rainford and Bickerstaffe Lyons is suggested by Daniel Lyon of Rainford witnessing the marriage licence application in 1684 of James and Sarah Lyon, both of Bickerstaffe.

The surname Lyon has been variously suggested as French (from Lyons, or Lyons la Foret) or Jewish (Leone) It seems likely that our Lyon line can be traced to Robert Lyon of Rainford, whose son Robert received non-conformist baptism at Rainford Chapel on 5th May 1700.

The Lyon family held land at Rainford under Lord Derby by circa 1574, when "George held a four-bay cottage and garden worth 10s (shillings) and in his own occupation, at 4½d (pence) rent; and Thomas had 5 acres worth 40s for a 5s rent.

Another Derby rental shows Thomas with a six-bay and 5-acre copyhold worth 10s; while George held the same 10s four-bay cottage and garden at will and the wife of John held two bays worth 4d."

The above extract is from the collection of data by a Thomas Steel and I have permission to reproduce – to see more go to; *(http://tsgf.pbworks.com/f/Lyon+of+Rainford+%26+Melling.pdf)*.

Lancashire is mainly rural nowadays and boasts two well-known holiday resorts; Blackpool and Southport. Most of the family still live in the south of the county and in North Cheshire and Merseyside.

I discovered these records on the web and have been able to contact Mr Thomas M Steele who owns the copyright for his genealogical efforts. I have his permission to use this research. There is some very interesting and challenging information about the family in Lancashire which has obviously been carefully researched.

Because this information being of interest to few readers I have posted the information. The genealogical challenge is for those who are interested in the Lyon family in Lancashire after the 1600's. The original transcript is hard to read so I have made it into a PDF that can be downloaded on my website. I may have time later to unscramble the families as they are quite local to me. *Visit www.thelyonfamily. org.uk/genealogy*

CHAPTER 13

THE EARLS OF KINGHORNE AND STRATHMORE TO THE PRESENT DAY.

The family were Roman Catholic as they were originally from Normandy and the rest of Scotland was Catholic by birth except for a few small groups who were in opposition to the Roman Church and its practices and beliefs. The Reformation and move to Protestantism was begun when Martin Luther posted a thesis in 1517 opposing the corruption of the church. This reform did not much effect Scotland until some years later. The Lyon family had not been outwardly religious people although in 1450 Glamis contained a chapel in common with most large houses in those days. This original chapel was replaced in the 17th century by the 3rd Earl of Kinghorne. To see details of the history of Glamis, a book by Harry Gordon Slade entitled 'Glamis Castle' is recommended reading and is beautifully illustrated. *(ISBN 0 85431 277 3 and no doubt available from any good booksellers through the web.)*

When Patrick Lyon became the first of this particular line of the Lyon family, Scotland and England were, as always it seems, in turmoil religiously and politically.

Nearly all the Scottish Lords, who were supporters of the executed Charles I, had their lands and titles sequestrated and often were fined large amounts of money for their disloyalty to their new ruler and the country.

This was known as the Act of Grace or more formally the Act of Pardon and Grace to the people of Scotland and was proclaimed at the Mercat (market) Cross in Edinburgh on 5th May 1654. General George Monck, the English Military Governor of Scotland, was present in Edinburgh, having arrived the day before for two proclamations also delivered at the Mercat Cross; the first declaring Oliver Cromwell to be the Protector of England, Ireland and Scotland, and the second that Scotland was united with the Commonwealth of England.

When Charles II took over most lands were restored but there was always a clear distinction between Royalists and those who stood with the Parliamentarians under Cromwell in the 1600s.

(http://en.wikipedia.org/wiki/Cromwell's_Act_of Grace)

The Reformation brought about massive changes to the country. Henry VIII had established the Church of England which still held sway with many. In Scotland the Presbyterian Church had been born with the leadership of John Knox. Later developments in Scotland saw other denominations spring to life but Scotland is still divided between the Catholics and the Protestants.

After the Reformation most of the descendants of the Lyon family were Protestant. There are many examples of Protestant Ministers of Religion coming from the family and the American story is of almost a total rejection of Catholicism.

The Earls stretch over a period of history that covers 18 kings and queens and one Protector of the Commonwealth. It saw the foundation of the Commonwealth in America, the conquest of India, Canada, Australia, New Zealand and Islands and countries in Africa too many to name.

1st Generation

Patrick Lyon, 1st Earl of Kinghorne, 9th Lord of Glamis

Patrick was born 1575 in Glamis Castle made Captain of the Guard, and one of the privy council of **King James VI** and was created Earl of Kinghorne 10th July 1606. His lordship married ANNE MURRAY daughter of John Murray, 1st Earl of Tullibardine, and had six children;

1. **John,** 2nd Earl Strathmore and Kinghorne – was born 13th August 1596 in Glamis, Angus died 12th May 1646. See 2nd Generation for more details.
2. **James,** of Auldbar, MP for Angus, was born 1600 a supporter of the Covenant, died before 13th August 1641.
3. **Patrick,** died young.
4. **Frederick,** of Brigton, MP was born 1602. A supporter of the Covenant; married, MARGARET daughter of Sir Patrick OGILVIE of Inchmartins. He later married JEAN STEWART widow of George Crichton of Arbeckle, but by her had no issue. He died 1660
5. **Anne,** born 3rd May 1598 in Perth Married 1618 William Hay afterwards 10th Earl of Erroll. She died 8th February 1637.
6. **Jean,** born 1600 she died 2nd October 1618.

Patrick Lyon followed James VI to London when he became King of England (as James I) following the death of Elizabeth I. The King made Patrick the first Earl of Kinghorne in 1606. It may well be that Patrick met William Shakespeare at the court of James I. If so, then James could be the one about whom the play MACBETH was probably written. The play was performed for King James I,

Shakespeare's patron. King James was fascinated by the occult and believed himself to be a descendant of Banquo, Macbeth's companion.

The Earl died 19ᵗʰ December 1615 and was succeeded by his eldest son John, his wife, Anne died 27ᵗʰ February 1618

King James VI of Scotland and James I of England. Born 19ᵗʰ June 1566 Edinburgh Castle. Father - Henry Stuart (Lord Darnley). Mother - Mary, Queen of Scots. Reign 24ᵗʰ July 1567 – 27ᵗʰ March 1625. Coronation 25ᵗʰ July 1603. Spouse Anne of Denmark. Died 27ᵗʰ March 1625 (aged 58) Theobald's House, England. Burial 7ᵗʰ May 1625 Westminster Abbey.

His children were; Henry Frederick, Prince of Wales; Elizabeth, Queen of Bohemia and Charles I of England, Scotland and Ireland.

His successor was Charles I and his predecessor was Queen Elizabeth I.

More about Glamis Castle

The history of Glamis is legendary, dating as far back as the 8ᵗʰ century when it was the home of St. Fergus and considered a holy place. In 1034, King Malcolm II was wounded in battle and taken to Glamis to die. Later, it became a Royal Hunting Lodge for the Kings of Scotland.

Glamis is probably best remembered as the place where Shakespeare's Macbeth murdered King Duncan. **That part of its story is pure fiction**. In fact, Shakespeare much maligned the historical Macbeth (ruled 1040-1057) who was never Thane of Glamis - the title did not even exist until 1264 - and he did not murder Duncan. He came to power after his rival Duncan was killed in battle and made a fairly good King, bringing peace and prosperity to the realm, until he himself was killed by Duncan's son Malcolm III.

Family tradition says that Shakespeare met Lord Glamis in London who told him about the castle (and probably the stories of its ghosts) and Shakespeare decided it was the perfect setting for his play. In 1040 Macbeth killed Duncan in battle near Elgin, to become King of Scotland. He was crowned at Scone and began his seventeen year reign. Macbeth's life had progressed far towards legend by the end of the 14ᵗʰ century, and it was historians that blackened Macbeth's name. Among them was Ralph Holinshed who spoke disparagingly of Macbeth in his *Chronicles of England, Scotland and Ireland, 1587*. It was on Holinshed's Chronicles which Shakespeare based his play Macbeth.

In the Scottish play, Macbeth is condemned as being "luxurious, avaricious, false, deceitful, sudden, malicious [and] smacking of every sin that has a name". In stark contrast to Duncan who was referred to as a "most sainted king", Macbeth's reign was said to have had a most negative impact upon Scotland; "think our country sinks beneath the yoke, it weeps, it bleeds and each new day a gash is added to her wounds".

In 1372 the castle was granted to Sir John Lyon by King Robert II and later became the family seat of the Earls of Strathmore & Kinghorne. Today the castle is home to the 18th Earl of Kinghorne and is famous for its many ghosts.

2nd Generation

John Lyon 2nd Earl of Strathmore and Kinghorne (Patrick) (1596 -1646)

John was born into one of the wealthiest families in Scotland and succeeded his father as Earl of Kinghorne in 1615. However, he spent much of the family wealth financing the Covenanting Army. Covenanters were people who strictly followed the Bible. John was a friend of James Graham, the Marquis of Montrose (1612-50), who helped frame the National Covenant in 1638.

John the 2nd Earl of Kinghorne and 10th Lord Glamis was born 13th August 1596. He was made heir of the lordship of Glamis, under a special dispensation from the King (James VI - 1567-1625) on 31st March 1617.

"In addition, he developed a great friendship with James Graham, Marquis of Montrose. Montrose was at first a fierce Covenanter but later became more of a Royalist. There came a point when John's conscience forced him to part company with Montrose who changed sides and took up arms against the Covenanters. John, who felt deserted considered that he had a moral obligation to the Covenanters cause, and contributed towards financing the army against his old friend Montrose, in the process committing himself to crippling debt."

He had married MARGARET ERSKINE on the 19th June 1618, third daughter of John, seventh Earl of Mar, they had a daughter:

1. **Marie**, born in 1620 in Kinghorne, Fife who died young 7th November 1639.

He later married ELIZABETH MAULE, second daughter of Patrick, the 1st Earl of Panmure. On 20th August 1641 he granted his future wife the barony of Bakie. They had three children;

1. **Patrick**, born 29th May 1643 in Glamis the 3rd Earl of Strathmore and Kinghorne. See details later.

2. **Joan,** born 10th February 1641 in Glamis, she died on 2nd July 1644 in Longforgan, Perthshire. She died young unmarried.

3. **Elizabeth,** (1626-1681), married on the 28th August 1665 Charles Gordon (1669-1702), first Earl of Aboyne.

John died 12th May 1647 and was succeeded by his only son Patrick. Elizabeth survived him, and married again, on 30th July 1650, George, third Earl of Linlithgow. She died at Castle Lyon in October 1659.

"Earl Patrick (the 3rd Earl) in lamenting his father's devotion to the cause of the Covenant, which did indeed bring the family to the verge of ruin, hints that it was all owing to the influence of his brother James Lyon of Auldbar, **Earl John** being a man 'easie to be intreated', but in justice to Auldbar and with deference to this filial explanation of what Earl Patrick regarded as a parent's weakness, it must be pointed out that such a view is nowhere countenanced by record. There is not in all these centuries of Lyon family history any example of facility to be found, least of all is any such weakness apparent in the career of Earl John.

From 1621 he took an active part in the public business of the country, siding with the great majority of the nation against the King, and the records of Privy Council and of Parliament team with testimonies to his energy. He served on all the important committees of State from 1627 onwards, and was the leading member of the commission to consider the proper sites for fortifications on the sea coast. On 22nd September 1638 the Privy Council in a body subscribed the Confession of Faith, and having set the example, proceeded to enforce it upon their fellow subjects.

The Earl, with Auldbar his brother and Montrose, formed three out of a committee of six appointed to enforce its acceptance upon the shire of Forfar with results which Sheriff Napier delights to record, and in the same year he accompanied Montrose in his Aberdeen campaign, and the energy and ability he then displayed, as well as the material aid he brought from his own estates, contributed largely to its successful issue, and it was an Aberdonian Homer who sang:

'God bliss Montrois our General,
The stout Earl of Kinghorne,
That we may long live and rejoyce that ever they were borne'.

The Earl's principles were now to be put to the severest test. The great Marquess of Montrose, one of his oldest friends, with whom he had contended in youthful emulation for the silver arrow on the Links of Barry and St. Andrews, and who had been in happier days his guest at Glamis, was now about to embark on that career of victory which shed its radiance over the sinking cause of the King. Perfectly aware of the importance of securing the help of so experienced and powerful a man as the **Earl of Kinghorne,** Montrose spared no effort to induce his old friend to join him. At first the Earl wavered, and with Montrose as suitor who can wonder? But the hesitation was temporary.

He was present in the Assembly of 1641 when the bound was denounced as unlawful, and members were required to sign a declaration to that effect. 'Kinghorne, being present, subscribed', writes Baillie, fully aware of the significance of the act'.

He died at St. Andrews 12th May 1646 of the plague, communicated by the Earl of Erroll's preceptor. By his will, dated at Glamis 15th January 1644, he 'ordaines our bodie to be buried honorablie conforme to our rank in our awand buriell in the kirk of Glamis', and nominated his wife sole executrix and tutrix to his son."

(www.electricscotland.com/History/kenneill/huntly/the_people.htm)

Frederick Lyon (Patrick) was born on 16th February 1602 in Angus. He was the brother of the 2nd Earl. He married MARGARET OGILVIE, daughter of James Ogilvy and Isabel Hamilton in 1627 in Brigtoune, Banffshire. She was born in 1606 in Lochmartine, Perthshire. Frederick Lyon and Margaret Ogilvie had the following children:

1. **Anna Lyon** was born in 1635 in Brigtoune, Banffshire. She married DAVID NEVAY. He was born in 1655.
2. **Patrick Lyon** was born in 1628 in Brigtoune, Banffshire.
3. **John Lyon** was born in 1637 in Brigtoune, Banffshire. He died on 23rd February 1671 in Edinburgh, Midlothian.

Margaret died in Scotland. Frederick died in 1660 in Scotland.

3rd Generation

Patrick 3rd Earl of Strathmore and Kinghorne (John, Patrick)

Patrick was born 29th May 1643 in Huntley Castle, near Dundee. Huntley Castle was for some time owned by the Lyon family and was for a while named Lyon Castle. It is now a prison and still in use.

Patrick inherited massive debts, but through determined hard work he managed to restore the family to solvency. He also made improvements to Glamis

Castle. In fact, his diary indicates he may have been involved in its architectural design. Patrick was the last noble in Scotland to keep a Jester, who's "motley" (outfit) is on display in Glamis Castle today. Unfortunately, the man had to be let go when he made an inappropriate proposal of marriage to the Lord's daughter.

Patrick was educated at the University of St. Andrews. On 12th April 1654 he was fined by Oliver Cromwell £1000 sterling, which sum was afterwards reduced to £250. Many details of his useful and happy life are to be found in the Glamis Book of Record.

"On 30th May 1672 Patrick obtained a new charter on his own resignation of the title and dignity of the **Earl of Kinghorne, Lord Lyon and Glamis,** and of the lands of the earldom, to himself and the heirs male of his body, whom failing, to any other persons whom he should please to nominate during his life, 'etiam in articulo mortis', as his heir.

This grant was ratified in Parliament. On 1st July 1677 he received an addition to his title, which in future was to be **Earl of Strathmore and Kinghorne, Viscount Lyon, Lord Glamis, Tannadyce, Sidlaw, and Stradichtie**, with the precedence of the former honour of **Earl of Kinghorne**.

To make headway against the enormous load of debt for which his father had become responsible, he was compelled to part with many of the family estates. Fothros and Schenwall, otherwise Tentsmuir, were sold by his tutors in 1649, and Inchsture and Holms were also sold during his minority. The barony of Belhelvies, in Aberdeenshire, he sold to his Uncle George, Earl of Panmure, 'at a just and equal price', as he gratefully records. He also parted with Bakie, Byreflatt, Newton and Nether Blackhall. In 1684 he sold the island of Inchkeith to Sir George Mackenzie. With the proceeds of these sales, added to strict economy and great business capacity, he was not only enabled to expend large sums on buildings and improvements at Glamis and Castle Lyon, now Castle Huntly, and wipe out a large part of his father's obligations, but to make substantial additions to the estates he retained.

He bought Glamis from Captain David Lyon 22nd June 1664; the barony of Reidie from Sir David Nevay of Reidie 1st August 1664; Drymmie from Sir George Kynnaird of Rossie 26th November 1664; Fofarty from William Gray of Invereightie. The lands of Thornton he purchased from John Seton of Thornton 25th August 1662; the Vicar's manse and Westhill of January 1670; Haystoun from William Gray of Haystoun also in January 1670; the barony of Kynnaird, with the church patronage, the Seamills of Dundee and Ferryboats and Admiralty of the River Tay, from James, Earl of Newburgh, 23rd June 1670; the

Castle of Kinghorne from Sir Robert Kirkcaldy of Grange the same year; Halltoun of Eassie and Balgownie Eassie from Donald Thorntoun of Balgownie 15th June 1671; the Office of the Constabulary of the Burgh of Forfar and the superiority of Nevay and Knap from William Gray of Carse 19th May 1672; the Preceptory of Balgownie Eassie and Chaplainry of Baikie from Mr John Lyon, Writer in Edinburgh, in the same year.

In 1662 he obtained an Act of Parliament for the holding of two yearly fairs in the town of Longforgan, 'a very populous place, far distant from any Royal burgh', to he held on the last Tuesday of July and the first Tuesday of October, in 1669 an Act for a weekly market and a yearly fair at Glamis; and in 1686 an Act for holding four free fairs in the year on his lands and baronies, the dates and places being unspecified."

The Earl no doubt supported Charles II who had come to the throne in 1660 after his previous unpleasant relations with Oliver Cromwell. In 1681 he received a pension of £500, 'in consideration of his loyalty and great charge in public employments' and in 1682 became a Privy Councillor. On 27th March 1686 he was appointed an Extraordinary Lord of Session from which post he was later removed. On 29th September 1668 he was appointed Captain of the second troop of Forfarshire Militia. This commission he held until 1682, when he voluntarily resigned it in favour of his eldest son.

In January 1678 he was nominated a member of the Western Committee appointed to superintend the operations of the 'Highland Host', which marched into the south western shires in the spring of that year, to compel the population to submit to the orders of the Privy Council in regard to the meeting in public to discuss religious matters. This was the time of King Charles II who wanted to return Scotland to Roman Catholic rule. The Highlanders were most Catholic by tradition and often opposed the work of the Protestant Reformation.

The 'Highland Host'

"The government were becoming desperate and in early 1678, nine thousand soldiers from the largely Catholic Highlands were brought south from their garrison in Stirling to Glasgow and the south-west. The town fathers of Ayrshire wrote to the Earl of Lauderdale, a senior official requesting him not to send so 'inhumane and barbarous a crew of spoilers' into that county. The appeal fell on deaf ears. Parties of Highland soldiers were quartered on land owned by suspected Covenanter sympathisers who were required to feed them and keep them for nothing. These were known as the 'Highland Host' who were Catholic and were responsible for many atrocities, robbing their Covenanter hosts of all belongings and livestock; rape, pillage and destruction. Thousands of pounds worth of damage and theft were done in the few months they were in residence." *(http://www.sorbie.net/covenanters.htm)*

As the Minutes of the Committee in question show, the 3rd Earl was by far the most regular attender of its meetings, being absent on only two occasions between 24th January and 20th March. The Highland Host was mustered at Stirling 24th January 1678, and numbered 590 horse and 6124 foot, of which Angus contributed 104 horse and 1000 foot, the horse in two troops, the first being commanded by the Earl of Airlie. Lord Strathmore's operations were chiefly in Ayrshire, where the memory of the Angus men was still green by reason of Woodrow's incessant references to their exploits.

He took no part in the campaign which terminated at Bothwell Brig in 1679, but in the Argyll Rising of 1685 he was again out with his Regiment, which escorted to Edinburgh the spoils of that campaign. Large quantities of meal and other victual were at this time purchased by the Government from the Earl, and stored at Stirling for the use of the troops. On 23rd July 1672 he received the commission of Lieutenant in the King's Life Guards, of which the Marquess of Atholl was captain; this employment he resigned 18th July 1680. His attitude towards the Reformation of 1688 was passively hostile, and he remained in Edinburgh up to January 1689, in the hope of preventing its success. But ultimately he accepted the new rule, and he is last noted as appearing in Parliament on 15th May 1693 at the time of King William of Orange."

The editor of the *Glamis Book of Record* justly sums up his character, "a man of strict integrity and uprightness, with a profound respect for the honour of his ancestors, and a deep sense of his responsibility to posterity".

Patrick married at Holyrood Palace on the 23rd August 1662 HELEN MIDDLETON, second daughter of John, Earl of Middleton, then Lord High Commissioner. The ceremony was performed on the same day by Archbishop Sharpe, the Earl being then nineteen years and four months of age. In that very human document, the *Glamis Book of Record*, no episodes make more delightful reading than those in which the Earl refers to his wife; these disclose a rare picture of domestic felicity, and they were sweethearts to the end. She died May 1708, having had children by him:

1. **John**, fourth Earl of Strathmore and Kinghorne, born 8th May 1663 in Huntley Castle.

2. **Patrick**, 1669-15, received the lands of Auchterhouse for his patrimony (an estate inherited from one's father or ancestor). He was the MP for Angus from 22nd September 1702 to the Union. He voted uniformly against the Treaty of Union with England. His name occurs in the list of persons for whose arrest warrants were issued on the occasion of the Jacobite scare of 1708 and he was present on the Braes of Mar, 9th September 1715, when the standard of King James VIII was raised. He, with the Earl of Aboyne, brought in the men of Aboyne, who were brigaded with the Panmure contingent and designated the Panmure Highlanders, Auchterhouse being lieutenant colonel.

He was killed at the battle of Sheriffmuir, fought 13th November 1715. 'A man of very great honour'. He married Margaret Carnegie, sister of that James Carnegie of Phinhaven who accidentally killed Charles, Earl of Strathmore. She died at Finhaven 14th April 1742.

3. **Charles**, born 12th February 1679 and died 1692.
4. **Grizel**, born 1669, married (contract 19th April and 8th May 1696) to David, third Earl of Airlie.
5. **Elizabeth**, born 1670, married her cousin Charles, 2nd Earl of Aboyne. She died January 1739.

Earl Patrick Lyon the 3rd Earl died on 15th May 1695.

John Lyon (Frederick, Patrick) was born in 1637 in Brigtoune, Banffshire. He married MARGARET NEVAY. She was born in 1641 in Aberdeen, Aberdeenshire. John Lyon and Margaret Nevay had the following children :
1. **David Lyon** was born in 1663.
2. **John Lyon** was born in 1665 in Brigtoune, Banffshire. He married Cecilia Dunsmore. She was born in 1669.

Margaret died in Scotland. John Lyon (1637) died on 23rd February 1671 in Edinburgh, Midlothian.

Elizabeth Lyon (John, Patrick) was born in 1626 in Glamis, Angus. She married CHARLES GORDON. He was born in 1669 in Glamis, Angus. Charles Gordon and Elizabeth Lyon had the following child:

1. John Gordon was born in 1702 in Aboyne, Aberdeenshire. He died on 7th April 1732 in Aboyne, Aberdeenshire.

Elizabeth died in 1681. Charles died in April 1702

4th Generation

John Lyon (Patrick, John, Patrick) 4th Earl of Strathmore and Kinghorne

John was born 8th May 1663 in Huntley Castle. He was the 3rd Earl's younger brother. The 12th Lord Glamis, was educated at the University of St. Andrews, he travelled abroad in his youth.

He was Captain of the second troop of Angus Militia 7th February 1682. He served as heir to his father on 29th October 1695. On 12th March 1696 he was appointed Sheriff of Forfar. He was a great horse breeder, and owned in his time several race horses. Among his memoranda is one dated 17th February 1702 – 'I went down this day to Barry Sands to see the race twixt my Red Rose and Sir James Kinloch's gelding, which I won'. He was an uncompromising opponent of the Whig party administrations of the period.

He subscribed £500 to the Darien Scheme. On 14th January 1701 he voted for the Act asserting the right of the nation to Darien, a proposal the Ministry in London succeeded in defeating.

The Darien Scheme

The colonization project that became known as the **Darien Scheme** or **Darien Disaster** was an unsuccessful attempt by the Kingdom of Scotland to become a world trading nation by establishing a colony called 'Caledonia' on the Isthmus of Panama in the late 1690s. From the outset, the undertaking was beset by poor planning and provision, weak leadership, lack of demand for trade goods, devastating epidemics of disease and increasing shortage of food; it was finally abandoned after a siege by Spanish forces in April, 1700.

John Lyon was consistently opposed to the Treaty of Union and wrote to the Earl of Mar, then Secretary of State of Scotland, asking for the protection for Episcopal ministers against Presbyterian zeal.

Wikipedia says; "The Treaty of Union is the name given to the agreement that led to the creation of the United Kingdom of Great Britain, the political union of the Kingdom of England (which included Wales) and the Kingdom of Scotland, which took effect on 1st May 1707. The details of the Treaty were agreed on 22nd July 1706, and separate Acts of Union were then passed by the Parliaments of England and Scotland to ratify the Treaty."

"In 1708, when many people were put under arrest in prospect of a Jacobite invasion, it was accounted as unusual that the Earl of Strathmore should be allowed to go about without guards. Macky wrote of him, "This gentleman is well bred and good natured, hath not yet endeavoured to get into the administration, being no friend to Presbytery. He hath two of the finest seats in Scotland, Glamis and Castle Lyon; is tall, fair and towards fifty years old."

To read more about the scheme visit;
(http://www.bbc.co.uk/history/british/civil_war_revolution/scotland_darien_01.shtml)

John was married on 21st September 1691 to ELIZABETH STANHOPE, daughter of Philip, second Earl of Chesterfield, by his second wife Lady Elizabeth Butler, daughter of James, Duke of Ormond. Elizabeth was a careful wife and mother, ample evidence of both facts being found in her household book 1706-24, still preserved at Glamis. Elizabeth and John had 11 children;

1. **John,** 5th Earl baptised 27th April 1690; who was slain in rebellion 18th November 1715 at the Battle of Sheriffmuir, and was succeeded by his brother Charles (16991728).
2. **Patrick,** Lord Glamis, born 1693. Educated at Edinburgh and Aberdeen. He died young, before 10th September 1709 in Glamis.
3. **Philip** born 29th October 1693. He was educated with his elder brother until the latter's death. He then proceeded to Oxford, where after an illness of nine days, he died on 18th March 1712.
4. **Helen,** Helen, baptized 3rd January 1695, married in 1714 to Robert, seventh Lord Blantyre, by whom she had no surviving issue. She died at Bath 19th December 1723.
5. **Mary,** Mary, baptized 16th April 1697, who died, unmarried at Glamis Castle 26th May 1780.
6. **Charles,** 6th Earl born 1699 in Glamis and died 11th May 1728 in Forfar, Angus. He became the 6th Earl.
7. **James** born 1702 in Glamis, died 18th January 1753 in Glamis. He became the 7th Earl.
8. **Hendrie,** she died at birth 1st July 1700.
9. **Elizabeth,** born 1701 in Glamis.
10. **Thomas** born 6th July 1704. He became the 8th Earl and died 18th January 1753
11. **Catherine,** baptized 24th April 1707; died young.

When John known as the 'Old Chevalier' left the Castle, he absentmindedly left his watch under the pillow. The maid who cleaned out the room after he had left, stole it. Many years later, that maid's great-great-great-granddaughter returned the watch to Glamis Castle. This, together with a sword which he presented to his host, are shown in the Family Exhibition.

John Lyon (1663) died 10th May 1712 Elizabeth died 24th April 1723.

The Jacobite cause

In 1688 King James II of England (King James VII) of Scotland was deposed as King. This was in the main due to his extreme Catholic tendencies. The English Convention (1689) was an irregular assembly of the Parliament of England which transferred the Crowns of England and Ireland from James II to William III and his wife Queen Mary II. Mary was the daughter of James II, but she and her husband were Protestants. The followers of King James were known as Jacobites and they were present in both England and Scotland

James II made one serious attempt to recover his crown from William and Mary, when he landed in Ireland in 1689 but, after the defeat of the Jacobite forces by the Williamite forces at the Battle of the Boyne in July 1690, James returned to France. He lived out the rest of his life as a pretender at a court sponsored by his cousin and ally, King Louis XIV. Following the death of Mary in 1694 and the later death of William in 1702, Anne became Queen of England. She was also a daughter of James II, but her Grandfather Charles II had ensured that she was raised as a protestant. In May 1707 under the Act of Union England and Scotland were combined into a single state, The Kingdom of Great Britain.

James II of England had died in 1701 but his followers now backed his son to become James VIII of Scotland and James III of England. He would be otherwise known as 'The Old Pretender'. Following the death of Queen Anne in 1714 and the accession of their cousin George of Hanover to the throne (George I) they saw a chance to take the throne back

Jacobite ideology

"Jacobites contended that **James II** had been illegally deprived of his throne, that the Convention Parliament and its successors were not legal. Scottish Jacobites resisted the Act of Union 1707, while not recognising Parliamentary Great Britain, Jacobites recognised their monarchs as Kings of Great Britain.

Jacobite ideology comprised four main tenets: The divine right of kings, the 'accountability of Kings to God alone, inalienable hereditary right, and the unequivocal scriptural injunction of non-resistance and passive obedience', though these positions were not unique to the Jacobites. What distinguished Jacobites from Whigs was their adherence

to 'right' as the basis for the law, whereas the Whigs held to the idea of 'possession' as the basis of the law. However, such distinctions became less clear over time, with an increase in the use of contract theory by some Jacobite writers during the reign of **George I** (1714-1727)."
(http://en.wikipedia.org/wiki/Jacobitism#Jacobite_ideology)

The Battle of Sheriffmuir in 1715

John Erskine, 6th Earl of Mar, standard-bearer for the Jacobite cause in Scotland, mustered Highland chiefs, and on 6th September 1715 declared James Francis Edward Stuart (the 'Old Pretender') as King of Scotland. (They were followers of King James I and his Stuart descendants).

With an army of about 12,000 men, John Erskine, the Earl of Mar proceeded to take Perth, and commanded much of the northern Highlands. Following unsuccessful skirmishes against John Campbell, 2nd Duke of Argyll (based at Stirling), Mar was eventually persuaded to lead his full army south, on 10th November. Spies informed Argyll of Mar's actions, and he moved his army of about 4,000 to Sheriffmuir, near Dunblane. The two armies met on the battlefield on 13th November 1715.

Argyll was seriously outnumbered by the Jacobite army (which was somewhat diminished from its previous numbers), and his left wing, commanded by General Whetham, was far shorter than the Jacobites' opposing right. Argyll's right wing attacked, and managed to drive the Highlanders back, but Whetham's soldiers were overpowered by a much larger force. Argyll came to the aid of Whetham's men. By evening, both armies were seriously reduced, and although Mar had a great advantage in numbers, he refused to risk the entirety of his army, allowing Argyll to withdraw. The battle was inconclusive with both sides claiming victory. However in strategic terms Argyll had halted the Jacobite advance. Those government regiments present that were titled Kings were awarded the White Horse of Hanover as a badge of battle honour. The engagement only served to demoralize the Jacobite army who, with their superior numbers, felt they should have decisively won. Mar's French and Spanish supporters in particular withdrew their forces.

The Earl of Strathmore at Sheriffmuir

When the Earl of Mar reached Perth in the end of September 1712 with the forces raised by him in support of the cause of James VIII, Lord Strathmore joined him with a battalion of 'Foot' raised from his estates. He steadily devoted himself to the training of his corps and it formed part of the force despatched by Mar to join Lord Kenmure and the Earl of Nithsdale in the south of Scotland. The command of the expedition was given to Brigadier Mackintosh of Borlum, who marched his force to Burnt-island, and leaving there a small party to make a feint of crossing, turned eastwards along the Fife coast, and on the night of the 12th and 13th October embarked his men in open boats at Elie, Pittenweem, the Ansters, and Crail.

The English men-of-war (ships) who were guarding the Forth concentrated their attention on Burnt-island, and did not discover that they had been outwitted until the greater part of Borlum's force was safely across, including four companies of the Strathmore regiment. The English ships now gave chase and captured two boats, the remaining part of the flotilla containing **Lord Strathmore**, his lieutenant-colonel, Walkinshaw of Barrowfield, and 200 men being driven on to the Isle of May, where they were attacked by the English longboats. They made a successful defence, and after maintaining themselves eight days on the island, succeeded in regaining the Fife coast, the **Earl** being the last man to enter the boats.

The opposing forces met at Sheriffmuir on 12th November 1715. The right wing of Argyll's army, commanded by the Duke in person, after a stubborn contest of three hours, compelled the left wing of the Highland army to give way, and drove it step by step across the Allan Water.

The Highlanders lost heavily, and among the slain was the Earl of Strathmore.

The last scene is thus described by a brother officer; "On our left the brave young Strathmore was killed after being wounded and taken, when he found all turning their backs he seized the colours, and persuaded fourteen or some such number to stand by him for some time, which drew upon him the enemy's fire, by which he was wounded in the belly, and going off was taken and murdered by a dragoon, and it may be said in his fate that a mill-stone crushed a brilliant soldier. He was the young man of all I ever saw who approached the nearest to perfection, and his least qualitie was that he was of a noble ancient familie and a man of qualitie".

On the 4th January following, King James VIII and the Earl of Mar arrived at Glamis Castle, where they remained several days, and from whence Mar addressed a circular letter of encouragement to his supporters, but his own incapacity and indecision were so manifest that the cause for which the young noble laid down his life collapsed a few weeks afterwards.

On 23rd December, the Old Pretender, who had been exiled in France, landed at Peterhead, his cause largely lost. He met with Mar at Perth, but was unable to rouse the disheartened army. Argyll, reinforced and invigorated, soon advanced north, while the Jacobite army fled to Montrose, and the Pretender returned to France. The Army moved to Ruthven, and dispersed. The period was fatal in the extreme to the Jacobite Pretender. His followers in the south had fallen into the hands of Generals Willis and Carpenter at Preston (Scotland), and Inverness, with all the adjacent country. This land had been recovered to the government, through the exertions of pro-government clans including the Earl of Sutherland, Fraser Lord Lovat, the Rosses, the Munros, and the Forbeses.

"The number of the slain on the side of the rebels has been stated to have been eight hundred, among whom were **John Lyon, 5th Earl of Strathmore and Kinghorne** and the chief of the Clan MacDonald of Clan Ranald, and several others of distinction. James Maule, 4th Earl of Panmure and Drummond of Logie were among the wounded. It meant that the Jacobite army had to withdraw to Perth. Argyll considered himself the victor and struck a medal to commemorate his feat. Of the government army there were killed, and wounded, upwards of six hundred. Archibald Douglas, 2nd Earl of Forfar was the only person of eminence killed on the government side."

A popular Jacobite song, "Will Ye Go to Sheriffmuir", was written about the battle. As with many such songs, the battle is presented as a noble victory for the Jacobite army. The song was collected by, and perhaps written by James Hogg in 1819.

Jacobite Claimants

(http://en.wikipedia.org/wiki/List_of_Scottish_monarchs#Jacobite_claimants)
"James VII continued to claim the thrones of England, Scotland, and Ireland. When he died in 1701, his son James inherited his father's claims, and called himself James VIII of Scotland and III of England and Ireland. He would continue to do so all his life, even after the Kingdoms of England and Scotland were ended by their merging as the Kingdom of Great Britain. In 1715, a year after the death of his sister, Queen Anne, and the accession of their cousin George of Hanover. James landed in Scotland and attempted to claim the throne; he failed, and was forced to flee back to the Continent. A second attempt by his son, Charles, in 1745 also failed. Both James's children died without legitimate issue, bringing the Stuart family to an end.

James VIII (Seumas VIII), also known as The Old Pretender, son of James VII, was claimant from 1701 until his death in 1766.
Charles III (Teàrlach III), also known as The Young Pretender and often called Bonnie Prince Charlie, son of James VIII, was claimant from his father's death until his own death in 1788 without legitimate issue.

Henry I (Eanraig I), brother of Charles III and youngest son of James VIII. Died unmarried in 1807.

After 1807, the Jacobite claims passed first to the House of Savoy (1807–1840), then to the Modenese branch of the House of Habsburg-Lorraine (1840– 1919), and finally to the House of Wittelsbach (since 1919). The current heir is Franz, Duke of Bavaria. Neither he nor any of his predecessors since 1807 have pursued their claim."

Some of the Lyon family members supported the Jacobites;

Lyon Jacobites of Angus

"**David Lyon**, a vintner in Montrose taken prisoner in Montrose and Carlisle

J Lyon taken prisoner after Sherriffmuir 13/11/1715 James Lyon, a tailor in Montrose, a prisoner in Arbroath.

James Lyon, innkeeper in Dundee, a soldier of Ogilvy's Regiment

John Lyon, Earl of Strathmore, born 1690, fought and died at Sheriffmuir 13/11/1715

Patrick Lyon of Auctherhouse, son of the Earl of Strathmore, Lieutenant Colonel of Panmure's Foot killed 13/11/1715

Patrick Lyon, a proprietor's son in Ogil, Tannadice, Lieutenant of Ogilvy's Regiment

Philip Lyon, transported from Liverpool to South Carolina on the Wakefield 21/04/1716

Robert Lyon, Ensign of Panmure's Foot, 1715

William Lyon, Lieutenant in Strathmore's Battalion, a prisoner in Preston, transported from Liverpool to Jamaica or Virginia on the Elizabeth and Ann 29/06/1716, landed in Virginia in 1716.

Lyon son of George Lyon minister of Tannadice, hung as a rebel at the age of 17."

John Lyon (John, Frederick, Patrick) was born in 1665 in Brigtoune, Banffshire. He married CECILIA DUNSMORE. She was born in 1669. John Lyon and Cecilia Dunsmore had the following child:

1.   **John Lyon** was born on 19th January 1684 in Glamis, Angus.

5th Generation

John Lyon the 5th Earl of Strathmore (John, Patrick, John, Patrick)
John was baptised on 27th April 1690; was slain in rebellion 18th November 1715 at the battle of Sheriffmuir, and was succeeded by his brother Charles (1699-1728).

John Lyon (John, John, Frederick, Patrick) was born on 19th January 1684 in Glamis, Angus. Notice the different lineage through Frederick. He married EUPHEMIA YOUNG. She was born about 1699 in Banffshire. John Lyon and Euphemia Young had the following children:
1. **Charles Lyon** was born in 1721 in Brigton. He died before 1754
2. **John Lyon** was born on 12th November 1723 in Forglen, Banffshire Scotland.

John was slain 18th November 1715.

Charles Lyon, 6th Earl of Strathmore (John, Patrick, John, Patrick) 14th Lord Glamis was baptised on the 12th July 1699. Charles married on 25th July 1725 SUSAN COCHRANE, daughter of John, Earl of Dundonald. After Earl Charles' death she married on 2nd April 1745, Mr. George Forbes, and died in the Roman Catholic faith at Chaventon, near Paris, 23rd June 1754. Charles and Susan possible had two children;

1. **Anne** born 1727 in Scotland
2. **James** born 1727 in Scotland

Charles served as heir general to his brother John on 9th April 1717. He took an active part in settling the disputes among the Episcopalian party in Scotland. He was one of the nobles who refused to take the oath of allegiance to the House of Hanover.

"It will be remembered that the family had been compelled to part with the Aberdeenshire estates in the time of Patrick, third Earl of Strathmore and Kinghorne, but the old connection was not forgotten, and in the Civil War of 1715 a body of Aberdeenshire men was placed under the command of Patrick Lyon of Auchterhouse, who fell at Sheriffmuir.

A still more striking episode occurred in the time of Earl Charles. Several families bearing the names of Bowman and in Glenmuick and Glenesk approached his Lordship in the autumn of 1723, setting forth that their forebears were truly and really of the surname of Lyon, who had come out of the shire of Angus on account of some troubles, and assumed the names Bowman and More, but being blood Lyons they now desired to resume their true surname.

The Earl acknowledged the kinship, and they accordingly entered into a bond with him as their chief and protector, and became bound to answer his call upon all occasions, the Earl on the other hand receiving them into his protection and acknowledging them to be of his clan and family. The contract, dated at Aboyne 2nd October 1723, was subscribed by 'twenty six heads of families taking the name of Lyon, together with one who subscribed'."

The death of the Earl

"On March 9th 1728 Mr Carnegie of Lour, residing in the burgh of Forfar, was burying his daughter. Before the funeral, he entertained the Earl of Strathmore, his own brother James Carnegie of Finhaven, Mr Lyon of Bridgeton, and some others, at dinner in his house.

After the funeral, these gentlemen adjourned to a tavern, and drank a good deal. Carnegie of Finhaven got extremely drunk. Lyon of Bridgeton was not so intoxicated, but the drink made him 'rude and unmannerly' towards Finhaven. Afterwards, the **Earl of Strathmore** went to call at the house of Mr Carnegie's sister, Lady Auchterhouse, and the others followed. The presence of a lady (even a lady who was a widowed sister-in-law) failed to make Bridgeton conduct himself discreetly. He continued his 'boisterous rudeness' towards Finhaven and even used some rudeness towards the lady herself.

About dusk, the party sallied forth into the street, and here Bridgeton pushed Carnegie of Finhaven into a 'deep and dirty kennel' (ditch), which covered him nearly head to foot with 'mire'. Incensed by Bridgeton's action, Carnegie of Finhaven, rose and drawing his sword, ran up to Bridgeton, with 'deadly design'. The earl, seeing him advance, pushed Bridgeton aside and unhappily received the lunge full in the middle of his own body. The Earl died forty-nine hours after the incident.

Carnegie of Finhaven was tried for murder in a famous trial which established the 'not guilty' verdict (in addition to 'proven' and 'not proven') in Scots Law and the right of Scots juries to try the whole case and not just the facts known as Jury Nullification." (*Main article: Carnegie of Finhaven*)

The Earl died on Saturday 11th May 1728

James Lyon, 7th Earl of Strathmore (John, Patrick, John, Patrick)

James was a Scottish peer and a Freemason. He was the son of John Lyon, 4th Earl of Strathmore and Lady Elizabeth Stanhope. He was christened on 24th December 1702.

He succeeded as the Earl of Strathmore following the stabbing of Charles Lyon, 6th Earl of Strathmore and Kinghorne in a drunken altercation in 1728. On 6th March 1731 he married MARY OLIPHANT, daughter of Charles Oliphant.

"He entered the Army and had a company in Barrell's Foot (22nd Regiment) 1732. In his time a sept (part) of the name of Breassauch, dwelling in Glenshee and Glenisla, entered into a contract similar to that between Earl Charles and the Bowmans and the Mores. They declared the sir name (surname) of Breassauch to be only their borrowed name, and they now desired to assume their true name of Lyon, and acknowledge the Earl to be their chief. The Earl admitted the claim and acknowledged them to be his kin and blood. The contract, dated at Glamis Castle 28th July 1731, is subscribed for the Clan by their leader Patrick Lyon, who is designed therein Captain Patrick Lyon, younger of Innerarity."

James was the Grand Master in 1733 of the Premier Grand Lodge of England that was founded on 24th June 1717 as the Grand Lodge of London and Westminster and it existed until 1813 when it united with the Ancient Grand Lodge of England to create the United Grand Lodge of England. It was the first Masonic Grand Lodge to be created. Its basic principles were inspired by the ideal of tolerance and universal understanding of the Enlightenment and by the Scientific Revolution of the 17th century.
(http://en.wikipedia.org/wiki/Premier_Grand_Lodge_of_England)

The reader may remember the connections between the Lyon family with Masonry in Scotland, then with the Knights Templar, then the Hospitallers and the Order of St John of Jerusalem. Freemasonry, many believe, was built upon the teachings of these and other Masonic orders. The family's connection with Freemasonry continues up to the present day.

James died without issue on 4th January 1735 at Edinburgh. The Earl was interred 18th January 1735, in the Abbey of Holyrood House. His wife had died at Glamis Castle 7th September 1731. He was succeeded as earl by his younger brother, Thomas (1704-53).

Thomas Lyon 8th Earl of Strathmore, (John, Patrick, John, Patrick)

Thomas was baptized 6th July 1704. He became sixteenth Lord Glamis. He married, 20th July 1736, JEAN, born 22nd September 1713, eldest daughter and one of the three co-heiresses of James NICHOLSON of West Rainton, County Durham, who died at Hetton in North Yorkshire 13th May 1778. Thomas and Jean had seven children:

1. **John,** ninth Earl of Strathmore and Kinghorne, born 17th July 1737,
2. **James Philip,** born at Rainton 2nd July 1738. Educated at Cambridge. His friends wished him to study for the bar, but he refused, and went out to India in the service of the East India Company. He was taken prisoner at Cossimbazaar by Mir Cossim, Nabob of Bengal, and with several other British officers put to death at Patna by order of the Nabob in February 1763, he was unmarried.
3. **Thomas** of Hetton House, Durham, born 1741. Educated at Cambridge. Candidate in a Parliamentary contest for the county of Forfar, in which he was defeated by the family of Panmure. The struggle was so exhausting to both sides that it resulted in a family compact by which it was settled that the House of Panmure and Strathmore should in future return a member alternately. After his defeat in the county he was elected member for the Montrose district of burghs 12th April 1768 to 30th September 1774.

    He was MP for Forfarshire 29th November 1774 to 11th January 1779. He married 13th June 1774, Mary Elizabeth, daughter of Farren Wren of Binchester, County Durham, and by her had issue. He died at Binchester 13th September 1796, and Mary died 13th June 1774.
4. **Susan,** married at Houghton-le-Spring, 5th September 1763 to General John Lambton of Harraton Hall County Durham, who died in 1794. She died at Nice 26th February 1769. They had issue.
5. **Anne,** married 15th July 1768 to John Simpson of Bradley County Durham.
6. **Mary,** died at Hetton born 1749, 2nd May 1767, aged eighteen.
7. **Janet,** born about 1776, died unmarried 22nd August 1836, aged sixty.

Thomas died 18th January 1753 at Glamis Castle and was succeeded by his eldest son John Lyon the 9th Earl.

6th Generation

John Lyon, 9th Earl of Strathmore and Kinghorne (Thomas, John, Patrick, John, Patrick). John was born 17th July 1737, a Representative Peer for Scotland 1767-76, he married 24th February 1767, MARY ELEANOR BOWES, only daughter and heiress of George Bowes, of Streatlam Castle and Gibside House, County Durham, and assumed by act of Parliament 1767, the surname of Bowes, due to a provision in her father's will that any suitor had to take the family name. This was a device to continue the Bowes lineage in the absence of a male heir. Mary and John had the following children;

1. **John**, born 14th April 1769 in Durham. **He became 10th Earl.**
2. **George Bowes**, born 17th November 1771 in Gibside, married 14th June 1805, Mary daughter of Edward Thornhill, of Kingston Lisle, Berkshire, and died without issue 31st January 1806.
3. **Thomas**, born May 1773 in Walden, Hertfordshire. Became the 11th Earl.
4. **Anne Maria**, born 1774 in Gibside, County Durham, died 22nd April 1832.
5. **Maria Janet**, born 1774 in Gibside and died 22nd April 1806.

John died of tuberculosis on route to Lisbon on the 7th March 1776 and was succeeded by his eldest son: **John Bowes-Lyon.**

Mary Eleanor Bowes remarried 17th January 1777, Andrew Robinson Stoney, MP for Newcastle on Tyne and High Sheriff, Durham the eldest son of George Stoney of Greyfort, County Tipperary, and from whom she obtained a divorce on 3rd March 1789, and she died 28th April 1800. Andrew inherited the following two large estates in County Durham as a result of his marriage to Mary Eleanor Bowes. The properties reverted to the Lyon family after his divorce from Mary Eleanor.

Streatlam Castle was a Baroque stately home located near the town of Barnard Castle in County Durham, England. Owned by the Bowes-Lyon family, Earls of Strathmore and Kinghorne, the house was one of the family's two principal seats, alongside Glamis Castle in Forfarshire, Scotland. Streatlam incorporated some 1,190 acres (4.8 km^2) of land, along with an estate consisting of some twenty farms. The last occupant was Lord Glamis, heir to the earldom, although the estate was owned by his father, the Earl of Strathmore.

The House came to the Bowes family in the mid-Eighteenth century. For much of the nineteenth century, it was owned by John Bowes, the eldest son of the 9th Earl of Strathmore who was illegitimate under Scottish law as his parents married after he was born, but was able to inherit the family's wealth and English properties. Following his death without issue, the estate was reunited with the Earldom in 1885. Unlike the fate of other properties which belonged to the Bowes-Lyon family, such as Gibside (which lay within a major coalfield near Gateshead and so was considered spoilt by pollution from the surrounding coal mines), Streatlam sat amidst the beautiful countryside of the Durham Dales. It has since been demolished.

Gibside is a country estate near Rowlands Gill, Tyne and Wear, North East England that was previously owned by the Bowes-Lyon family. It is now a National Trust property. The main house on the estate is now a shell, the property is most

famous for its chapel. The stables, walled garden and Banqueting House are also intact.

The Blakiston family acquired the estate by marriage in about 1540. William Blakiston replaced the old house with a spacious mansion between 1603 and 1620. The property came into the possession of the Bowes family when Elizabeth Blakiston married Sir William Bowes of Streatlam Castle.

In 1767 the Bowes heiress Mary Eleanor Bowes had married John Lyon, 9th Earl of Strathmore and Kinghorne. *(http://en.wikipedia.org/wiki/Gibside)* *(http://en.wikipedia.org/wiki/File:Gibside_House_pic_3.JPG)*

There is much could be written about the Bowes family but this would make another book, to see more follow the next hint:

A letter has surfaced revealing how the Queen Mother's ancestor escaped an abusive marriage. She suffered eight years of marriage to a 'despicable rogue' who imprisoned and tortured her for her fortune.

"Mary   Eleanor Bowes, the   Countess   o   f Strathmore and Kinghorne, became known as the 'Unhappy Countess' after being fooled into marriage by the self-styled 'Captain' Andrew Robinson Stoney in the late 18th century.

Bowes, who was said to be the richest heiress in Britain, was an attractive 37year-old widow with five children when Stony hatched his plan to win her affection. He arranged to have scurrilous stories about her published in the Morning Post newspaper, and then contacted his damsel offering to challenge the editor to a duel. But unknown to Bowes, the two men were in cahoots. He faked the duel, pretending to be mortally wounded with the aid of lashings of animal blood, and asked her to marry him as a dying wish.

The countess – who appeared prone to strange affairs, and was at the time pregnant by another man – fell in love and agreed. But before the hastily arranged marriage Stony underwent a seemingly miraculous recovery. After the ceremony he proceeded to overturn a prenuptial agreement protecting her vast fortune – which included Glamis Castle in Scotland, the childhood home of the late Queen Elizabeth, the Queen Mother, whose maiden name was Elizabeth Bowes-Lyon. Stony, who had no rightful claim to the title, imprisoned the countess in her home, squandered her wealth, raped the maids and he also fathered many illegitimate children.

She only escaped after some of the maids helped her, and in 1785 filed for divorce in a London court on the grounds of adultery, 'beating, scratching, biting, pinching, whipping, kicking, imprisoning, insulting, provoking, tormenting, mortifying, degrading, tyrannising, cajoling, deceiving, lying, starving, forcing, compelling, and … wringing of the heart'. Stony, who by then had become an MP, did not give up easily: he kidnapped her and carried her around the country on horseback, threatening to rape and kill her to keep her compliant. He was eventually captured after publicity about the outrage swept the country.

The letter which has just come to light was written on 26th March 1785 to her lawyer Charles Wren. In it, she wrote of her 'almost miraculous escape after eight years of unprecedented misery'. She also apologised for not writing to Wren sooner due to the 'extreme hurry of business in which I have been involved ever since I left Mr Bowes.'

It (the letter) is being sold at Mullocks auctioneers in Ludlow, Shropshire, on Tuesday, where it is expected to fetch £150. Richard Westwood-Brookes, from Mullocks discovered the letter while clearing out the office of a Northumberland legal firm which had been run by Wren. He said: 'It is written in a beautiful hand despite the countess having been a prisoner of her husband for eight years.' Stoney's plot to marry her was breath-taking in its audacity, but it worked and he married her to gain access to her fortune. He was a despicable rogue without any morals and put his wife through nearly a decade of extreme torment. Bowes died in 1800, living her final years in isolated houses in Hampshire and Dorset where she said she could feel 'out of the world'. Stony Bowes, as he became after the marriage, was jailed for three years for abducting her. He died in 1810."

(http://www.telegraph.co.uk/culture/7344587/Letter-surfaces-telling-how-Queens-ancestorescaped-the-marriage-from-hell.html)

During the 18th century much of the present Glamis village was developed by the 9th Earl, and the rural community is still supported by the Royal estate. Modernisation, refurbishment and occasional additions to the main structure of Glamis Castle continued into the 20th century, when it entered into the most significant phase of its Royal connections, and established a lasting union between Scotland and the English Royal Family. The village of Glamis is small and unspoiled by the years. It supports a very interesting Folk Museum and fascinating Farm Museum. This small museum gives insight into what life was like in the last three centuries. It is owned and run by the Scottish National Trust.

James Lyon (Charles, John, Patrick, John, Patrick) was born in Scotland in 1727. He had two children; Robert Lyon, Cicely Lyon.

7th Generation

John Lyon-Bowes, 10th Earl of Strathmore (John, Thomas, John, Patrick, John, Patrick). John was born on the 14th April 1769 and succeeded his father as Earl of Strathmore and Kinghorne when the latter died at sea on 7th March 1776.

From 30th June 1796 to 24th October 1806 and again from 9th June 1807 to 29th September 1812, he sat as a Scottish Representative peer in the House of Lords. The family crest was quartered with the Bowes family crest with the three bows representing the Bowes family and the lion rampant the Lyon family. It is most unusual that two families should share a crest.

The 10th Earl did much restoration work on Glamis Castle besides managing estates in England. He built what is now the Bowes Museum in Barnard Castle and  maintained homes at Gibside and Streatlam. He had a long affair with the commoner MARY MILNER, the beautiful daughter of a gardener; according to some stories he went through a false ceremony of marriage with her. They had one son: John Bowes in 1811

John was known as Lord Glamis from his birth until 1820. The Earl was created Baron Bowes on 1815 and held this as a subsidiary title to his death. He married Mary on 2nd July 1820, a mere day before his death on the 3rd of July 1820. John attempted to legitimize his son by this marriage and his will named his son as his heir. According to his will (dated 3rd July 1817), all his real estate was left to Mary and five other trustees in the name of his son. The trustees were also required to pay Mary £1,000 per annum for life.

This deathbed marriage did not prevent his primary title from being inherited by his younger brother Thomas Lyon-Bowes, 11th Earl of Strathmore and Kinghorne. Records show the name sometimes as Bowes-Lyon and sometimes as Lyon-Bowes. The Scottish courts agreed that by marrying Mary, John had been legitimized under Scottish law, but since both parties (notably the father) were domiciled in England, English law would prevail. And Scottish law required Scottish domicile of the parents for the son to have been legitimated. It was on the point of domicile that John's legitimation failed.

A bitter court case followed over the terms of the Earl's will, and after five years, it was decided that the Earl's son John would inherit his English estates, including Gibside, Streatlam Castle and St Paul's Walden Bury in Hertfordshire, the latter estate has been in the possession of the Bowes-Lyon family since 1725, while his brother would inherit the Scottish estates. His secondary title as Baron Bowes became extinct.

Mary, now Dowager Countess of Strathmore, remarried in 1831 to her son's tutor William Hutt, and died in 1860. Her son John Bowes married twice, but had no issue. He is best known today as the founder of the Bowes Museum. On his death, all his wealth and properties were inherited by the family of his uncle, reuniting the Scottish and English estates of the Bowes-Lyon family.

(http://en.wikipedia.org/wiki/John_Lyon-Bowes,_10th_Earl_of_Strathmore_ and Kinghorne)

Thomas Bowes-Lyon, 11th Earl of Strathmore, (John, Thomas, John, Patrick, John, Patrick). Thomas was born on the 3rd May 1773 in Walden, Hertfordshire; he married, MARY ELIZABETH LOUISA RODNEY CARPENTER, who was born 1783, the only daughter and heiress of George Carpenter of Redbourn, Hertfordshire. They married on the 1st January 1800 and had two children;

1. **Thomas George**, Lord Glamis born 6th February 1801. He became the 12th Earl.
2. **Mary Isabella** born 8th August 1802 and married John Walpole Willis, a barrister and had issue.

Thomas was the High Sherriff of the county of Leicester in 1810. His first wife died on 1st June 1811. He then married ELIZA NORTHCOTE, the daughter of a Colonel of the British Army. They had a daughter: **Sarah** Bowes-Lyon born 8th August 1813, who married George Augustus Campbell and later Charles Philip Ainslie.

On 8th December 1817, Thomas married his third wife MARIANNA CHEAPE, daughter of John Cheape. This marriage was childless. Thomas had succeeded his brother John on his death in 1820.

Thomas died at the Palace of Holyrood on 27th August 1846. Thomas BowesLyon, the 11th Earl was succeeded by his grandson Thomas Bowes-Lyon, 12th Earl of Strathmore and Kinghorne.

8th Generation

Thomas George Bowes-Lyon (Thomas Bowes-Lyon, John Lyon, Thomas Lyon, John Lyon, Patrick Lyon, John Lyon, Patrick Lyon). Thomas was born on 6th February 1801 in Walden, Hertfordshire. He married CHARLOTTE GRIMSTEAD on 21st December 1820 in Westminster, London, Middlesex. She was born in 1797 in Redbourne, Hertfordshire. Thomas and Charlotte had the following children:

1. **Thomas George Bowes-Lyon** became the 12th Earl of Strathmore & Kinghorne was born on 28th September 1822 in St Paul's Walden Hertfordshire.
2. **Claude Bowes-Lyon** became the 13th Earl of Strathmore and Kinghorne was born on 21st July 1824 in Redbourn, Hertfordshire.
3. **Charlotte** born 15th May 1826, died 22nd October 1844.
4. **Herbert Bowes-Lyon** was born in 1828, died as infant.
5. **Arthur Bowes-Lyon** was born in 1830, died as infant.
6. **Frances Lyon Bowes** was born on 20th April 1832 in Edinburgh, Midlothian. Married HUGH CHARLES TREVANION. She died on 27th January 1903 in London.

Thomas later married Mary Isabella on 8th August 1824. Thomas George died on 27th January 1834 in Honfleur, Lesieux, Normandy, France. Charlotte died on 19th January 1881 in Leatherhead, Surrey.

9th Generation

Thomas George Lyon-Bowes, 12th Earl of Strathmore, 20th Lord Glamis

(Thomas George, Thomas, John Lyon, Thomas, John, Patrick, John, Patrick).

Thomas George was born 28th September 1822; married 30th April 1850, CHARLOTTE MARIA BARRINGTON the eldest daughter of 6th Viscount BARRINGTON, 1st Life Guards and a Representative Peer 1852-65. With the death of his father on 27th January 1834, Thomas became the heir of his paternal grandfather. He inherited his titles and most of his estate on the death of said grandfather on 27th August 1846. Thomas and Charlotte had no children.

He was a keen amateur cricketer and played amateur first-class cricket for the Marylebone Cricket Club from 1844 to 1857 and Gentlemen of England (1846), Surrey Club (1857), Hertfordshire (1844-1856), I Zingari (1845-1857), Lord Strathmore's XI (1848), R Grimston's XI (1853) Earl of Stamford's Team (18551857), Scotland (1855-1857), Melton Mowbray (1856), Old Harrovians (1856), Lords and Commons (1857-1858).
(http://www.cricketarchive.com/Archive/Players/37/37753/37753.html)

Charlotte died 3rd November 1854. Thomas died 13th September 1865, when he was succeeded by his brother.

Claude Bowes-Lyon, 13th Earl of Strathmore and Kinghorne (Thomas

George[8] Bowes-Lyon, Thomas[7] Bowes-Lyon, John[6] Lyon, Thomas[5] Lyon, John[4] Lyon, Patrick[3] Lyon, John[2] Lyon, Patrick[1] Lyon).

Claude was born on 21st July 1824, he was styled; 'The Honourable Claude Bowes-Lyon' from 1847 to 1865, and was a British peer. He was born in Redbourn, Hertfordshire.

Claude carried out much work at Glamis to make it a comfortable home for his large family. He introduced gas in 1865 and central heating in 1866, much of this was replaced by electricity in 1929. He built a five acre wall garden in 1866 to provide food and flowers for the castle and its occupants and re-built the chapel. He also made many improvements to the Castle and the servant's quarters over many years.

Born Claude Lyon-Bowes, he altered the family name to **Bowes-Lyon.** "He was a Representative Peer for Scotland 1870-87; Lord-Lieutenant of Forfarshire, City of Dundee; Justice of the Peace. Sussex; sometime an officer 2nd Life Guards;

created Lord Bowes of Streatlam Castle, Co. Durham and of Lunedale, Yorkshire, in the peerage of the United Kingdom, 1st July 1887."

Claude married, FRANCES DORA on 28th September 1853 the daughter of OSWALD SMITH of Blendon Hall, Kent, they had eleven children.

1. **Claude George**, born 14th March 1855 who became the **14th Earl.**

2. **Francis**, born 23rd February 1856 of Ridley Hall, Bardon Mill, Northumberland educated at Eton, married 23rd November 1883, Lady ANNE CATHERINE SYBIL LINDSAY who died 15th December 1936, she was the 5th daughter of the 25th Earl of Crawford and Balcarres, He was Deputy Lieutenant and Justice of the Peace. Forfarshire and Northumberland, Colonel Commanding 2nd Voluntary Battalion the Black Watch (Royal Highlanders); sometime Provincial Grandmaster in Freemasonry. Forfar, and died 18th February 1948, having had issue.

3. **Ernest** born 4th August 1858. 2nd Sec. Her Majesty's Diplomatic Service; married 23rd November 1882, ISOBEL HESTER she died 15th July 1945 the daughter of Harvey Drummond, of Iping, Sussex, and Ernest died 27th December 1891, having had issue:

4. **Herbert Bowes-Lyon** born 8th October 1860 in Glamis Castle, Angus. He died 14th April 1897.

5. **Patrick Bowes-Lyon**, born 1863 died 5th October 1946 married ALICE WILTSHIRE (died 1953) had issue:

6. **Constance Frances Bowes-Lyon** born 1865, died 19th November 1951. Married Robert Francis Leslie Blackburn she died 1944, they had three children;

7. **Kenneth Bowes-Lyon**, born 26th April 1867; died unmarried 9th January 1911.

8. **Malcolm Bowes-Lyon Lieutenant Colonel,** born 23rd April 1874. Educated at Eton, and Trinity Hall, Cambridge. He married Winifred Gurdon-Rebow, who was born 23rd April 1874, married 28th September 1907. Formerly Captain 2nd. Life Guards, served in South African War 1899-1900 and 1902, and in World War I 1914-18 (wounded). Lt-Colonel late 5th Battalion the Black Watch (TF). Winfred died 30th May 1957. Malcolm died 23rd August 1957.

9. **Mildred Marion Bowes-Lyon** born 6th October 1868; married 1st July 1890 to Alfred E Jessup of Torquay and died 9th June 1897 leaving issue.

10. **Maud Agnes Bowes-Lyon** born 12th June 1870, she died 28th February 1941.

11. **Evelyn Mary Bowes-Lyon** born 16th July 1872; died 15th March 1876.

Claude's eldest son Claude George was the father of the late Queen Mother. For those who are interested in studying Claude George's family in more detail see the entry under the 14th Earl. Claude Bowes-Lyon died on the 16th February 1904, and was succeeded by his eldest son. Frances Dora died on the 5th February 1922.

10th Generation

Claude George, 14th Earl of Strathmore and Kinghorne, Knight of the Garter, Knight of the Thistle., Knight Grand Cross of the Royal Victorian Order, (Claude[9] Bowes- Lyon 13th Earl of Strathmore and Kinghorne, Thomas George[8], Thomas[7] Bowes-Lyon, John[6] Lyon, Thomas[5] Lyon, John[4] Lyon, Patrick[3] Lyon, John[2] Lyon, Patrick[1] Lyon).

Claude George was born on the 14th March 1855. President of the Territorial Army Association; Deputy Lieutenant Dundee, Justice of the Peace and CC., Hertfordshire., Hon. LL.D., St Andrews; received Freedom of the Burgh of Arbroath 1932; Lord Lieutenant of Angus 1904-36; Hon. Colonel 4th/5th Bn. The Black Watch (Territorial Decoration.); formerly Lieutenant 2nd Life Guards; Knight of St. John, created Knight Grand Cross of the Royal Victorian Order. 26th April 1923, Knight of the Thistle. 11th October 1928, Knight of the Garter. 11th May 1937, and Earl of Strathmore and Kinghorne in the United Kingdom, 1st June 1937.

Claude George married 16th July 1881, NINA CECILIA CAVENDISHBENTINCK, Knight Grand Cross of the Royal Victorian Order, Dame of Grace, Most Venerable Order of the Hospital of St. John of Jerusalem, a daughter of Reverend Charles William Frederick Cavendish-Bentinck.

The Cavendish-Bentinck's

This family had many notable ancestors including: Alfred the Great (849-899), Charlemagne (747-814), Hugh Capet (c 940-996), Rurik (c 832-879), Henry II of England (1133-1189), and William I of England (1027-1087). Their ancestors came from the United Kingdom, France, Germany, Russia, Spain, Byzantium, Belarus, the Netherlands and Belgium.

The family tree takes us back to King William of Orange who came from Holland and the family is related to the Dukes of Devonshire and Dukes of Portland. The British press took great pleasure sometimes in reporting some members of the upper classes who claimed that Elizabeth Bowes-Lyon was a commoner. They obviously rather overlooked her pedigree; her father directly related to the monarchs for centuries and her mother who also had an impressive amount of 'royal blood'.

Cecilia was a gregarious and an accomplished hostess who played the piano exceptionally well. Her houses were run with meticulous care and a practical approach, and she was responsible for designing the Italian Garden at Glamis. She was deeply religious, a keen gardener and embroiderer, and preferred a quiet family life. Claude and Cecilia had the following children;

1. **Violet Hyacinth Bowes-Lyon**, born 17th April 1882, died 17th October 1893.

2. **Mary Frances Bowes-Lyon,** born 30th August 1883, married 14th July 1910, 16th Baron Elphistone, Knight of the Thistle, and died 8th February 1961, he died 28th November 1955, leaving issue three daughters and one son.

3. **Patrick**, 15th Earl. Born 1884 See details later.

4. **John Herbert**, born 1st April 1886. Deputy Lieutenant. Forfar, Lieutenant 5th Bn. the Black Watch, served in World War I. (wounded); Honourable Fenella Hepburn Stuart-Forbes-Trefusis (19th August 1889 – 19th July 1966), the younger daughter of the Charles Hepburn-Stuart-Forbes-Trefusis, 21st Baron Clinton. They had five children, all girls.

   Before the outbreak of World War I, John worked as a stockbroker in the City of London for the firm Rowe and Pitman. In 1915, he was posted with the Black Watch and just prior to the Battle of Aubers Ridge that year, he accidentally shot himself in his left forefinger. It was amputated the following day and while receiving treatment in the UK, he admitted having experienced a nervous breakdown in 1912 and also suffered from neurasthenia.

   Later that year, he was posted to the Ministry of Munitions and then in the Territorial Army in 1916. After the war, he was twice threatened with court-martial after having failed to appear on parade for demobilisation and later returned to his job in the City. Jock, as he was known, died at the family home of Glamis Castle just after midnight on the morning of 7th February 1930 of pneumonia, aged 44, leaving his widow to care for their four young children alone. (Two of them, Nerissa and Katherine, were severely mentally disabled). Three days later he was buried at St Paul's Walden Bury. See the full story later.

   His widow was a leading guest at the 1947 wedding of *Princess Elizabeth* and *Philip, Duke of Edinburgh*.

5. **Alexander Francis**, born 14th April 1887; died unmarried 19th October 1911.

6. **Fergus Henry**, born 18th April 1889 married 17th September 1914, LADY CHRISTIAN NORAH DAWSON-DAMER Fergus was born

at Glamis Castle in Angus and educated at Eton College, Berkshire. During the First World War he served with the 8th Battalion, Black Watch and was killed in the opening stages of the Battle of Loos. As he led an attack on the German lines, his leg was blown off by a barrage of German artillery and he fell back into his sergeant's arms. Bullets struck him in the chest and shoulder and he died on the field. He is commemorated on the Loos Memorial.

His mother, Cecilia Bowes-Lyon, Countess of Strathmore and Kinghorne, was severely affected by the loss of her son, and after his death she became an invalid. (She withdrew from public life until the marriage of her daughter ELIZABETH to the future King in 1923.) Fergus was killed in action 27th September 1915, leaving a daughter. Lady Christian died on the 29th March 1959.

7. **Michael Claude Hamilton**, born 1st October 1893, was educated at Eton and Magdalen College, Oxford. Deputy Lieutenant and Justice of the Peace. Bedfordshire., Vice-Lieutenant from 1945, Captain late 3rd Battalion Royal Scots, served in World War I - 1914-17 (prisoner), and in World War II as Lieutenant Colonel Horse Guards; married 2nd February 1928, ELIZABETH MARGARET CATO, MEMBER OF THE BRITISH EMPIRE. (1945) the only daughter of John Cato, of Woodbastwick Hall, Norfolk. Michael died 1st May 1953, leaving a daughter. Elizabeth died 19th January 1959.

8. **Rose Constance**, born 6th May 1890; married 24th May 1916, Vice-Admiral William Spencer Leveson-Gower, 4th Earl Granville, Knight of the Garter, Knight Commander of the Royal Victorian Order, Companion of the Order of the Bath, Distinguished Service Order. Knight Grand Cross of the Royal Victorian Order. (1953), Dame Commander of the Royal Victorian Order. (1945), Hon. LLJB, Queen's University, Belfast (1951), Companion, Order of St. John of Jerusalem. Rose and William had 2 children. Granville James Leveson-Gower who became the 5th Earl. Rose died 24th May 1916. William died 25th June 1953

9. **ELIZABETH ANGELA MARGUERITE,** born 4th August 1900 (see the Royal Family).

10. **David (Hon. Sir)**, Knight Commander of the Royal Victorian Order (1959), Justice of the Peace, Hertfordshire, Lord Lieutenant 1952-61, High Sheriff 1950; Captain Hertfordshire Regt. (Territorial Army), appointed to Min. of Economic Warfare 1940, employed in British

Embassy, Washington 1942-44, Dir. Royal Exchange Assoc., The Times Publishing Co., Martins Bank Ltd., and Dunlop Rubber Co., born 2nd May 1902, educ. Eton and Magdalen College, Oxford (MA); married 6th February 1929, Rachel Pauline (St. Paul's Walden Bury, Hitchin, Hertfordshire), younger daughter of late Lt-Colonel Rt.Hon. Herbert Henry Spencer Clay, PC, CMG, MC, MP, and died 13th September 1961, leaving a daughter, Davina Katherine (1930) and Simon Alexander (1932).

Nina Cecilia died on the 23rd June 1938. Claude George, 14th Earl of Strathmore and Kinghorne died on the 7th November 1944, and was succeeded by his eldest son.

Ernest Bowes-Lyon (Claude[9] Bowes-Lyon 13th Earl, Thomas George[8], Thomas[7] Bowes-Lyon, John[6] Lyon, Thomas[5] Lyon, John[4] Lyon, Patrick[3] Lyon, John[2] Lyon, Patrick[1] Lyon).

Ernest was born on 4th February 1858 in Glamis, Angus. He married ISOBEL HESTER DRUMMOND on 23rd November 1882 in London, Middlesex. She was born on 21st May 1860 in Long Ditton, Surrey. Ernest Bowes-Lyon and Isobel Hester Drummond had the following children:

1. **Hubert Ernest Bowes-Lyon** was born on 6th October 1883 in Glamis, Angus. He married MARY AGNES SMEATON on 14th January 1905 in St Giles, London. She was born on 16th October 1885 in Edinburgh, Midlothian. Hubert and Mary had 3 children Constance Mary (1904), Hubert Malcolm Ernest (1907) and Douglas Ian Gordon (1912). Mary died on 5th March 1914 in Edinburgh, Midlothian. Hubert later married MARGARET MAY NUTTALL on 13th August 1919. She was born in 1895. Hubert died on 28th April 1959 in Jersey, Channel Islands. Margaret died on 25th May 1966.

2. **Susan Frances Bowes-Lyon** was born on 25th October 1884 in London, Middlesex. She died on 28th October 1885 drowned in the wreck of SS Sidon off Corunna, Spain.

3. **Dorothea Marion Bowes-Lyon** was born on 12th April 1886 in London. She died on 10th July 1886 in London, Middlesex.

4. **Joan Isobel Margaret Bowes-Lyon** was born on 30th April 1888. She died on 6th July 1954 in Jersey, Channel Islands.

5. **Marjorie Effie Bowes-Lyon** was born on 7th May 1889. She died on 23rd December 1981 in Yeovil, Somerset.

6. **Ernestine Hester Maud Bowes-Lyon** was born on 19th December 1891. She married RONALD CHARLES GRANT on 4th October 1918

in Eton, Buckinghamshire. He was born on 13th March 1888 in Pau, Pyrenees-Atlantiques, Aquitaine, France. He died in 1959 in Navarrenx, Pyrenees-Atlantiques, Aquitaine, France. She then married FRANCIS WINSTONE SCOTT on 23rd November 1910 in Kensington, London. He was born in 1882 in Hendon, Middlesex. He died on 14th May 1948 in Tonbridge, Kent. Ernestine died in 1981 in Pau, Pyrenees Atlantiques, Aquitaine, France.

Ernest died on 27th December 1891 in Belgrade, Yugoslavia. Isobel died on 15th July 1945 in Eton, Buckinghamshire.

Malcolm Bowes-Lyon Lt. Colonel (Claude[9] Bowes- Lyon, Thomas George[8], Thomas[7] Bowes-Lyon, John[6] Lyon, Thomas[5] Lyon, John[4] Lyon, Patrick[3] Lyon, John[2] Lyon, Patrick[1] Lyon).

Malcolm was born on 23rd April 1874 in Glamis Castle, Glamis, Angus. He married WINIFRED GURDON REBOW on 28th September 1907 in London, Middlesex. She was born in 1880. Malcolm Bowes-Lyon Lt. Colonel and Winifred had a daughter

Clodagh Pamela Bowes-Lyon who was born on 15th July 1908.

Winifred died on 30th May 1957. Malcolm died on 23rd August 1957.

Patrick Bowes-Lyon Major (Claude Bowes-Lyon, Thomas George (Lord Glamis) Bowes-Lyon, Thomas George Bowes-Lyon, Thomas[7] Lyon-Bowes, John[6] Lyon-Bowes, Thomas Strathmore[5] Lyon, John[4] Lyon, Patrick[3] Lyon, John[2] Lyon, Patrick[1] Lyon).

Patrick was born on 5th March 1863 in London. He married ALICE WILSHIRE on 9th August 1893 in Northamptonshire. She was born in April 1868. Patrick Bowes-Lyon Major and Alice had the following children:

1. **Gavin Patrick Bowes-Lyon** Lieutenant was born on 13th December 1895 in South Kensington, London. He died on 27th November 1917 in Cambrai, Nord, Nord-Pas-de-Calais, France, World War I death.
2. **Angus Patrick Bowes-Lyon** was born on 22nd October 1899 in South Kensington, London. He died on 9th July 1923 in Chertsey, Surrey.
3. **Jean Barbara Bowes-Lyon** was born on 9th October 1904 in Sevenoaks, Kent. She died on 7th January 1963 in Battle, Sussex.
4. **Margaret Ann Bowes-Lyon** was born on 19th June 1907 in England. She died on 14th August 1999 in Camden, London.

Patrick died on 5th October 1946 in Tonbridge, Kent. Alice died on 1st March 1953 in Marylebone, London.

Ernest Bowes-Lyon, Hon. was born on 4th August 1858 in Chelsea, London. He married ISOBEL HESTER DRUMMOND on 23rd November 1882 in London, London. She was born on 21st May 1860 in Malden, Surrey. Ernest Bowes-Lyon and Isobel Hester Drummond had the following children:

1. **Hubert Ernest Bowes-Lyon** was born on 6th October 1883 in Gravenhage, Zuid Holland, Netherlands. He married MARY AGNES HAY-SMEATON on 14th January 1905 in St Giles, London. She was born about 1886 in Edinburgh, Midlothian, and died on 5th March 1914. He then married MARGARET MAY NUTTALL on 13th August 1919 in Kensington, London. She was born about 1887. Hubert died on 28th April 1959 and Margaret died on 25th May 1966 in Camelford, Cornwall.

2. **Susan Frances Bowes-Lyon** was born on 25th October 1884 in London, London. She died on 28th October 1885 at sea, near Corunna, Spain.

3. **Dorothea Marion Bowes-Lyon** was born in December 1886. She died on 10th July 1886 in London.

4. **Joan Isobel Margaret Bowes-Lyon** was born on 30th April 1888. She died on 6th July 1954 in Jersey, Channel Islands.

5. **Marjorie Effie Bowes-Lyon** was born on 7th May 1889. She died on 23rd December 1981 in Somerset.

6. **Ernestine Hester Maud Bowes-Lyon** was born on 19th December 1891. She died in 1981 in Pau, Pyrenees-Atlantiques, Aquitaine, France.

Ernest died on 27th December 1891 in Belgrade, Yugoslavia. Isobel died on 15th July 1945 in Buckinghamshire.

Constance Frances Bowes-Lyon was born on 08th October 1865 in London. She married ROBERT FRANCIS LESLIE BLACKBURN on 21st December 1893 in St Stephen, Kensington, London. He was born on 27th April 1864 in Selkirk, Selkirkshire. Robert and Constance had the following children:

1. Phyllis Frances Agnes Blackburn was born on 24th October 1894 in Edinburgh, Midlothian.

2. Leslie Herbert Blackburn was born on 11th January 1901 in Edinburgh, Midlothian.

3. Hilda Constance Helen Blackburn was born on 10th March 1902. She died on 14th January 1986 in Newbury, Berkshire.

4.   Claudia Katherine Angela Blackburn was born in 1908. She died on 8th February 2001 in Scotland, United Kingdom.

Robert died on 21st March 1944. Constance died on 19th November 1951 in Edinburgh, Midlothian.

11th Generation

Francis Bowes-Lyon (Claude[10] Bowes-Lyon, Thomas George (Lord Glamis)[9] Bowes-Lyon, Thomas George Bowes- Lyon Lord Glamis, Thomas[7] Lyon-Bowes, John[6] Lyon (Bowes, Thomas Strathmore[5] Lyon, Patrick[3] Lyon, John[2] Lyon, Patrick[1] Lyon).

Francis was born on 23rd February 1856 in Glamis, Angus. He married ANNE CATHERINE SYBIL LINDSAY on 22nd November 1883 in Durham. She was born in 1858 in London. Francis Bowes-Lyon and Anne Catherine Sybil Lindsay had the following children:

1.   **Muriel Frances Margaret Bowes-**Lyon was born on 29th September 1884 in Bedfordshire, Hertfordshire, United Kingdom. She died on 31st October 1968.

2.   **Charles Lindsay Claude Bowes-Lyon** was born on 15th September 1885 in Scotland. He died on 23rd October 1914 in Ypres, Belgium.

3.   **Geoffrey Francis Bowes-Lyon** Captain was born on 30th September 1886 in Luton, Bedfordshire. He married Edith Katherine Selby-Bigge on 31st October 1914 in Southampton, Hampshire. She was born on 31st March 1889 in St Giles, Oxfordshire. She died on 19th September 1971 in Lewes, Sussex. He died on 30th August 1951 in Sussex.

4.   **Doris Cicely Bowes-Lyon** was born on 16th December 1887 in London, Middlesex. She died on 27th October 1918 in Warwickshire.

5.   **Winifred Geraldine Bowes-Lyon** was born on 18th December 1889 in Netherlands. She died on 9th January 1968 in London, London.

6.   **Ronald George Bowes-Lyon,** Captain, was born on 22nd June 1893 in Northumberland, United Kingdom. He married MARY CLAIRE RUSSELL. She was born in 1895. He married an unknown spouse in March 1925 in Chelsea, Middlesex. He died on 17th April 1960 in London, London.

7.   **Lillian Helen Bowes-Lyon** was born on 22nd December 1895 in Northumberland, United Kingdom. She died on 25th July 1949 in London, London.

Anne died on 15ᵗʰ December 1936 in Haltwhistle, Northumberland. Francis died on 18ᵗʰ February 1948 in Northumberland.

Geoffrey Francis Bowes-Lyon Captain (Francis*¹⁰*, Claude*⁹* Bowes- Lyon)
Geoffrey was born on 30ᵗʰ September 1886 in Luton, Bedfordshire. He married EDITH KATHERINE SELBY-BIGGE on 31ˢᵗ October 1914 in Southampton, Hampshire. She was born on 31ˢᵗ March 1889 in St Giles, Oxfordshire. Geoffrey Francis Bowes -Lyon Captain and Edith had the following children:

1.   **Anne Caroline Lindsay Bowes-Lyon** was born on 7ᵗʰ May 1916 in Chelsea, London. She died on 17ᵗʰ March 2004 in Portugal.
2.   **Francis James Cecil Bowes-Lyon** was born on 19ᵗʰ September 1917 in Chelsea, London. He married MARY DE TRAFFORD on 22ⁿᵈ April 1941 in Kensington, London. She was born on 23ʳᵈ February 1920 in London He died in 1977 in Northumberland West, Northumberland. She died on 28ᵗʰ October 2007.
3.   **Sarah Susannah Bowes-Lyon** was born on 20ᵗʰ May 1920 in Kensington, London. She died on 13ᵗʰ December 2002.

Geoffrey died on 30ᵗʰ August 1951 in Chichester, Sussex. Edith died on 19ᵗʰ September 1971 in Lewes, Sussex.

Ernestine Hester Maud Bowes-Lyon (Ernest*¹⁰* Bowes-Lyon, Claude*⁹* Bowes- Lyon).
Ernestine was born on 19ᵗʰ December 1891. She married FRANCIS WINSTONE SCOTT on 23ʳᵈ November 1910 in Kensington, London. He was born in 1882 in Hendon, Middlesex. Ernestine and Francis had the following children:

1.   Anthony Leonard Scott was born on 11ᵗʰ September 1911 in Buckinghamshire. He died in November 2000.
2.   Patrick Drummond Winstone Scott was born on 5ᵗʰ February 1913 in Buckinghamshire. He died on 25ᵗʰ October 1985 in Kidderminster, Worcestershire.

She then married RONALD CHARLES GRANT on 4ᵗʰ October 1918 in Eton, Buckinghamshire. He was born on 13ᵗʰ March 1888 in Pau, Pyrenees-Atlantiques, Aquitaine, France. Ernestine and Ronald had the following children:

1.   Raoul Charles Grant was born on 7ᵗʰ June 1919. He died in 1942.

2.   Raymond David Grant was born on 3rd September 1921 in Navarrenx, Pyrenees-Atlantiques, France. He died on 13th February 2005 in Navarrenx, Pyrenees

Francis died on 14th May 1948 in Tonbridge, Kent. Ronald died in 1959 in Navarrenx, Pyrenees-Atlantiques, Aquitaine, France. Ernestine died in 1981 in Pau, Pyrenees-Atlantiques, France.

Hubert Ernest Bowes-Lyon (Ernest Bowes-Lyon, Claude Bowes- Lyon)

Hubert was born on 6th October 1883 in Glamis, Angus. He married MARY AGNES SMEATON on 14th January 1905 in St Giles, London. She was born on 16th October 1885 in Edinburgh, Midlothian. Hubert and Mary had the following children:

1.   **Constance Mary Bowes-Lyon** was born on 24th December 1904.
2.   **Hubert Ernest Malcolm Bowes-Lyon** was born on 17th May 1907 in Bourne End, Buckinghamshire. He married Fay Rose Jacobs on 12th July 1943 in Johannesburg, Gauteng, South Africa. She was born on 8th November 1909. She died on 27th July 1969 in Westminster, London. He died on 9th April 1995 in Torbay, Devon.
3.   **Douglas Ian Gordon Bowes-Lyon** was born on 30th June 1912 in Folkestone, Kent. He married Charlotte Gardner on 20th June 1942. She died on 11th March 1988. He died on 6th September 1997.

Mary died on 5th March 1914 in Edinburgh, Midlothian.

Hubert then married MARGARET MAY NUTTALL on 13th August 1919. She was born in 1895. Hubert and Margaret had one child:

1 **Sonia Gabrielle Bowes-Lyon** was born on 1st October 1922.

Hubert died on 28th April 1959 in Jersey, Channel Islands. Margaret died on 25th May 1966.

Michael Claude Hamilton Bowes-Lyon (Claude George[10] Knight of the Garter, Claude[9] Bowes- Lyon).

Michael was born on 1st. October 1893 in St Pauls Walden, Hertfordshire. He married ELIZABETH MARGARET CATOR on 2nd February 1928 in St George Hanover Square, London, England, United Kingdom. She was born on

30th September 1899 in Woodbastwick, Norfolk. Michael and Elizabeth had the following children:

1. **Fergus Michael Claude Bowes-Lyon 17th Earl of Strathmore & Kinghorne** was born on 31st December 1928 in St George Hanover Square, London. He married MARY PAMELA MCCORQUODALE. She was born about 1930. He married an unknown spouse in June 1956 in Westminster, Middlesex. He died on 18th August 1987 in Glamis Castle, Glamis, Angus.
2. **Patricia Maud Bowes-Lyon** was born on 30th January 1932. She died on 01st April 1995 in Norwich, Norfolk.
3. **Michael Albermarle Bowes-Lyon** was born on 29th May 1940
4. **Mary Cecilia Bowes-Lyon** was born on 30th January 1932

Michael died on 1 May 1953 in Bedfordshire. Elizabeth died on 19th January 1959 in St Pancras, London.

Mary Frances Bowes-Lyon Lady (Glennis) (Claude George[10] Bowes-Lyon Knight of the Garter, Claude[9] Bowes- Lyon).

Mary was born on 30th March 1883 in Glamis Castle, Angus. She married SIDNEY HERBERT BULLER-FULLERTON-ELPHINSTONE 16th Lord Elphinstone on 14th July 1910 in Westminster, London. He was born on 27th July 1869 in Musselburgh, Midlothian. Sidney and Glennis had the following children:

1. Mary Elizabeth Elphinstone was born on 2nd July 1911 in Musselburgh, Lothian. She died on 16th May 1980 in Perthshire.
2. John Alexander Elphinstone 17TH EARL ELPHINSTONE was born on 22nd March 1914 in Scotland, he died on 8th February 1961 in Musselburgh, Midlothian. He died on 15th November 1975.
3. Jean Constance Elphinstone was born on 3rd April 1915 in London, Middlesex. She died on 29th November 1999 in Lambeth, London.
4. Reverend the Hon Andrew Charles Victor Elphinstone was born on 11th November 1918 in St George Hanover Square, London. He died on 19th March 1975 in Worplesdon, Surrey

Sidney died on 28th November 1955 in Carberry Tower, Musselburgh, Midlothian. Glennis died 8th February 1961 in Musselburgh, Midlothian.

ELIZABETH ANGELA MARGUERITE BOWES-LYON - (Claude George[10] Knight of the Garter, Claude[9] Bowes- Lyon 13th Earl of Strathmore and Kinghorne, Thomas George[8], Thomas[7] Bowes-Lyon 11th Earl of Strathmore and Kinghorne, John[6] LYON 9th Earl Strathmore & Kinghorne, Thomas[5] Lyon 8th Earl of Strathmore & Kinghorne, John[4] Lyon 4th Earl of Strathmore and Kinghorne, Patrick[3] Lyon 3rd Earl of Strathmore & Kinghorne, John[2] Lyon 2nd Earl of Strathmore and Kinghorne, Patrick[1] Lyon 9th Lord Glamis and 1st Earl of Kinghorne)

Elizabeth Bowes-Lyon

Elizabeth was born on August 4th, 1900. She was the ninth of 10 children born to Claude Bowes-Lyon and Cecilia Cavendish-Bentinck, a vicar's daughter and a descendant of the Dukes of Portland. Four years after her birth, her parents became Lord and Lady Strathmore.

"From an early age, Elizabeth and her younger brother David – referred to affectionately by their mother as the "two Benjamins" - exhibited a great sense of fun and mischief, a quality that she was known to possess in abundance."

(http://newsgroups.derkeiler.com/Archive/Alt/alt.talk.royalty/2006-msg00887.html)

The Strathmores lived at St Paul's Walden Bury which has a celebrated Grade I listed landscape garden, laid out in the early 18th century, covering about 50 acres. The surrounding St Paul's Walden Bury Estate, with its arable and livestock farm and its ancient woodland, is a traditional country estate set in the heart of the beautiful Hertfordshire countryside. This was the birth place and childhood home of Queen Elizabeth the Queen Mother. Her family, the Bowes-Lyons, still live here as they have since 1725.

The daughter of the Scottish Lord Glamis, who became the 14th Earl of Strathmore and Kinghorne, Elizabeth was educated at home. She was a descendent of the Scottish King, Robert the Bruce. Brought up to duty, she worked to nurse troops in World War I when her home was used as a hospital for the wounded.

Elizabeth married ALBERT FREDERICK ARTHUR GEORGE, WINDSOR on 26th April 1923. He was born on 14th December 1895 in York Cottage, Sandringham, Norfolk.

In 1936, Albert's brother, King Edward VIII, abdicated to marry Wallis Simpson, a divorcee, and Albert was crowned King of Great Britain and Ireland as George VI. Elizabeth thus became queen consort and they were crowned May 12, 1937. Neither had expected these roles, but they fulfilled them dutifully.

When Elizabeth refused to leave England during the London Blitz in World War II, even enduring the bombing of Buckingham Palace, where she was residing with the king, her spirit was an inspiration to many who continued to hold her in high regard until her death.

Prince Albert and Elizabeth Bowes-Lyon had the following children:

1. **ELIZABETH ALEXANDRA MARY WINDSOR** was born on 21st April 1926 in London, Middlesex. Still living.
2. **Margaret Rose Windsor** was born on 21st August 1930 in Glamis Castle, Glamis, Angus. She died on 9th February 2002 in King Edward VII Hospital, London.

HRH King George died on 5th February 1952 in Sandringham, Norfolk. The Queen Mother died on 30th March 2002 in Royal Lodge, Windsor and Maidenhead, Berkshire.

Patrick Bowes-Lyon 15th Earl Of Strathmore & Kinghorne (Claude George[10] Bowes-Lyon Knight of the Garter, Claude[9] Bowes- Lyon, Thomas George[8] Bowes-Lyon, Thomas,[7] John[6] Lyon, Thomas[5] Lyon, John[4] Lyon, Patrick[3] Lyon, John[2] Lyon, Patrick[1] Lyon).

Patrick was born on 22nd September 1884 in St Pauls. He married DOROTHY BEATRIX GODOLPHIN OSBORNE on 21st November 1908 in Warwickshire. She was born on 3rd December 1888 in Kensington, London. Patrick and Dorothy had the following children:

1. **John Patrick Bowes-Lyon** was born on 1st January 1910 in Westminster, London. He died on 10th September 1941 in North Africa.
2. **Cecilia Bowes-Lyon** was born on 28th February 1912 in Glamis, Angus. She died on 20th March 1947 in Switzerland.
3. **Nancy Moira Bowes-Lyon** was born on 18th March 1918 in Glamis, Angus. She died on 11th February 1959 in London, London.
4. **Timothy Patrick Bowes-Lyon 16th Earl of Strathmore & Kinghorne** was born on 18th March 1918 in Teesdale, Durham. He married MARY BRIDGET BRENNAN on 18th June 1958 in Glamis Castle, Angus. She was born in March 1923 in Ireland. She died on 8th

September 1967 in Glamis, Angus. He died on 13th September 1972 in Glamis Castle, Angus.

Dorothy died on 16th June 1946 in East Grinstead, Sussex. Patrick died on 25th May 1949 in Glamis Castle

John Herbert Bowes-Lyon (Claude George[10] Bowes-Lyon Knight of the Garter, Claude[9] Bowes- Lyon, Thomas George[8] Bowes-Lyon, Thomas[7], John[6] Lyon, Thomas[5] Lyon, John[4] Lyon, Patrick[3] Lyon, John[2] Lyon, Patrick[1] Lyon).

John was born on 1st April 1886 in St Pauls Walden, Hertfordshire. He married FENELLA HEPBURN STUART FORBES TREFUSIS on 29th September 1914. She was born on 19th August 1889 in Fettercairn, Kincardineshire. John and Fenella had the following children:

1. **Patricia Bowes-Lyon** was born on 6th July 1916 in Glamis Castle, Angus. She died on 18th June 1917 in Glamis Castle, Angus.
2. **Anne Ferelith Fenella Bowes-Lyon** was born on 5th December 1917 in Washington City, District Of Columbia, District of Columbia, United States. She died on 26th September 1980 in London, Middlesex.
3. **Nerissa Janet Irene Bowes-Lyon** was born on 18th February 1919 in Glamis, Angus. She died in 1986 in Surrey.
4. **Diana Cinderella Mildred Bowes-Lyon** was born on 14th December 1923 in London. She died on 20th May 1986 in Glamis Castle, Angus.
5. **Kathryn Bowes-Lyon** was born on 4th July 1926 in St George's Square, Greater London. She died in 1961.

Hubert Ernest died on 07th February 1930 in Glamis Castle, Angus. Fenella died on 19th July 1966 in Westminster, London.

12th Generation

Patrick Bowes-Lyon 15th Earl Of Strathmore & Kinghorne (Claude George 14th Earl of Strathmore and Kinghorne Knight of the Garter, Claude 13th Earl of Strathmore and Kinghorne, Thomas George (Lord Glamis), Thomas George Bowes-Lyon (Lord Glamis), Thomas Lyon-Bowes 11th Earl of Strathmore & Kinghorne, John Lyon (Bowes) 9th Earl of Strathmore & Kinghorne, Thomas Lyon 8th Earl Strathmore, John Lyon 4th Earl of Strathmore and Kinghorne, Patrick Lyon 3rd Earl of Strathmore & Kinghorne, John Lyon 2nd Earl of Strathmore and Kinghorne, Patrick Lyon 9th Lord Glamis and 1st Earl of Kinghorne).

Patrick was born on 22nd September 1884 in St Pauls Walden, Hertfordshire. He married DOROTHY BEATRIX GODOLPHIN OSBORNE on 21st November 1908 in Warwickshire. She was born on 3 December 1888 in Kensington, London. Patrick and Dorothy had the following children:

1. **John Patrick Bowes-Lyon** was born on 1st January 1910 in Westminster, London. He died on 19th September 1941 in North Africa on war service.
2. **Cecilia Bowes-Lyon** was born on 28th February 1912 in Glamis, Angus. She died on 20th March 1947 in Switzerland.
3. **Nancy Moira Bowes-Lyon** was born on 18th March 1918 in Glamis, Angus. She died on 11th February 1959 in London, London.
4. **Timothy Patrick (16th Earl of Strathmore) Bowes-Lyon** was born on 18th March 1918 in Teesdale, Durham. He died on 13th September 1972 in Glamis Castle, Angus. He married Mary Bridget Brennan on 18th June 1958 in Glamis Castle, Angus. She was born about 1923 in Ireland. She died on 8th September 1967 in Glamis, Angus.

Dorothy died on 16th June 1946 in East Grinstead, Sussex. Patrick died on 25th May 1949 in Glamis Castle, Angus

Fergus Bowes-Lyon (Claude George 14th Earl of Strathmore and Kinghorne Knight of the Garter, Claude 1, Thomas George (Lord Glamis), Thomas George Bowes- Lyon Lord Glamis)
Fergus was born on 18th April 1889 in St Pauls Walden, Hertfordshire. He married CHRISTIAN NORAH DAWSON-DAMER on 17th September 1914 in Sussex. She was born on 7th August 1890 in London, Middlesex. Fergus and Christian had the following child:
1. **Rosemary Luisa Bowes-Lyon** was born on 18th July 1915 in Uckfield, Sussex. She died on 18th January 1989 in Ringwood and Fordingbridge, Hampshire.

Fergus died on 27th September 1915 in Loos, Pas-de-Calais, Nord-Pas-de Calais, France. Christian died on 29th March 1959 in Weymouth, Dorset.

Geoffrey Francis Bowes-Lyon Captain (Francis, Claude Bowes-Lyon 13th Earl of Strathmore and Kinghorne, Thomas George (Lord Glamis)[2] Bowes-Lyon, Thomas George Bowes-Lyon Lord Glamis).
Geoffrey was born on 30th September 1886 in Luton, Bedfordshire. He married EDITH KATHERINE SELBY-BIGGE on 31st October 1914 in Southampton,

Hampshire. She was born on 31st March 1889 in St Giles, Oxfordshire. Geoffrey and Edith had the following children:

1. **Anne Caroline Lindsay Bowes-Lyon** was born on 7th May 1916 in Chelsea, London. She died on 17th March 2004 in Portugal
2. **Sarah Susannah Bowes-Lyon** was born on 20th May 1920 in Kensington, London. She died on 13th December 2002
3. **Francis James Cecil Bowes-Lyon** MAJOR-GENERAL MC was born on 19th September 1917 in Chelsea, London. He married Mary de Trafford on 22nd April 1941 in Kensington, London. She was born on 23rd February 1920 in London. She died on 28th October 2007. Francis died in 1977 in Northumberland West, Northumberland.

Geoffrey died on 30th August 1951 in Sussex. Edith died on September 1971 in Lewes, Sussex.

David Bowes-Lyon Sir Knight Commander of the Royal Victorian Order was born 2nd May 1902. He was the sixth son of Claude Bowes-Lyon, 14th Earl of Strathmore and Kinghorne, and Cecilia Nina Cavendish-Bentinck. He was the younger brother of the Queen Mother.

During World War II, David was a member of the secret propaganda department Political Warfare Executive. He was High Sheriff of Hertfordshire in 1950 and Lord Lieutenant of Hertfordshire from 1952 until his death. Also, he became President of the Royal Horticultural Society in 1953. In 1960, he commanded the third World Orchid Conference. On 6th February 1929, he married RACHEL PAULINE CLAY and they had two children;

1. **Davina Katherine Bowes-Lyon** was born on 2nd May 1930
2. **Simon Alexander Bowes-Lyon** was born on 17th June 1932

He died at his sister's home, Birkhall, on the Balmoral estate, of a heart attack after suffering from hemiplegia. The Queen Mother discovered him dead in bed. The funeral was held at Ballater, and he was buried at St Paul's Walden Bury. David died 13th September 1961. Rachel died 21st January 1996.

Douglas Ian Gordon Bowes-Lyon (Hubert Ernest Bowes-Lyon, Ernest Hon, Claude Bowes-Lyon 13th Earl of Strathmore and Kinghorne, Thomas George (Lord Glamis) Bowes-Lyon, Thomas George Bowes- Lyon Lord Glamis).

Douglas was born on 30ᵗʰ June 1912 in Folkestone, Kent. He married CHARLOTTE GARDENER. She was born in 1914. Douglas and Charlotte had the following children:

1. Charlotte Mary Diane Bowes-Lyon was born on 19ᵗʰ April 1943
2. Douglas Malcolm Bowes-Lyon was born on 17ᵗʰ August 1946.
3. David Gordon Bowes-Lyon was born on 7ᵗʰ August 1949.
4. Deborah Janet Bowes-Lyon was born on 9ᵗʰ June 1958

He married MARGARET MAY NUTTALL (GRAHAM). She was born in 1904. Douglas and Margaret had the following child:

Sonia Gabrielle Bowes-Lyon was born on 1ˢᵗ October 1922.

Margaret died on 28ᵗʰ April 1966. Douglas died on 6ᵗʰ Sep 1997

Patricia Maud Bowes-Lyon (Michael Claude Hamilton Lieutenant Colonel, Claude George Bowes-Lyon 14ᵗʰ Earl of Strathmore and Kinghorne Knight of the Garter, Claude³ Bowes-Lyon 13ᵗʰ Earl of Strathmore and Kinghorne', Thomas George (Lord Glamis) Bowes-Lyon, Thomas George Bowes- Lyon Lord Glamis).

Patricia was born on 30ᵗʰ January 1932 in Biggleswade, Bedfordshire. She married OLIVER ROBIN TETLEY on 10ᵗʰ June 1964 in London. He was born on 16ᵗʰ April 1929 in East Grinstead, Sussex. Olive and Patricia had the following child:

1. Alexander Tetley was born on 4ᵗʰ March 1965.

Oliver died in September 1972 in Wantage, Berkshire. Patricia died on 1ˢᵗ April 1995 in Norwich, Norfolk, England (Age: 63).

Anne Ferelith Fenella Bowes-Lyon (John Herbert, Claude George 14ᵗʰ Earl of Strathmore and Kinghorne Knight of the Garter, Claude 13ᵗʰ Earl of Strathmore and Kinghorne, Thomas George (Lord Glamis), Thomas George Bowes- Lyon Lord Glamis).

Anne was born on 5ᵗʰ December 1917 in Washington DC, District of Columbia, USA. She married GEORGE VALDEMAR CARL AXEL GLÜCKSBURG on 16ᵗʰ September 1950 in Glamis, Angus. He was born on 16ᵗʰ April 1920 in Gentofte, Kobenhavn, Denmark.

She then married THOMAS WILLIAM ARNOLD ANSON on April 1938 in Westminster, London. He was born on 4th May 1913 in Chelsea, London. Thomas and Anne had one child;

Thomas Patrick John Anson was born on 25th April 1939 in Chelsea, London. He died on 11th November 2005 in Oxford, Oxfordshire.

Thomas died on 18th March 1958 in London, London. Anne died on 26th September 1980 in London, Middlesex. George died on 29th September 1986 in København, Kobenhavn, Denmark.

Francis James Cecil Bowes-Lyon Major-General MC (Geoffrey Francis Captain, Francis, Claude Bowes-Lyon 13th Earl of Strathmore and Kinghorne, Thomas George (Lord Glamis) Bowes-Lyon, Thomas George Bowes- Lyon Lord Glamis).

Francis was born on 19th September 1917 in Chelsea, London. He married MARY DE TRAFFORD on 22nd April 1941 in Kensington, London. She was born on 23rd February 1920 in London. Francis and Mary had the following children:

1. John Francis Bowes-Lyon was born on 13th June 1942.
2. Davis James Bowes-Lyon was born on 21st July 1947.
3. Fiona Ann Bowes-Lyon was born on 3rd July 1944.

Francis died in 1977 in Northumberland West, Northumberland. Mary died on 28th October 2007.

Timothy Patrick Bowes-Lyon, 16th Earl of Strathmore and Kinghorne (1918-1972). Was born on the 18th June 1918, Teesdale, Durham. He married MARY BRIDGET BRENNAN (1923-1967) who was born about 1923 in Ireland. They married on the 18th June 1958 in Glamis Castle. Their only child, Caroline Frances Bowes-Lyon was born 8th December 1959, died 1st January 1960.

He was a first cousin of Queen Elizabeth II and Princess Margaret. After the death of his older brother in 1941 in World War II, he was styled **Lord Glamis**. On 25th May 1949, he succeeded his father Patrick as Earl of Strathmore and Kinghorne. Mary Bridget Brennan died on 8th September 1967. Timothy died on the 13th September 1972.

Michael Claude Bowes-Lyon, 17th Earl of Strathmore and Kinghorne
Michael was born 31st December 1928 he married 10th April 1956 MARY PAMELA McCORQUODALE, born on the 31st May, 1932, 2nd daughter of Brigadier Norman Duncan McCorquodale, MC, of King's Head House, Winslow,

Co. Buckingham, by his wife Barbara Helen de Knoop, daughter of Captain Jersey de Knoop. Michael and Mary's children were:

1. Hon. Michael Fergus Bowes-Lyon, later 18th Earl of Strathmore and Kinghorne.
2. Lady Mary Cecilia Bowes-Lyon (born 23rd December 1959), married 1990 Antony Richard Leeming, of Skirsgill Park, Penrith, Cumbria, 1st son of Richard Leeming, and had issue.
3. Lady Diana Evelyn Bowes-Lyon (born 29th December 1966), March 8th April 1995 Christopher Godfrey-Faussett, 1st son of Richard Godfrey-Faussett, of Badlesmere, Kent, and has issue. Died 1987 succeeded by her son.

Michael died in 1987

Michael Fergus Bowes-Lyon, 18th Earl of Strathmore and Kinghorne, 16th Viscount Lyon, 26th Lord Glamis, 16th Lord Glamis, Glamis, Tannadyce, Sidlaw and Strathdichtie.

Michael was born on the 17th June 1957. Earl Strathmore has been married twice. In 1984, he married ISOBEL CHARLOTTE WEATHERALL and had his first three sons:

1. Hon. Simon Patrick Bowes-Lyon, Lord Glamis (born 18th June 1986) (heir)
2. The Hon. John Fergus Bowes-Lyon was born 1988.
3. The Hon. George Norman Bowes-Lyon was born 1991.

The Strathmores separated in 2003 and a year later became embroiled in a divorce suit much publicised in the press. The Countess hoped to continue to live at Glamis Castle and to receive a lump settlement of five million pounds...for whom the continued stress of the case posed a health danger.

The divorce between the Earl and the first Countess was finalised in January 2005. He married for a second time on 24th November 2005 to Dr. Damaris E. Stuart-William at the family seat of Glamis Castle. The couple had one son, born in March 2005:

1. The Hon. Toby Peter Fergus Bowes-Lyon was born 2005.

The Earl separated from his second wife in June 2007, later filing for divorce, which was granted in August 2008. On 8th September 2011 he announced his intention to marry his partner Karen Baxter.

Summary of the Earls of Strathmore

1606-1615 - Patrick Lyon, 1st Earl of Kinghorne.

1615-1646 - John Lyon, 2nd Earl.

1646-1695 - Patrick Lyon, 3rd Earl.

1695-1712 - John Lyon, 4th Earl.

1712-1715 -John Lyon, 5th Earl.

1699-1728 -Charles Lyon, 6th Earl.

1702-1735 -James Lyon, 7th Earl of Strathmore and Kinghorne.

1735-1753 -Thomas Lyon, 8th Earl.

1753-1776 -John Bowes, 9th Earl.

1776-1820 -John Lyon-Bowes, 10th Earl.

1820-1846 -Thomas Lyon-Bowes, 11th Earl.

1846-1865 -Thomas Lyon-Bowes, 12th Earl.

1865-1904 -Claude Bowes-Lyon, 13th Earl.

1904-1944 -Claude George Bowes-Lyon, 14th Earl.

1944-1949 -Patrick Bowes-Lyon, 15th Earl.

1949-1972 - Timothy Patrick Bowes-Lyon, 16th Earl.

1972-1987 -Fergus Michael Claude Bowes-Lyon, 17th Earl.

Current Chief -Michael Fergus Bowes-Lyon, Deputy Lieutenant, 18th Earl.

CHAPTER 14
THE BRITISH ROYAL FAMILY

The Royal family are undoubtedly the best known family in the world. Let us just begin a few generations before the Queen with her Windsor family from:

King George V who was born in 1865 and married Princess Mary daughter of the Duke of Teck, she was born in 1867. Their children were;

1   Edward VIII, the Duke of Windsor who was born in 1894.
2   George VI who was born in 1895.
3   Mary, Princess Royal who was born in 1897.
4   Henry, Duke of Gloucester who was born in 1900.
5   George, Duke of Kent who was born in 1902.
6   Prince John born in 1905, died 1919.

King George V died in 1936 and Princess Mary in 1953.

The Next Generation

Edward VIII, Edward Albert Christian George Andrew Patrick David, the Duke of Windsor, on the death of his father. He later married Wallis Simpson who was born in 1896 – she was the daughter of Teackle Wallis Warfield. The Duke abdicated in 1936 – they had no children.

George VI, Albert Frederick Arthur George, was born in 1895 and married Elizabeth Bowes-Lyon (1900-2002), the daughter of the Earl of Strathmore and Kinghorne and became the Queen of England with the coronation on the 12th May 1937. They had two children, Elizabeth (1926) and Margaret (1930). King George died in 1952 and the Queen Mother in 2002.

Mary, Princess Royal, Victoria Alexandra Alice Mary, was born in 1897. She married Henry Lascelles (1922-1947), the Earl of Harwood. They had two sons; George Lascelles (1923) and Gerald Lascelles (1924). Henry died in 1947 and Princess Royal in 1965.

Henry, William, Frederick Albert, Duke of Gloucester who was born in 1900 married Lady Alice Montagu Douglas Scott, Princess Alice, Duchess of Gloucester. She was born in 1901. They had two children; William Henry Andrew Frederick of Gloucester (1941) and Richard Alexander Walter George (1944). Henry died in 1974 and Alice in 2004.

George, Edward Alexander Edmund, Duke of Kent who was born in 1902. He married Princess Marina of Greece. They had 3 children, Edward (1935), Alexander (1936), Michael (1942). George died in 1942 in WW II. Marina died in 1968.

The Next Generation

ELIZABETH ALEXANDRA MARY WINDSOR - QUEEN OF ENGLAND. Her mother was Elizabeth Angela Marguerite Bowes-Lyon and her father was Prince Albert Frederick Arthur George who became King George VI in 1936.

Princess Elizabeth was born on 21st April 1926 in London, Middlesex. She married PHILIP MOUNTBATTEN on 20th November 1947 in Westminster, London. He was born on 10th June 1921 in Kérkyra, (Corfu), Ionian Islands, Greece. Prince Philip and Princess Elizabeth had the following children:

1. **Charles Philip Arthur George Windsor, Prince** was born on 14th November 1948 in Buckingham, London, England
2. **Anne Elizabeth Alice Louise Windsor, Princess** was born on 15th August 1950 in St James Park, London.
3. **Andrew Albert Christian Edward Windsor, Prince** was born on 19th February 1960 in Buckingham Palace, London.
4. **Edward Anthony Richard Louis Mountbatten Windsor, Prince** was born on 10th March 1964 in Buckingham, London.

MARGARET ROSE WINDSOR - PRINCESS OF THE UK COUNTESS OF SNOWDON - Her mother was Elizabeth Angela Marguerite Bowes-Lyon and her father was Prince Albert Frederick Arthur George who became King George VI in 1936.

Princess Margaret was born on 21st August 1930 in Glamis Castle, Glamis, Angus. She married ANTHONY ARMSTRONG-JONES 1st Earl of Snowdon 1st Viscount Linley in May 1960 in Westminster Abbey, Westminster, London, Middlesex. He was born in 1930. Lord Snowdon and Princess Margaret had the following children:

1.   **David Albert Charles Armstrong-Jones, Viscount Linley** was born on 3rd November 1961.
2.   **Sarah Frances Elizabeth Armstrong-Jones** was born on 1st May 1964.

Princess Margaret died on 9th February 2002 in King Edward VII Hospital, London.

Prince William Henry Andrew Frederick; (Henry Windsor, George V), born 18th December 1941, he died on 28th August 1972 and was never married.

Prince Richard Alexander Walter George, (Henry Windsor, George V) was born 26th August 1944. He became the Duke of Gloucester on the death of his father Henry. He married Brigitte van Deurs in 1972 and they have 3 children;

1.   Alexander (1974), Earl of Ulster, married Claire Booth 22nd June 2002. They have issue; Xan Windsor (Lord Culloden), Lady Cosima Windsor.
2.   Davina Lewis (1977) Lady, married Gary Lewis on the 31st July 2004. They have issue; Senna Lewis, Tane Lewis.
3.   Rose Gilman (1980) Lady. She married George Gilman on the 19thJuly 2008. They have issue; Lyla Gilman, Rufus Gilman.

Edward George Nicholas Paul Patrick, Duke of Kent. (George Windsor, George V) was born on 9th October 1935. Duke of Kent. He married Katherine Worsley on the 8th June 1961. They have issue;

1.   George, Earl of St Andrews, born 26 June 1962; married Sylvana Tomaselli.
2.   Lady Helen Taylor, born 28 April 1964; married Timothy Taylor.
3.   Lord Nicholas Windsor, born 25 July 1970; married, 2006, Paola Doimi de Lupis de Frankopan, in Vatican City, becoming the first British royal in history to do so.

Alexandra Helen Elizabeth Olga Christabel, Princess; (George Windsor, George V) was born on the 25th December 1936. She married Angus James Bruce Ogilvy (1928). She is the widow of Sir Angus Ogilvy. He died 26th December 2004. They have issue;

1.   James Ogilvy was born in 1964. James married Julia Rawlinson, they had issue; Flora (1994) and Alexander (1996).

2.   Marina Ogilvy was born in 1965. She married Paul Mowatt. They have issue; Zenouska Mowatt (1990), Christian Mowatt (1993).

Michael George Charles Franklin, Prince; born 4th July 1942, (George Windsor, George VI). On 30th June 1978, Prince Michael was married, at a civil ceremony, at the Rathaus, Vienna, Austria, to Baroness Marie-Christine von Reibnitz. They have issue;

1.   Frederick (1979).
2.   Gabriella (1981).

The Next Generation

CHARLES PHILIP ARTHUR GEORGE WINDSOR, PRINCE was born on 14th November 1948 in Buckingham, London. The Prince, as Heir to The Throne, took on the traditional titles of The Duke of Cornwall under a charter of King Edward III in 1337; and, in the Scottish peerage, Duke of Rothesay, Earl of Carrick, Baron Renfrew, Lord of the Isles, and Prince and Great Steward of Scotland.

He was invested as Prince of Wales by The Queen on 1st July 1969 in a colourful ceremony at Caernarfon Castle. Before the investiture The Prince had spent a term at the University College of Wales at Aberystwyth, learning to speak Welsh.

On 29th July 1981, The Prince of Wales married LADY DIANA SPENCER in St Paul's Cathedral who became HRH the Princess of Wales. The Princess was born on 1st July 1961, at Park House on The Queen's estate at Sandringham, Norfolk. She lived there until the death in 1975 of her grandfather, the 7th Earl, when the family moved to the Spencer family seat at Althorp House in Northamptonshire. Prince Charles and Princess Diana had two sons;

1.   Prince William, Duke of Cambridge born on 21st June 1982. He is now married to Catherine Middleton born on the 9th January 1982, they have a son – George Alexander Louis who was born 22nd July 2013.
2.   Prince Harry of Wales born on 15th September 1984.

The marriage was dissolved on 28th August, 1996. The Princess was still regarded as a member of the Royal Family. She continued to live at Kensington Palace and to carry out her public work for a number of charities. Princess Diana was killed in a car crash in Paris on 31st August 1997.

On 9th April 2005, The Prince of Wales and MRS CAMILLA PARKER-BOWLES were married in a civil ceremony at the Guildhall, Windsor. After the wedding, Mrs Parker Bowles became known as HRH the Duchess of Cornwall.

Anne Elizabeth Alice Louise Windsor, Princess was born on 15th August 1950 in St James Park, London. She married Captain Mark Phillips, they were divorced in 1992. They have issue;

1.   Peter Phillips who was born in in 1977 and married Autumn Kelly.
2.   Zara Phillips born in 1981. Married Mike Tindall on the 30th July 2011 and they have a daughter, Mia Grace born on the 17th January 2014.

Andrew Albert Christian Edward Windsor, Prince (Elizabeth, George VI, George V) was born on 19th February 1960 in Buckingham Palace, London. He married Sarah Ferguson in 1986, they were divorced in 1996. They have issue;

1.   Beatrice Elizabeth Mary of York, Princess; born 8th August 1988
2.   Eugene Victoria Helena of York, Princess; born 23rd March 1990.

Edward Anthony Richard Louis Mountbatten Windsor, Prince (Elizabeth, George VI, George V) was born on 10th March 1964 in Buckingham, London. He is the Earl of Essex. He married Sophia Rhys-Jones and they have issue;

1.   Louise Alice Elizabeth Mary Mountbatten-Windsor, Lady was born 8th November 2003.
2.   James Alexander Philip Theo Mountbatten-Windsor, Viscount Servern; was born 17th December 2007.

The British Royal family has survived like no other such families despite wars, political decisions, the press and countless enemies and opponents over the centuries. The Queen has reigned magnificently since 1951, an impressive 63 years as I write.

The Lyon family can claim millions of descendants since William the Conqueror came to England in 1066 and there are over a million still bearing the name Lyon or a direct relationship today. To see more about the Royal family visit the website; where there is an enormous amount of information available.

(http://www.royal.gov.uk/hmthequeen/hmthequeen.aspx)

APPENDIX A

The Norman Conquest in 1066

The Invasion of England in 1066 by Duke William of Normandy (William the Conqueror) was one of the most significant events in British history. It influenced events hundreds of years into the future and was the cause of many wars. It had a significant effect on the relations between England and Scotland.

We can also say that no record exists of any member of the Lyon family in Britain before this date.

The main cause of the Norman Conquest of England was that the English King Edward (known as the Confessor), did not have an heir to succeed him. In 1057 King Edward found that his half-brother's son (known as Edward the Exile) and his son Edgar were living in Germany. These were the only other male members of the Royal House of Wessex who were still alive.

He arranged for them to be brought to England so that he could resolve the succession. Shortly after arriving in England, Edward the Exile died. This left Edgar (known as the Atheling or Royal Prince) as the only other living male member of the family. The problem was that Edgar was born in 1051 and so was only 6 years old in 1057.

When Edward died in 1066 there were several candidates for the English throne. These were:

Edgar (the Atheling), who was the only male relative living of the house of Wessex. He was the great nephew of King Edward. However he was only 15 years old in 1066.

William, Duke of Normandy (the Conqueror). He apparently was related to King Edward through the maternal line. He had been expecting to succeed Edward for many years. In 1064 when Harold Godwinson, then the Earl of Wessex was shipwrecked in France he was rescued by Duke William. He claimed that Harold was so grateful that he swore on a holy relic that he would support William as the next King of England. This account is portrayed in the 'Bayeux Tapestry' which was created after the Norman invasion. Whether it was true or done to justify his actions will never be known.

Harold Godwinson, the Earl of Wessex (Southern England). After the death of Edward, the Witenagemot (The Witan) met. They were an Anglo Saxon Council made up of the top members of the ruling classes. This council voted to support Harold to be King. The Witan felt that Edgar was too young to become King and would not have the support needed in the country.

Sweyn II Estridsson, King of Denmark also believed that he should have the English throne. He was the nephew of King Canute the Great (1016-1035) who had once ruled England. However he had had a long standing feud with Harold Hardrada, the King of Norway over the throne of Denmark. For the time being he did nothing, he was not going to support Harold Hardrada in his attempt for the English Throne.

Harold Hardrada, King of Norway. He thought he had a claim because his father and the English King Canute had agreed that they should have the throne of England if either died without an heir. Tostig Godwinson, the brother of the newly chosen English King Harold Godwinson had been making raids along the English coast and joined Harold Hardrada in his quest for the English Crown. Hardrada invaded England in 1066 but King Harold (1022-1066) marched north and met him in battle. Hardrada and Tostig were defeated and killed at the battle if Stamford Bridge in northern England on 25th September 1066.

King Harold (1022 – 1066) then marched south again, where he learnt that Duke William had landed a force at Pevensey in Sussex. He had subsequently moved to Hastings where he had erected a fort. William then started to attack and burn the local settlements. King Harold believed that he had no choice but to march to meet Duke William in Sussex. He positioned his army on Senlac Hill just north of Hastings and the two armies met in battle on 14th October 1066. Harold was killed in the battle leaving the way clear for William to march on London.

Following Harold's death at the Battle of Hastings, the Witan assembled in London and elected Edgar as King, however he never got to be crowned. The commitment of these men to Edgar's cause, men who had so recently passed over his claim to the throne, must have been doubtful from the start. Their resolve to continue the struggle against William of Normandy was questionable and the military response they organized to the continuing Norman advance was ineffectual. When William crossed the Thames at Wallingford he was met by men, who now abandoned Edgar and submitted to the invader. As the Normans closed in on London, Edgar's key supporters in the city began negotiating with William. In early December the remaining members of the Witan in London met and resolved to take the young uncrowned King out to meet William to submit to him at Berkhamsted, quietly setting aside Edgar's election.

William was crowned as William 1st of England at Westminster Abbey on Christmas Day 1066. William kept Edgar in his custody and took him, along with other English leaders, to his court in Normandy in 1067, before returning with them to England. Edgar may have been involved in the abortive rebellion of the Earls Edwin and Morcar in 1068; in any case, in that year he fled with his mother and sisters to the court of King Malcolm III Canmore of Scotland. Malcolm married Edgar's sister Margaret and agreed to support Edgar in his attempt to reclaim the English throne.

In early 1069 a major rebellion broke out in Northumbria. Edgar left Scotland and joined the rebels as a figurehead for the revolt. After early successes the rebels were defeated at York by King William and Edgar again fled to Scotland.

Later in 1069 King Sweyn II of Denmark arrived in England and a fresh uprising broke out. Edgar sailed south again to link up with Northumbrian rebels and the Danes. The combined force was sufficient to capture York and Northumbria. Later in the year King William fought his way north and retook York. He used the tactic of buying off the Danes under Sweyn. He subsequently devastated the surrounding countryside as a lesson to the rebels.

Early in 1070 he moved against Edgar and other English leaders who had taken refuge with their remaining followers in a marshy region, perhaps Holderness, and put them to flight. Edgar returned to Scotland.

He remained there until 1072, when William invaded Scotland and forced King Malcolm to submit to his overlordship. The terms of the agreement between them probably included the expulsion of Edgar. He therefore took up residence in Flanders, whose count, Robert the Frisian, was hostile to the Normans. However, in 1074 he was able to return to Scotland. Shortly after his arrival there he received an offer from Philip 1, King of France, who was also at odds with William, of a castle and lands near the borders of Normandy from which he would be able to raid his enemies' homeland. He embarked with his followers for France, but a storm wrecked their ships on the English coast. Many of Edgar's men were hunted down by the Normans, but he managed to escape with the remainder to Scotland by land. Following this disaster, he was persuaded by Malcolm to make peace with William and return to England as his subject, abandoning any ambition of regaining his ancestral throne.

This invasion in 1072 and the forcing on King Malcolm of King William's overlordship had huge implications for the future. The treaty was interpreted differently by future Kings of England and Scotland. It resulted in King Edward I of England insisting that Scotland was his and his becoming 'the Hammer of the Scots'.

APPENDIX B

Genealogy problems

There are many challenging problems for those trying to trace their family tree through various branches.

1. First we have to choose from the finding of various other amateur and professional genealogists and historians from the many sources that are available on the web and on various sites that specialise in the subject.
2. We then have to enter the information about the person accurately and correct any obvious errors.
3. We need to be as accurate as possible about the dates of birth, marriage and death and the place that they were born, is this Manchester, Kentucky or Manchester, England.
4. We need to say something about these place names such as the county which may have changed over time. For example Manchester, England was once in Lancashire but is now part of Greater Manchester. In the USA particularly there are many duplications of town names in the various states.
5. We need to make sure of the spelling of all names as original records can be difficult to read and census entries have commonly been damaged by people using the original records for their own tabulations.
6. We will need to make intelligent guesses sometimes about the accuracy of dates or spellings, these cannot be avoided but we must be willing to be corrected, despite the fact that the new information may spoil our claim to fame.
7. It is very important to find an **anchor** for your research, someone whose dates and information are well attested, this provides springboard for research.

In the first case we will examine we have a problem with at least three John Lyon members of the family and the relationships with each other. I will state that the information below is correct, despite the fact that most historians and genealogists in the past have come to other conclusions.

Sir John de Lyons (1289-1346) was born in Great Oakley in Northamptonshire and married ALICE DE ELIZABETH (1300-1374) from Grafton Regis in Northamptonshire. They married when she was 15 and they had two children;

1. **John Lyon** (1314- unknown) who was born in Scotland.
2. **Elizabeth** (1324-1371) was born in Warkworth, Northamptonshire.

John Lyon (1314) (John de Lyons) married MARGERY ST JOHN (born in 1330?).

Some records say that Margery was born in Plumpton in Northamptonshire her father was John St John III who was born in Scotland in 1296 and was living in Scotland at the time in the early 1300's. He died in 1355. If this date of birth is correct she was NOT the mother of John Lyon born in Scotland in 1340.

John Lyon (1340) was a very famous member of the family who married a daughter of King Robert II of Scotland JEAN STEWART. He is an ANCHOR in any family search. There is much proof of his existence and it is easier to work forward and backward when we have a solid footing for research.

He became the Lord Chamberlain of Scotland, second to the King in terms of power and importance so that records are available, see chapter 4 for more details. We know of his death in November 1382.

Hindrances to our research in this matter;

1. The Lyon Memorial books made mistakes because it was often unable to verify the data provided by its participants in America in 1905. Most records had been passed down over many generations and the written data was in England and Scotland. The three volumes are priceless in many ways and invaluable to researchers but most people follow the information as if it is the gospel.
2. We have an almost crippling problem of the key persons all being mostly named John Lyon. In those days second names rarely appear in records. Even the name Lyon becomes 'de Leonne' or 'Lyons'. These are left-over names from the Norman influences and the French language which was then used in court.
3. The family had moved to Glamis by the time of John (1340) but as his grandfather Sir John (1289) was named 'Sir John of Forteviot', the old Scottish capital, and his son John (1314) also it seems to be 'Sir John of Forteviot' we have a problem.

The Lyon Memorial *(The Lyon Memorial- Massachusetts Families by A B Lyons 1905, page 11)* states;

"Baron John's children were Sir Adam (1285), Richard (1287), Sir John. This last Sir John of Forteviot settled in Scotland. His son, Sir John of Forteviot was a favourite of (King) Robert II and married his daughter Jean, he was killed in a duel in 1383".

This is erroneous on several counts, the problem is we are talking about two or three John Lyon's.

1. 'Baron John I' (1250-1316) had three children, the latter being 'Sir John II' (1290), and says that 'he settled in Scotland'.
2. His son, 'Sir John III of Forteviot' (1314) 'was a favourite of Robert II .....' This really refers to the John IV (1340) who married the daughter of King Robert II and was not 'killed in a duel in 1383' but was actually murdered in his bed according to all other records, see chapter 4 for the details.
3. This misses out the third John III (1314) who was born somewhere in Scotland and lived there until his death. He was the father of John IV (1340).
4. The last of all these errors in the two sentences of the above quote is that 'Sir John (1289/90) settled in Scotland' – this is not correct, he returned to England by 1321 and his daughter Elizabeth Lyon was born in 1324 in Warkworth, Northamptonshire, England.

Many other genealogists support the idea that John (1314) was actually a John (1320) and that he was the future Chamberlain of Scotland. This is not likely as he was described as;

"He was a young man of very good parts and qualities, a very graceful and comely person and a great favourite of the King".
(www.archive.org/stream/.../lyonmemorial00lyon_djvu.txt)

This was said by King Robert II in 1372. It is unlikely he was describing the father John (1314) who would have 58 years of age at the time but might be a good description of John (1340) who at that time who would have been 32 years of age!

In the Northamptonshire we have even more confusion. Sir John de Lyons born in 1320 was the son of Richard de Lyons (1289) who was the brother or possibly the twin of Sir John de Lyons (1289/90) who had also named his son John.

"The tomb of this <u>last</u> Sir John Lyons (1320) is in the parish church. He is in plate armour; each elbow gusset is decorated with a lion's face; his shield, charged with a lion rampant, is on his left arm: and the upper part of it is sustained by a small lion seated on his breast: his feet rest on a couchant lion. He reposes on his helmet, surmounted by his crest, a talbot's head issuing out of a ducal coronet."—*George Baker, Northamptonshire Records.*

Sir John de Lyons (1320) died in or about 1371 in Warkworth, Northamptonshire.

Believing and knowing

When tracing members of families we have to be like detectives trying to solve a crime. We gather information from any relevant source that we can find and then have to discern whether that information is pertinent or whether it will lead us nowhere. It is all too easy to jump to a conclusion and to think that we **know** the answer to a problem when in fact we only **believe** that we have reached the correct conclusion.

The two family lines that qualify for research purposes are the Norfolk line and the Northamptonshire lines both of which claim the fatherhood of this John Lyon (1314) at the beginning of the 14th century. No one, to my knowledge, has claimed that there is any other family lineage that is verifiable in any way in this matter. To see the whole table go to Maps and Illustrations in the front of the book.

	The Norfolk Line
10	Sir John de Leonne was born 1225-1316 – married Marjory de Ackle (Northampton) sons John (13) Adam (12)
13	Sir John de Lyons born 1250-1316 – sons Adam (14), Richard (15) and John (16), he died Warkworth.
16	**Sir John Lyon born 1289 in Warkworth. Lived in Scotland for a few years – son John (20) see Northamptonshire line.**
20	**John Lyon born 1314 see Northamptonshire line (14)**

A quick look at the John Lyons in the extract from the Norfolk line shows No. 13 as the father of Adam and Richard, both born in Norfolk. John on the other hand and was born in Northamptonshire at Warkworth. His father, John (1250) died at Warkworth so he would in all probability have moved to Warkworth before the birth of his son John (16).

Sir John born in 1289 No. 16 in Warkworth had a son John No.20 who was born in Scotland in 1314. He also had a daughter, Elizabeth who was born in 1324 at Warkworth.

	The Northamptonshire Lyons
9	Sir John de Lyons was born in 1268 married Margery de Oakley, he died 1312 – sons Adam (1285), Richard (11), John (10)
10	*Sir John de Lyons was born in 1289/90 married Alice de Liz, he died 1346 - son John Lyon (14), Elizabeth (15)*
11	Richard de Lyons was born about 1289 married Elizabeth de Senlis (St. Liz) died after 1349 – son John (12), Elizabeth (13)
12	Sir John de Lyons born 1320 – 1385 – no known issue – died in Northamptonshire.
13	Elizabeth Lyons 1330 – 1371 daughter of Richard (11)
14	*Sir John Baron Of Forteviot Forgandenny And Drumgawan Lyon was born in 1314 in Scotland*
15	*Elizabeth Lyons was born in 1324 married Sir Nicholas Chetewode and Richard de Wydeville sister of John (14) born in Warkworth.*

Lyon Memorial says; "The last Sir John No. 10 in the chart above *(1289?)* is the one who has been mistaken for John of Glamis. The John de Lyons (1314) who in 1334 was summoned to attend the King with horses and arms at Roxburgh". *[Rot. Scot., I. 306]*, and "in 1343 had charters for lands in Perth and Aberdeen, who obtained the return of Glamis, and **whose son was the Grand Chamberlain of Scotland, was a descendant of Richard of Northampton (1242)**" – *(Lyon Memorial New York families descended from the immigrant Thomas Lyon, of Rye with introductory chapter by dr. G. W. A. Lyon on the English Lyon families 1907)*

King David had possessions there (in Northamptonshire) - and may have been a cousin of the last Sir John (1314).

Problems about Sir John Lyon (1289)

Wikipedia says; "Sir John Lyon was the son of John Lyon (c. 1290 - ?), feudal Baron of Forteviot and Forgandenny, who was born in Norfolk, England. Sir John is widely accepted as being the progenitor of Clan Lyon, a claim verified by renowned historian Sir Iain Moncreiffe of that Ilk. His origins were French, his surname being an anglicised version of the Norman - de Leonne".

(http://en.wikipedia.org/wiki/John_Lyon,_Lord_of_Glamis)

I must disagree with Sir Iain who states that Sir John No. 10 above (1289) 'was born in Norfolk', this is unfounded as has been shown in chapters 1 and 2. He was born in Warkworth, Northamptonshire. He states that Sir John is widely accepted as the 'progenitor of the Clan Lyon'.

There are so many John Lyons at this time it is almost impossible in the context to state which one. No John Lyon in my opinion has ever headed a Lyon clan. The Lyon family were Normans originally and Scottish clans are not usually Normans, they were Celts. They have no claim to be a Scottish clan which might hurt some people's feelings but would find full support from any true Scot. Some of the ill-feeling generated against the family by members of Scottish clans such as instigated the murder of John Lyon (1340) may well have been partly caused by a distrust and dislike of the 'foreigners and outsiders' from Normandy!

The Lyon Memorial also states; "Baron John's No. 9 above *(1250)* children were Sir Adam (1285), Richard (1287), Sir John *(1290)*. This last, Sir John of Forteviot settled in Scotland. His son Sir John of Forteviot *1320*, was the favourite of Robert II and married his daughter Jean, he was killed in a duel 1383 and it is from this John that have descended the Scottish Earls of Strathmore, whose lineage is found in Burke and whose reference is made in the preface of the Rolfe edition of Macbeth". *(The Lyon Memorial p.11)*

I hope that this clarifies the problems and the suggestions for solving the conundrums of the early days of the Lyon family.

Even professional genealogists find these types of problems baffling. I hope this helps the amateurs like myself to simply apply logic to such problems. I could not find my great, great grandfather James Hewitt for months. He was listed on his son Charles's marriage certificate as being deceased in 1851. His name was in the Holy Trinity Parish register in Hull, East Yorkshire, in 1821 as Charles' father. I could not find him anywhere until someone said have you looked in the criminal registers?

I soon found him, imprisoned for seven years for stealing a shirt in Northampton in 1833. He was sent to Van Dieman's Land, now Tasmania, to do his time. He was killed in 1837 and never returned to England, his wife died in a mental institution in 1861 in Hull, and she never attended her son Charles's wedding. There are many Hewitts in Tasmania today, I wonder how many are my relatives?

APPENDIX C

The Middlesex Line

The names in brackets after the name are the ancestors of the person. EOL means end of line when known all the children were without issue.

John Lyon (Sir Henry Lyon (1355)) born 1380 in Ruislip, Middlesex, he died in 1425

Henry Lyon (John, Sir Henry) born in 1410 in Ruislip, he married ELIZABETH DENNIS BERKLEY born in 1412. They had four children;
1.   Henry Lyon born1440 -1477, Norfolk.
2.   John Lyon born 1450, Preston, Middlesex.
3.   Thomas Lyon born 1453 -1550,
4.   William Lyon born 1460 -1508 – no children.

Henry died in1460 in Perifere, London.

Henry Lyon (Henry, John, Sir Henry) was born in 1440 in Norfolk he married ELIZABETH DENNIS BERKELEY in 1449, she was born in 1442 in Berkeley, Gloucestershire. He had two children;

1   John Lyon born 1470-1528 born Ryslippe, Middlesex, 4 sons,
2   William Lyon born 1475, Ryslippe, Middlesex – no children. EOL.
3   Elizabeth died 1470. Henry died in Upton, Berkshire in 1477.

There seems to be a bit of a muddle here, a father and son claim to have married an Elizabeth Dennis Berkeley one born in 1412 and the other one in 1442 but the latter married in 1449 – something is wrong with the dates.

John Lyon (Henry, John, Sir Henry) born in 1450, he married EMMA HEDDE born about 1470. They had one son;
John Lyon born in 1500 – 1592 in Preston, Middlesex.

Thomas Lyon (Henry, John, Sir Henry) 1453-1550 married ANNE HYDE in Berkshire. They had two sons;
1. **Sir John Lyon** 1490 – 1564, 2.
2. **Henry Lyon** born1495 Middlesex.

John Lyon (Henry, Henry, John, Sir Henry) born in 1470 Ryslippe, Middlesex. He married EMMA HEDDE in 1500 in Ruislip, she was born in 1474 in Ruislip They had four children;
1. Henry Lyon born 1500 – no children.
2. Thomas Lyon born 1503 – no children.
3. Richard Lyon born1505 – no children.
4. John Lyon 1510-1592 - 3 children.

Emma died in 1509. John died 8th April 1528 in Leith, Midlothian, Scotland.

Sir John Lyon (Thomas, Henry, John, Sir Henry) born in 1490 in Middlesex, he married ALICIA, they had three sons,
1. Richard Lyon 1532-1579 - 3 children.
2. Henry Lyon 1550-1590 – no children.
3. John Lyon 1550-1620 – no children.

Sir John died 6th Nov. 1564.

Henry Lyon (Thomas, Henry, John, Sir Henry) born in 1495 in Middlesex. Married DOROTHY born 1490, they had two sons;
1. Henry Lyon 1535 - no children.
2. Richard Lyon 1532-1579 – no children.

John Lyon (John, Henry, John, Sir Henry) born in 1500 in Preston, Middlesex, married JEAN unknown He was the founder of Harrow School. They had three children,
1. Mary Lyon 1540-1568 – no children.
2 Jean Lyon 1545-1559 – no children.
3. Zackery Lyon 1560-1583 – no children.

John died 3rd October 1592 in Harrow on the Hill, Middlesex. She died 30th August 1608 in Harrow on the Hill, Middlesex.

John Lyon (John, Henry, John, Sir Henry) born 1510 Ryslippe, married JEAN LYON in 1555 she was born in 1514 Ryslippe. They had three children;

1. William Lyon 1540-1624 – 7 children.
2. Elizabeth Lyon 1545 –1606 – no records,
3. Thomas Lyon 1550.

Jean died 5th April 1575(?) in London. John died 3rd October 1592 in London.

Richard Lyon (Sir John, Thomas, Henry, John, Sir Henry) born in 1532 in West Twyford, Middlesex, married AGNES born in 1520 then ISABELLA MILLET born in 1535, they had four children;
1. Henry Lyon 1555- (AGNES) – 1 son,
2. John Lyon 1560-1615, (ISABELLA) – no children,
3. Dorothy Lyon 1565 (ISABELLA).
4. Catherine Lyon 1570

Richard died 17th March 1579 in Twyford.

Henry Lyon (Richard, Sir John, Thomas, Henry, John, Sir Henry) was born 1535. No children.

Richard Lyon (John, Henry, John, Sir Henry) born in 1540? No children. He died 17th March 1579 in Twyford, Middlesex.

Henry Lyon (Richard, John, Henry, John, Sir Henry) born 1555 in Roxley, Lincolnshire. Married CATHERINE RITHE born in 1555. Then later married MABILLA DORNELL, born in 1557 in Lincolnshire. One son;
George Lyon born 1580 – no children.

John Lyon (Richard, Sir John, Thomas, Henry, John, Sir Henry), born in 1560, died in 1615 – no children.

Up until now there is little disagreement with the Middlesex tree families.

William Lyon (John, John, Henry, John, Sir Henry) born in 1540 in Little Stanmore, Middlesex, He married (1) ISABELL WIGHTMAN on 17th June 1576 in Heston, Middlesex, born 1559 in Harrow on the Hill. He later married AUDREY DEERING, born 1543. William and ISABELL's children:

1. John Lyon 1568 in Heston – no children,
2. William Lyon 1580 - 1634 in Stanmer Parva, mother Audrey- 3 children,
3. Isabelle Lyon 1582 in Heston – no children,
4. Audrey Lyon 1584 in Heston – no children,

5. Thomas Lyon 1585- 1634 in Little Stanmer – no children,
6. Richard Lyon 1590 in Heston – 1678 death in Connecticut – <u>see note</u> <u>below</u> – 8 children,
7. Robert Lyon 1590 – 1678 born in Stanmer Parva, mother Audrey – no children. Died Fairfield, Connecticut, America?

Isabell died in 1593. William died 7th September 1624 in Little Stanmore.

William Lyon (William, John, John, Henry, Henry, Sir John) born in 1580 in Stanmer Parva, Middlesex, He maybe had a son by an unknown wife in 1600;

1. Thomas Lyon born 1600 in London, mother unknown.

William later married ANNE CARTER, born in 1594 in London. He had 3 more children:
2. Katherine Lyon born 25th October 1616 in London, she died 1720 in Picardie, France,
3. John Lyon (1617-1617) died as infant.
4. William Lyon born on 13th December 1620 in Cambridge (?), England and died on 16 May 1692 in Roxbury, Massachusetts, America.

William died 1634 in London. Anne Carter also died in 1634 in London.

He is in reality the son of a William Lyon (1580), the grandson of William Lyon (1555), and great grandson of John Lyon the 7th Lord Glamis.

Richard Lyon (William, John, John, Henry, Henry, John) born 1590 in Heston, he married MARGARET unknown, born 1630 in Fairfield, Connecticut. They had 8 children all born in Fairfield; Samuel (1644-1723), Richard (1653-1740), Esther (1658), Elizabeth (1659), William (1660-1699), Hannah (1661-1743), Samuel (1665-1733), Abigail (1673-1698)

Richard died 17th October 1678 in Fairfield, Connecticut, America. Margaret died 23rd March 1705 in Fairfield, CT. The ages of some of these children are a bit fanciful as Abigail would have been born when Richard was 83 years of age!

This must be another **Richard Lyon** (1590) because the Richard that concerns us had two or three sons according to most opinions, that is another story;

1. Thomas Lyon born 1621 at Heston, Middlesex.
2. Henry Lyon born 1625 at Heston, Middlesex.

3.   Richard Lyon born 1624 at Heston, Middlesex.

Many people following their hopes claim that these boys were the three who migrated to America in 1649. They came from a different line connected to the 7th Earl of Glamis. They were born in Heston and dates are correct but the line is wrong in my opinion.

APPENDIX D

Lands acquired by John Lyon (1340)

In the book in Chapter 3 the life of John Lyon (1340) was explained and on some occasions the quoted text listed long lists of titles and land that he inherited after his marriage to King Robert II daughter. For those who are interested in such details I have included the sometimes defunct names of his lands in Scotland.

"He further received from the Crown on 9th August 1378 the Loch of Forfar with the fishings thereof and eel chest; on 27th September 1379 certain lands in Thuriston, Wodhall and Wodoley, in the constabulary of Haddington on 24th. December 1381 the whole burgh of Kinghorne with the manor place, lands, rents and forests belonging to the King in the Constabulary of Kinghorne, reserving only the whole great customs of the burgh due from wool, skins and hides; on 30th August 1382 an annual rent of four chalders of victual and £10 sterling, out of the lands of Doune in Banffshire, in the gift of the Crown, and on the same date a charter of the lands of Glendowachy. He had in addition to these lands several grants of escheats from the Crown.

The lands of Longforgan he (John Lyon) acquired in three separate portions; the first or Pyngle's part was acquired from Adam de Pyngle, burgess of Aberdeen, the discharge of the purchase price being dated 20th March 1374; the second or Bruce's part of Longforgan he got in excambion (exchange) for certain other lands, from Agnes, wife of Sir Robert de Ramesay, Knight, on 28th April 1377; the third or Scarlet's part was resigned by Thomas Scarlet on 6th June 1377, and confirmed to John Lyon 14th July 1378; these lands were erected into a barony by charter from Robert II on the 2nd October 1378.

His first acquisition from the Crown was the lands of Courtastoune in the territory of Garioch and the shire of Aberdeen, granted him on 9th July 1368 by King David II.

On 22nd February 1371, however, David II died unexpectedly at his castle of Edinburgh before his marriage to Agnes could take place."

This the first mention of Kinghorne which eventually became a title of the Lyon family when Patrick was made the 1st Earl of Kinghorne and Strathmore later in time. Other lands that he owned are listed in Chapter 3.

APPENDIX E

"At this time he (John Lyon (1544) the 8ᵗʰ Lord Glamis) corresponded with Beza, the famous theologian on questions of church government, supporting the maintenance of Bishops."

Theodore Beza, "French Théodore de Bèze was born June 24ᵗʰ 1519 in Vézelay, France. He was an author, translator, educator, and theologian who assisted and later succeeded John Calvin as a leader of the Protestant Reformation centred at Geneva.

After studying law at Orléans, France (1535–39), Beza established a practice in Paris, where he published *Juvenilia* (1548) a volume of amorous verse that earned him a reputation as a leading Latin poet. On recovering from a serious illness, he underwent a conversion experience and in 1548 travelled to Geneva to join Jean Calvin, then deeply involved with his reforms of Swiss political and educational institutions. A year later Beza became a professor of Greek at Lausanne, where he wrote in defence of the burning of the anti-Trinitarian heretic Michael Servetus who died 1553. For several years Beza travelled throughout Europe defending the Protestant cause. He returned to Geneva in 1558.

There, in 1559, with Calvin, he founded the new Geneva academy, destined to become a training ground for promotion of Calvinist doctrines. As its first rector, Beza was the logical successor to Calvin upon the Reformer's death in 1564. Beza remained the chief pastor of the Geneva church for the rest of his life, contributing numerous works that influenced the development of Reformed theology.

In most matters, he reiterated Calvin's views, though with greater stress on ecclesiastical discipline and rigid obedience to authority. Beza's sermons and commentaries were widely read in his time; his Greek editions and Latin translations of the New Testament were basic sources for the Geneva Bible and the King James Version (1611). His *De jure magistratum* (1574; "On the Rights of the Magistrate"), defending the right of revolt against tyranny, grew out of the Massacre of St. Bartholomew's Day (1572), from which many surviving French Protestants were welcomed by Beza in Geneva. Beza's book overthrew the earlier Calvinist doctrine of obedience to all civil authority and subsequently became a major political manifesto of Calvinism.

In 1581 Beza donated to the University of Cambridge from his library the celebrated Codex Bezae, an important manuscript from about the 5th century bearing Greek and Latin texts of the Gospels and Acts and supplemented by Beza's commentary based on the Calvinist viewpoint. Other works among Beza's own writings include anti-Catholic tracts, a biography of Calvin, and the *Histoire ecclésiastique des Églises réformées au royaume de France* (1580; "Ecclesiastical History of the Reformed Church in the Kingdom of France"). Both as a theologian and as an administrator, despite occasional charges of intolerance made against him, Beza is considered not only Calvin's successor but also his equal in securing the establishment of Calvinism in Europe." See Wikipedia for more information.

Theodore died October 13th 1605 in Geneva, Switzerland.

APPENDIX F

William Tyndale

The Reformation in England was started by a man little known in today's world. William Tyndale was born in 1494 in Gloucestershire where his father was a cloth trader. He was brought up on a farm as a committed Roman Catholic and at the age of 12 went to Oxford where he joined Magdalene School which later became Magdalene College. He spent eight years there and also studied at Cambridge University. After graduating he came a priest in Gloucestershire serving a local landowner.

At this time he became aware of Martin Luther and his charge against the Roman Catholic Church that it was unscriptural in many of its teachings. As a scholar he realised that the Bible was not available to the common man as it was written in Latin. Because of this the Roman Catholic Church was able to control its members by denying them the right to translate the Bible into their own language and members had to rely on their priests to translate the Bible from Latin.

William was inspired by Erasmus and his humanistic teachings and began to learn Greek and eventually Hebrew so that he could translate the Bible into English allowing the common man to be able to find his own salvation through faith according to the teachings of the New Testament. This also followed the teachings of Martin Luther in Germany where he had translated the Bible into German. He taught that becoming a Christian was an individual matter where no priest would be necessary and a reliance on the teachings of the church to achieve salvation was pointless.

When Bishops of the church in London, such as Thomas More and Cardinal Wolsey, heard about Tyndale's beliefs they tried to arrest him but he fled to Germany for his own protection. He moved to Worms where he continue to translate the New Testament into English. Despite being a hunted man he persisted from 1524 until 1526 where he found a printer willing to produce copies of his translation of the New Testament. Copies were smuggled into England where Henry VIII gave orders that all copies should be destroyed and many people who had handled them were arrested and tortured. Bishop Tunstall, the Bishop of London, said that there were over 2000 errors in the new translation and that Tyndale was a heretic.

In 1528 Henry VIII wanted a divorce from Catherine of Aragon on the grounds that he had married his brother's wife and asked the Pope to annul his marriage. He sought to marry Anne Boleyn who happened to be a Protestant but the Pope refused his request. Tyndale agreed with the King that the Old Testament supported his argument and asked Henry to allow him to print the Bible in English, Henry refused. By 1530 Tyndale had translated the first five books of the Old Testament, commonly known as the Pentateuch. In 1534 Thomas More fell out of favour and was eventually executed in 1535. Tyndale had by now moved to Antwerp in Belgium and King Charles V of France heard about his endeavours and wanted to destroy him for heresy. He set a trap for Tyndale and he was captured and burned at the stake as a martyr. He had translated the whole of the New Testament and part of the Old Testament. The same year Henry allowed the Bible to be printed in English and used a scholar named Miles Coverdale to carry out the translation with no mention of the work that Tyndale had done over the years. Coverdale plagiarised Tyndale's translation and took the credit. Henry later ruled in 1538 that every parish in the kingdom should have a copy of the English Bible in every church, this involved the printing of over 8000 copies.

APPENDIX G

The Warrington Lyon family

Thomas Lyon, left Scotland and settled at Warrington, Lancashire, where he purchased property. He was born about 1626, the youngest son of **George Lyon** of Balmuchtie, Angus, youngest of Cossins. History does not tell us why Thomas left Scotland but we know that many members of the family moved to Lancashire where other Lyon family members settled at that time. He served in the Royal Scots Greys, and settled eventually at Warrington in Lancashire.

1st Generation

Thomas Lyon was born in 1626 in Scotland. He married DOROTHY who was born in 1630. Thomas Lyon and Dorothy 1630 had the following child:

Thomas Lyon was born in 1656.

Thomas died in 1694 in Warrington, Lancashire.

2nd Generation

Thomas Lyon (Thomas) was born in 1656. He married FRANS JONES. She was born about 1660. Thomas Lyon and Frans Jones had the following child:

John Lyon was born in 1688 in Warrington, Lancashire.

Thomas died in 1694 in Appleton, Warrington.

3rd Generation

John Lyon (Thomas, Thomas) was born in 1688 in Warrington, Lancashire, England. He bought land in Warrington and purchased estates in Appleton. He married MARGARET EDWARDSON. She was born about 1692 in Prescot, Lancashire, England. John Lyon and Margaret had the following children:

1. **Thomas Lyon** was born in 1714 in Warrington, Lancashire. He died on 29th December 1776.
2. **Matthew Lyon** was born in 1716 in Warrington, Lancashire, England. He married ELLEN FAIRCLOUGH. She was born about 1720 in Lancashire, England. She died about 1770. He died in 1783 in Warrington, Lancashire.
3. **Ellen Lyon** was born in 1717 in Appleton Hall, Cheshire.

John died in July 1752 in Appleton, Warrington, Cheshire.

4th Generation

Matthew Lyon (John, Thomas, Thomas) was born in 1716 in Warrington, Lancashire, England. He married ELLEN FAIRCLOUGH. She was born about 1720 in Lancashire. Matthew Lyon and Ellen Fairclough had the following children:

1. **Thomas B Lyon** was born on 28th Jul 1759 in Huyton, Lancashire. He died in 1818.
2. **Ellen B Lyon** was born in 1762.
3. **James Lyon Rev.** was born in 1758 in Lancashire. He married MARY RADCLIFFE. She was born in 1760 in Manchester, Lancashire. She died in Jan 1841 in Lancashire. He died on 13th Aug 1836 in Prestwich, Lancashire.

Ellen died about 1770. Matthew died in 1783 in Warrington, Lancashire.

5th Generation

Ellen Lyon (Matthew, John, Thomas, Thomas) was born in 1762. She married JOSEPH PARR. He was born on 29th December 1755 in Warrington, Lancashire. Joseph Parr and Ellen B Lyon had the following children:

1. Joseph Parr. He died in 1824.
2. Thomas Parr was born in December 1792. He married ALICIA CHARLTON. She died on 20th May 1858. He died in January 1870 in Lancashire.
3. Isabella Parr.

Joseph died on 18 Nov 1820.

James Lyon Rev. (Matthew, John, Thomas, Thomas) was born in 1758 in Lancashire, England. He was the Rector of Prestwich, Lancashire. He married MARY RADCLIFFE. She was born in 1760 in Manchester, Lancashire. James Lyon Rev. and Mary Radcliffe had the following children:

1   **James Radcliffe Lyon**

2   **Thomas B. Lyon** was born on 2nd Dec 1786 in Prestwich, Cheshire.

3   **Sarah Ann Lyon** was born on 14th September 1793 in Prestwich, Lancashire.

4   **John Lyon** was born on 5th Feb 1797 in Prestwich, Lancashire. He died on board the HMS Minden in 1820 serving as a Midshipman.

5   **Matthew Nathan Lyon** was born on 12th July 1800 in Prestwich, Lancashire. He married Frances. She was born about 1805 in Stafford, Staffordshire. 6 **George Lyon** was born on 4th October 1801 in Prestwich, Lancashire.

James died on 13th August 1836 in Prestwich, Lancashire. Mary died in January 1841 in Lancashire.

6th Generation

Thomas Parr (Ellen B Lyon, Matthew Lyon, John Lyon, Thomas Lyon, Thomas Lyon) was born in Dec 1792. He married ALICIA CHARLTON. Thomas Parr and Alicia Charlton had the following children:

1   Thomas Philip Parr was born in February 1834.

2   Frederick Parr was born in October 1835.

3   Joseph Charlton Parr was born in 1837. He died in 1920.

4   Raymond William Parr was born in 1843.'

5   Cecil Francis Parr was born in 1847.

Alicia died on 20 May 1858. Thomas died in January 1870 in Lancashire.

Thomas B. Lyon (James Rev., Matthew, John, Thomas, Thomas) was born on 2nd December 1786 in Prestwich, Cheshire. He married ELIZABETH CLAYTON in June
1820. She was born on 15th October 1792 in Lostock Hall, Preston, Lancashire. Thomas Lyon Esquire, of Appleton Hall, was a magistrate and Deputy Lieutenant for the counties of Chester and Lancaster. Thomas B. Lyon and Elizabeth Clayton had the following children:

1   **Thomas Lyon** was born in 1820 in Appleton Hall, Cheshire. He married HELENA POSSE OF ALSPONGA. She was born in 1820 in Sweden.

2   **Thomas Henry Lyon** was born on 28th February 1825 in Appleton Hall, Cheshire. He died on 13th Feb 1914 in Appleton Hall, Cheshire.

3   **Eliza M Lyon** was born about 1825 in Great Budworth, Cheshire. She married RICHARD GREENALL Reverend. He was born about 1807 in Great Budworth, Cheshire.

4   **Georgiana Lyon** was born on 22nd January 1828 in Great Budworth, Cheshire. She died on 20th January 1907 in Ulverston, Lancashire.

5   **Agnes Lyon** was born about 1830.

6   **Francis Lyon Colonel** was born on 11th January 1834 in Stretton. Cheshire. He died on

26th February 1885 in Shoeburyness, Essex.

Thomas died on 17th August 1859 in Warrington, Lancashire.

James Radcliffe Lyon (Rev), (James Rev., Matthew, John, Thomas, Thomas). He was the Rector of Pulford, Cheshire born 11th July 1785. He married 18th May 1814, FRANCES "FANNY" daughter of George CLAYTON. She was born about 1786 in Lostock Hall, Preston, Lancashire. James Radcliffe Lyon Rev and Frances Clayton "Fanny" had the following children:

1.   **John Radcliffe Lyon** was born on 3th August 1818 in Christleton, Cheshire. He married CHRISTINA NEWCOME of Aldenham about 1845 in Cheshire. She was born about 1820 in Shenley, Hertfordshire. She died on 22nd September 1895 in Elstree, Hertfordshire. He died on 10th October 1906 in Sunninghill, Berkshire.

2.   **Sophia Lyon** was born about 1820 in Pulford, Cheshire. She died in July 1909 in London.

3.   **Samuel Edmund Lyon** was born on 18th February 1822 in Pulford, Cheshire. He died in October 1899 in Stratton, Dorset.

4.   **William Barrie Lyon** was born in 1823 in Preston, Lancashire. He died in July 1899 in East Court, Finchamstead.

5.   **Edward Lyon** was born on 21 Nov 1826 in Pulford, Cheshire. He married ALICE H J LYON. She was born about 1828 in India.

Frances died on 11th January 1869 in Pulford, Cheshire. James died on 6th December 1869 in Pulford, Cheshire.

Matthew Nathan Lyon (James Rev., Matthew, John, Thomas, Thomas) was born on 12 July 1800 in Prestwich, Lancashire. He married FRANCES LYON. She was born about 1805 in Stafford, Staffordshire. Matthew Nathan Lyon and Frances Lyon had the following children:

1. **Mary Lyon** was born about 1835 in Broughton Manchester, Lancashire.
2. **Frances D.[7] Lyon** was born about 1836 in Broughton Manchester, Lancashire.
3. **Eliza Lyon** was born about 1838 in Manchester, Lancashire.
4. **Catherine Lyon** was born about 1839 in Broughton Manchester, Lancashire.
5. **Charlotte E Lyon** was born about 1840 in Manchester, Lancashire.
5. **James L Lyon** was born about 1842 in Manchester, Lancashire.
6. **George Lyon** was born about 1845 in Broughton Manchester, Lancashire. He married LAURA HASLOPE LYON. She was born about 1842 in Hateley Heath, West Bromwich Staffordshire.
7. **Nathan Lyon** was born about 1847 in Upholland, Lancashire.

Matthew died in 1883 in Broughton, Manchester.

7th Generation

Georgiana Lyon (Thomas B., James Rev., Matthew, John, Thomas, Thomas) was born on 22 Jan 1828 in Great Budworth, Cheshire, England. She married RICHARD ASSHETON CROSS 1st Viscount Cross, son of William Cross and Ellen Chaffers on 4th May 1852 in Stretton, Cheshire. He was born on 30th May 1823 in Preston, Lancashire. Richard Assheton Cross 1st Viscount Cross and Georgiana Lyon had the following children:

1. Thomas Richard Cross was born on 23rd April 1853 in London. He died on 22nd September 1873 in Bridlington, Yorkshire.
2. Thomas R Cross was born about 1854 in St. George, Hanover Square, London.
3. William Henry Cross was born on 22nd Aug 1856 in Great Budworth, Cheshire. He died on 11th December 1892 in London.
4. John Edward Cross was born on 5th September 1858 in Great Budworth, Cheshire. He died on 26th June 1921 in High Legh, Cheshire.
5. Charles Francis Cross was born on 22nd September 1860 in Northwich, Cheshire. He died on 28th March 1937 in Warrington, Lancashire.
6. Georgiana Harriet Cross was born in 1862 in Stretton, Cheshire. She died on 15th March 1957 in Millom, Cumberland.

7. Mary Dorothea Cross was born in 1864 in Stretton, Cheshire. She died on 2nd April 1921 in Uttoxeter, Staffordshire.
8. Anne Margaret Cross was born in 1873 in London. She died on 8th July 1962 in Cheadle, Staffordshire.

Georgiana died on 20th January 1907 in Ulverston, Lancashire. Richard died on 8th January 1914 in Ulverston, Lancashire.

Francis Lyon, Colonel (Thomas B., James Rev., Matthew, John, Thomas, Thomas) was born on 11th January 1834 in Stretton. Cheshire. He married FLORA MARY ANNESLEY on 23rd June 1863 in London. She was born about 1841 in Scotland. Francis Lyon and Flora Mary Annesley had the following children:

1. **Charles Lyon** LIEUT COL was born in 1865 in East Indies, Murest. He died in March 1944 in Chelsea, London.
2. **Francis Lyon** BRIG-GEN. DSO CVO CMG was born in April 1868 in Northwich, Cheshire. He died on 21st February 1953.
3. **Arthur Lyon** MAJOR was born on 25th January 1869 in Woolwich St Mary Magdalene. He married GLADYS STUART. She was born in 1870. He died in March 1920 in Runcorn, Cheshire. She died in 1954.
4. **Mary Lyon** was born on 11th Oct 1870 in Stretton (Near Warrington), Cheshire.
5. **Henry Lyon** was born on 10th August 1872 in Woolwich Arsenal. He died on 22nd November 1940 in Horley, Surrey.
6. **Florence**^{8} **Lyon** was born on 5th May 1875 in Woolwich, Kent. She died in September 1944 in Chard, Somerset.

Francis died on 26th February 1885 in Shoeburyness, Essex. Flora died on 4th August 1924 in Amersham, Buckinghamshire.

Thomas Henry Lyon (Thomas B., James Rev., Matthew, John, Thomas, Thomas) was born on 28 Feb 1825 in Appleton Hall, Cheshire. He married EDITH GRACE BRANKER. She was born on 8th May 1849 in Billinge, Lancashire. They had a son and a daughter:

1. **Thomas Henry Lyon** was born in 1869 in Appleton Hall, Cheshire.
2. **Dorothy Lyon** was born on 4th January 1876 in Mayfair, London. She died on 1st March 1953.

Thomas Henry died on 13th February 1914 in Appleton Hall, Cheshire. She died on 12 March 1929 in St George, Hanover Square, London.

Samuel Edmund Lyon (James Radcliffe Rev, James Rev., Matthew, John, Thomas, Thomas) was born on 18th February 1822 in Pulford, Cheshire. He married CAROLINE LYON. She was born about 1831 in Preston, Lancashire.

1. **Edmund Hubert Lyon** was born about 1862 in East Stratton, Hampshire.
2. **Blanche C Lyon** was born about 1863 in East Stratton, Hampshire.

Samuel died in October 1899 in Stratton, Dorset, England.

Edward Lyon (James Radcliffe Rev, James Rev., Matthew, John, Thomas, Thomas) was born on 21st November 1826 in Pulford, Cheshire. He married ALICE H J LYON. She was born about 1828 in India. He later married EDITH LYON. She was born about 1832 in St. Pancras, London. Edward and Edith had the following children:

1. **Moore S Lyon** was born about 1863 in Windlesham, Surrey.
2. **Mabel O Lyon** was born in 1863 in Windlesham, Surrey.
3. **Ashton Edward Lyon** was born about 1866 in Windlesham, Surrey.

Edward and Alice had the following children:

1. **Alice M Lyon** was born about 1860 in Hannover, St Georges, London.
2. **Edith F Lyon** was born about 1861 in Ealing, Middlesex.

Edward died in Dec 1917 in Chertsey, Surrey.

8th Generation

George Lyon (Matthew Nathan, James Rev., Matthew, John, Thomas, Thomas) was born about 1845 in Broughton, Manchester, Lancashire. He married LAURA HASLOPE. She was born about 1842 in Hateley Heath, West Bromwich, Staffordshire. George Lyon and Laura Haslope had the following children:

1. **Ethel Lyon** was born about 1873 in Alden, Hertfordshire.
2. **Winifred Lyon** was born about 1875 in Alden, Hertfordshire.
3. **Claude Darcy George Lyon** was born about 1878 in Kaising Ho, St Mary Abbot, Middlesex. He died in March 1956 in Taunton, Somerset. He married Evelyn M Mount on 3rd October 1905 in Berkshire. She was born in June 1877 in London.

Dorothy Lyon (Thomas Henry, Thomas B., James Rev., Matthew, John, Thomas, Thomas) was born on 04 Jan 1876 in Mayfair, London, England. She married RICHARD MAXIMILIAN (2nd BARON ACTON OF ALDENHAM) LYON-DALBERG-ACTON, son of John Emerich Edward Dalberg-Acton Baron and Marie Anna Ludomilla Euphrosina von Arco auf Valley, Countess on 7th June 1904 in Kensington, London. He was born on 7th August 1870 in Bavaria, Germany. Richard Maximilian (2nd Baron Acton of Aldenham) Lyon-Dalberg-Acton and Dorothy Lyon had the following children:

1. **Marie Immaculate Antoinette Lyon-Dalberg-Acton** was born on 1st April 1905. She died on 5th April 1994 in Abingdon, Berkshire.

2. **Dorothy Elizabeth Anne Pelline Lyon-Dalberg-Acton** was born on 25th June 1906 in London. She died on 11th April 1998 in Westminster, London.

3. **John Emerich Henry (3rd Baron Acton of Aldenham) Lyon-Dalberg-Acton** was born on 15th December 1907. He married Daphne Strutt on 25th November 1931. She was born on 5th November 1911 in Kensington, London. He died on 23rd January 1989. She died in February 2003 in Warwickshire.

4. **Richard William Herbert Peter Lyon-Dalberg-Acton** was born on 21st February 1909 He married Jill Lyon Dalberg-Acton on 16th December 1937 in Bridgnorth, Shropshire. She died on 7th September 1946 in Near Bathurst, Gambia. . He died on 7th September 1946 in Banjul, Gambia.

5. **Helen Mary Grace Lyon-Dalberg-Acton** was born on 21st May 1910 in Runcorn,
    Cheshire. She died on 6th June 2001 in Brighton, Sussex.

6. **Gabrielle Marie Leopoldine Lyon-Dalberg-Acton** was born on 15th December 1912. She died on 2nd August 1930.

7. **Joan Henrica Josepha Mary Clare Lyon-Dalberg-Acton** was born on 7th August 1915. She died on 14th November 1995 in Westminster, London.

8. **Margaret Mary Teresa Lyon-Dalberg-Acton** was born on 27th May 1919 in
    Switzerland. She died on 9th December 1997 in Westminster, London.

9. **Aedgyth Bertha Milburg Mary Antonia Frances Lyon-Dalberg-Acton** was born on 15th December 1920 in Bridgnorth, Shropshire. She died in June 1994 in Hackney, London.

Dorothy died on 17th March 1923 in Bridgnorth, Shropshire. Richard died on 16th June 1924 in St George, Hanover Square, London

9th Generation

John Emerich Henry (3rd Baron Acton of Aldenham) Lyon-Dalberg-Acton (Dorothy Lyon, Thomas Henry Lyon, Thomas B. Lyon, James Lyon Rev., Matthew Lyon, John Lyon, Thomas Lyon, Thomas Lyon) was born on 15th December 1907. He married DAPHNE STRUTT on 25th November 1931. She was born on 5th November 1911 in Kensington, London. John Emerich Henry (3rd Baron Acton of Aldenham) Lyon-Dalberg-Acton and Daphne Strutt had the following child:

Charlotte Lyon-Dalberg-Acton was born on 6th December 1934. She died on 1st March 1935.

John died on 23rd January 1989. Daphne died in February 2003 in Warwickshire.

APPENDIX H

Early Grand Masters the Guild of Masons in Scotland

1	Malcolm III	1031 - 1093	King of Scotland
2	Alexander I	1078 - 1124	King of Scotland
3	David I	1084 - 1153	King of Scotland
4	William the Lion	1143 - 1214	
5	Henry Wardlaw	- 1440	Henry Wardlaw, Bishop of Andrews was Grand Master of Scotland until James VI, I, was ransomed from the English. Wardlaw was also founder of the University of Glasgow
6	James 1	1394 – 1437	King of Scotland
7	William Sinclair	1404 - 1484	
8	William Turnbull	? - 1454	
9	Sir Robert Cockeran	? - 1482	
10	Alexander Lord Forbes	? - 1491	
11	William Elphinston	1431 - 1514	
12	Gavin Dunbar	1455 - 1532	Gavin Dunbar (c1490-1547) was Archbishop of Glasgow and Chancellor of the University, 1524-1547. Dunbar was born in Wigtownshire and studied canon and civil law in Glasgow and Paris. He was appointed tutor to the infant James V in 1517 and it was on Dunbar's advice that James founded Scotland's Supreme Court, the Court of Session, in 1532. He held several high offices in the Church before becoming Archbishop of Glasgow in 1524. He is believed to have died in the Bishop's Palace at the top of High Street.
13	Gavin Douglas	1474 - 1522	Gavin Douglas was the Bishop of Dunkeld and famous for being an advanced theologian of his age.
14	George Creighton	?	

15	Patrick, Earl of Lindsay	? - 1526	Patrick Lindsay, 4th Lord Lindsay of the Byres was the son of John Lindsay, 1st Lord Lindsay of the Byres and Agnes Stewart. He died in 1526. Patrick Lindsay, 4th Lord Lindsay of the Byres gained the title of *4th Lord Lindsay of the Byres*
16	Sir David Lindsay	1551 - 1610	Lord Ochiltree
17	Andrew Stewart	1548 - 1593	
18	Sir James Sandilands	? - 1579	
19	Claud Hamilton	1543 - 1622	Lord Paisley
20	James VI & I	1566 - 1625	King of Scotland and England

APPENDIX I

DNA—the problem

DNA could well be the biggest aid to genealogists since the computer. However when I found the following statement about the Lyon brothers in a genealogical magazine it needs some explanation.

"As to the myth of Richard, Henry and Thomas being brothers, I am afraid that always was a myth with **no paper documentation ever having been found to support it** and now Y-DNA evidence has debunked it." The author goes on to say: I'm sorry to be playing the unpopular role of 'egghead at the party' here but I think we are better off on the trail of the truth and the evidence is unequivocal." *(Egghead is an intellectual or bookish person)*

These are two rather strong statements and they deserve some comment. First of all we are talking about the claim that Richard, Henry and Thomas Lyon were not brothers because there is no paper documentation to support it. No genealogist would expect there to be documentation such as birth certificates in the 1500s. It is generally accepted by many genealogists that they were the sons of Richard Lyon born 1580 in Middlesex. Genealogists obtain their information from Parish Registers, County or town records, family records etc. I can find no information which suggests that this generally accepted view is incorrect.

I am certainly no expert on DNA but have tried to get some answers to some basic questions how it can be used to establish relationships hundreds of years ago. I presume that there would be no samples of tissue or other remnants available from all the brothers from which DNA could be extracted. They lived in the 17th Century in England and America.

One would need to find descendants, who could probably claim to be descendants of each of the brothers – this would take us from about twelve generations to the present day. We would have to be 100% certain that these were legitimate births and that the fathers' claims of son-ship were correct. We would arrive at a position where we had enough descendants to give a DNA reading that matched. It would be impossible to say with certainty that they were brothers or not using DNA. The experts say that in this situation it would be impossible to say definitively that these were or were not brothers.

"Both males and females have mitochondrial DNA because mitochondria are essential to life, so both males and females can take an mtDNA test. Still, both genders inherit their mtDNA *only from their mother*, because it's transmitted in the body of the egg, not in the sperm. Like the DNA in the Y-chromosome, the DNA in mitochondria is passed on unchanged (except for rare mutations), so mtDNA analysis can reveal ancestry on your matrilineal line."

Patrilineal and Matrilineal Lines

"Between the two tests — a Y-DNA test and an mtDNA test — only two of the ancestral lines are being tested, that is, either an unbroken chain of male ancestors or an unbroken chain of female ancestors, and any one person has only one each of these lines. All the rest of your ancestral lines zig - zag between males and females, so these lines cannot be revealed with your test results alone. To test all your ancestral lines, you need to share results with others whose ancestry you share. For example, to test your mother's patrilineal line, you need to find and test a male relative of her father (*e.g.*, a brother or uncle or male first cousin with that surname). By finding and testing cousins, you can eventually piece together a complete picture of your yDNA and mtDNA ancestry. This dependence of the testing of cousins is the reason sharing information is so important because, while you are depending on others to test surnames in your 'zig-zag' lines of inheritance, *they are depending on you* to test yours for them."

http://dgmweb.net/DNA/Lyon/LyonDNA-Introduction.html

Taken from the website of 'Egghead' who states that Thomas, Henry and Richard are not brothers and that 'the evidence is unequivocal.'?"

In the future genealogy has the potential not only to help with a family tree, but also to confuse. When you use such a tool you have to be sure that the DNA comes from a wide enough cross section so that you can screen out instances where outside DNA was maybe introduced. In the case under discussion we have twelve generations where we are assuming the couples were absolutely faithful to each other. We hope that this was the case.

Genealogy also has a possible problem when in the future it may be proved that young children were taken in and became part of the family. In this sort of case we could have the problem where a person was raised as a member of a family and took the family name. We may eventually be able to prove that many historic families have breaks in their gene record.

BIBLIOGRAPHY

Lyon Memorial, Vol. I -- Families of William of Roxbury, Peter and George of Dorchester (MA) families

Lyon Memorial, Vol. II -- Families of Connecticut and New Jersey including the descendants of Richard Lyon of Fairfield and Henry Lyon of Fairfield

Lyon Memorial, Vol. III -- Families of New York including the descendants of Thomas Lyon of Rye

The Lyon Memorial books are available free online courtesy of the Open Library and other sources.
http://openlibrary.org/search?q=lyon+memorial) or *(http://freepages.genealogy.rootsweb.com/~lyonfamilies/)*

Barbarians – an alternative Roman history – Terry Jones – ISBN 978-0-563-539162 - © Fegg Features and Sunstone Films 2006

Edward I, A great and terrible king – Marc Morris- ISBN 978-0-09-348175-1 © Marc Morris 2008

Edward III – W.M. Ormrod – ISBN 0 75243320 2 - © Dean & Chapter of York 2005

Everyday life in Medieval England – Christopher Dyer - ISBN 1-85285-201-1 - © Christopher Dyer, 2000

Freemasonry – A journey through ritual and symbol – W Kirk MacNulty - © Thames and Hudson, London – ISBN 0-500-81037-0

Glamis – a village history. ISBN 9 780953 749409. © Glamis Publishing Group 2000

Glamis Castle –Various authors. ISBN 1 874670 4. © Pilgrim Press Ltd 2000

Glamis Castle – Harry Gordon Slade. ISBN 0 85431 277 3. © The Society of Antiquities of London 2000

Medieval Lives – Terry Jones. ISBN 978 0 563 52275 1. © Fegg Features and Sunstone Films 2004

Scone Palace - Jamie Jauncey and others. ISBN 0845101 3775. © Scone Palace 2003

Streatlam & Gibside. - © Durham County Council

The Isles – a history – Norman Davies – ISBN 0-333-76370-X © Norman Davies 1999

The Knights Templar in Yorkshire – ©Diane Holloway & Trish Colton, 2008 - The History Press – ISBN 978-0-7509-5087-9

The Lyons of Cossins & Wester Ogil, Cadets of Glamis – Andrew Ross. ISBN 978 1 150 01875 born General Books 2010

The Lyon Family of Appleton Hall and Stretton Parish Church – Clare Furneaux – 1996 – Alfresco Books.

The Secret History of Freemasonry covering 1000 years of rituals and rites – Jeremy Harwood - © Anness Publishing Ltd. 2009 – ISBN -13-978-84477-965-9

POSTSCRIPT

All of this detailed and enthusiastic work, by Mike on the Lyon Family started with just two photographs; one of the nine children of Hester (nee Blackburn) and Walter Lyon taken in the 1920's in West Derby, Lancashire and one of Peter Lyon

the Horticulturist, who was the grandfather of the nine children and my great grandfather.

The district of West Derby is no longer included in the county of Lancashire, instead it has become part of the expanded city of Liverpool, Merseyside.

Croxteth Hall, where the photograph of Peter was taken in his Victorian greenhouse, is now owned by Liverpool City Council, and the old Hall and its grounds are open to the public. One can still go and visit the greenhouses where Peter worked. One can even see the actual greenhouse where the photo was taken. He looks so proud of his greenhouse, and rightly so. To be a Horticulturist in charge of using one of the Victorian products of the day, relatively cheaply made glass, was cutting edge technology.

Today in 2014, Peter's great grandchildren, the children of the nine are now the "older generation". Of the 23 great grandchildren, 13 are alive today, a few in their fifties, but most in their seventies with children and grandchildren of their own. Most of them live within 50 miles radius of West Derby, Liverpool with one living in France, two in Australia and one in America.

The saying passed down the generations, "that one should always put your money into land and property if you can and be proud of the name Lyon" seems to still be up held, as all but two of Peter's great grandchildren and many of his great, great grandchildren, own their own property with a "little bit of land" and are proud to be called Lyon. We have omitted from Chapter 12 all generations who may still be living.

Thank you Mike for telling our story.
Sylvia Dillon (nee Lyon)

283